Changing Course
in Washington

☆ ☆ ☆

HOLY SPIRIT LIBRARY

CABRINI COLLEGE, RADNOR, PA.

CHANGING COURSE
IN
WASHINGTON

☆ ☆ ☆

Clinton and
the New Congress

RICHARD E. COHEN

Congressional Reporter, *National Journal*

Macmillan College Publishing Company
New York

Maxwell Macmillan Canada
Toronto

Maxwell Macmillan International
New York   Oxford   Singapore   Sydney

E
885
.C64
1994

28890049

Editor: Robert B. Miller
Production Supervisor: Anthony VenGraitis
Production Manager: Paul Smolenski
Text Designer: Eileen Burke
Cover Designer: Robert Freese
Cover illustration: Mike Theiler/Reuters/The Bettmann Archives
Photographs: The photographs for this book were
taken by Richard A. Bloom.
This book was set in Modern 880 by Compset Inc.,
and was printed and bound by Book Press, Inc.
The cover was printed by New England Book Components, Inc.

Copyright © 1994 by Richard E. Cohen

Printed in the United State of America

All rights reserved. No part of this book may be reproduced or transmitted
in any form or by any means, electronic or mechanical, including
photocopying, recording, or any information storage and retrieval system,
without permission in writing from the Publisher.

Macmillan College Publishing Company
866 Third Avenue, New York, New York 10022

Macmillan College Publishing Company is part of
the Maxwell Communication Group of Companies.

Maxwell Macmillan Canada, Inc.
1200 Eglinton Avenue East
Suite 200
Don Mills, Ontario M3C 3N1

Library of Congress Cataloging-in-Publication Data

Cohen, Richard E.
    Changing course in Washington : Clinton and the New Congress /
    Richard E. Cohen.
        p.   cm.
    Includes bibliographical references and index.
    ISBN 0-02-323195-5 (pbk)
    1. United States—Politics and government—1993–   2. Clinton,
Bill, 1946–   I. Title.
    E885.C64   1994
973.929—dc20   93–36191
                                                       CIP

Printing: 1234567   Year: 4567890

To Lyn, for her encouragement
and patience in a difficult year

Contents

☆ ☆ ☆

Preface

In writing this book about how President Clinton and the Democratic-controlled Congress sought to change the direction of government during their early months, I have explored three basic themes that highlight the sweeping results of the 1992 election.

The new president: The election of a new president, especially one who has defeated the incumbent, provides an infrequent opportunity to reshape the way Washington works and what it produces. Clinton's fresh ideas and his team of leading players brought both new substance and style to the nation's policy-making and to the Capitol's politics.

The new Congress: Along with accommodating the largest number of new members since the 1940s, Congress faced a dual challenge: restoring its good name and helping the new president achieve his goals. Democratic congressional leaders welcomed these arduous tasks, which sometimes required delicate balancing. Their help would prove vital to whatever success Clinton attained. In addition, the enthusiasm and perspectives of new lawmakers freshened the institution's human nature and the direction of the diverse nation whom they represent.

Changing course: Although the new players can find it difficult to learn the ropes, the results yield a dynamic period that is a reminder that our government's policies are subject to change at any time. Such an infrequent spurt of activity captures the attention of the nation at large and its many factions, but the public does not always embrace the results.

The early months of any new presidency typically are a time of great change in Washington. When that transition is led by a young leader with lots of ideas who is intent on getting things done and one who succeeded Presidents Reagan and Bush—two leaders of an older generation who were less committed to overhauling and expanding domestic policy—the prospects for dramatic shifts, and even turmoil, loom larger. Add to that the pent-up frustrations of the Democratic party and its legislative leaders who had had little opportunity for creative governing in more than a decade and many Republicans' relief that they no longer shared responsibility for the results. All sides knew that the end of divided party control of government, in short, created a period of accountability they could not escape.

In contrast to other recent presidencies, however, Clinton's initial months were rarely referred to as a "honeymoon," the early period of cooperation that members of Congress from both parties typically have granted to a new president. As would soon become clear, Clinton entered office with a series of political burdens that would handicap his performance. He had won only 43 percent of the vote and had campaigned on a promise of change that was vague, for the most part. As a leader new to Washington, he also had little experience with its culture or its personalities. And he faced a series of national problems that would have burdened any new president. But the notion of a honeymoon also may have become a victim of other factors, such as the deepening national cynicism toward Washington and the public's media-driven impatience for action. Whether that reflected a more mature view of the relationship between the president and Congress or the problems that they faced is less important than that the sense of excitement quickly disappeared as the new players quickly settled to work on a range of problems.

The early centerpiece of legislative action was Clinton's economic-reform agenda, designed to stimulate the limp economy and to reduce the soaring budget deficit—a major legacy of the 1980s that had hamstrung government's ability to respond to public problems. Although Clinton did not achieve everything that he wanted and the margin of victory was exceedingly tight, his early success was a sign that Washington could address the nation's needs. The contrast to the frequent posturing and the grenade-firing between Congress and the White House that had marked the previous decade was striking. For the players—government officials, lobbyists, reporters and the public—it took time and often required a second look to adjust to the renewed activism.

Surprisingly, perhaps, studies of such a period of change at the start of a new presidency are scant. There have been the largely biographical reviews, such as William Greider's *The Education of David Stockman and Other Americans,*[1] which dealt with the young budget director's efforts to reshape government during the Reagan presidency in 1981. My former colleague Lawrence Haas's *Running on Empty*[2] explored how President Bush and Congress managed budget issues in 1989. By focusing chiefly on the handling of a single major bill, this book includes elements of the conventional legislative case-study method. But I also have sought to take a broader look at how the institutions of government, as a whole, cope with sweeping change.

Writing a book about how Washington works is a challenging enterprise. I have been a journalist in the nation's capital for more than two decades. But I have found that the effort can be educational and stimulating for the author as well as, I hope, the reader. Both in this book and in my earlier book about the enactment of the 1990 Clean Air Act, *Washington at Work: Back Rooms and Clean Air,*[3] I have been reminded that those of us who work as Washington reporters usually only skim the surface in our daily or weekly efforts—no matter how much we credit ourselves for presenting the inside story. Even in a book such as this, which involves scores of interviews and includes tens of thousands of words that allow me to dig several layers deeper than the traditional level of journalistic reporting, I know that some questions remain unanswered or even unasked. There are many causes for the remaining ambiguities: conflicting views or lack of knowledge by the main players, the occasional complexity of the subject matter and the fact that some questions—such as an individual's motivation or intention—cannot be fully resolved or explained. However incomplete, I firmly believe that the public benefits from a fuller presentation of how our government works. And if public officials also learn something in the process, that would be welcome, as well.

I have reported and written this book in the period mostly between the November 1992 election and the August 1993 congressional recess. Some of the reporting and analysis appeared concurrently in the weekly issues of *National Journal,* where my bosses generously permitted me to work on this book while I continued to write for the magazine. In contrast to the retrospective reporting of my earlier book, this case study offers a greater sense of immediacy—both for better and worse. Although the major players kindly fulfilled my original expectation that Congress and the White House would reach a form of closure by my August deadline, I have sought to maintain a currency and flow to the storytelling without bogging down in a strict chronology.

As in the past, I thank the countless sources without whose help a reporter's task is far more difficult. The members of Congress and administration officials, their aides, lobbyists, and outside observers all play a role in how Washington functions. Most of them have been generous with their time and observations and in tolerating sometimes overbearing or dumb questions. Unless otherwise noted, all quotes—some of which have already appeared in *National Journal*—are taken from my own interviewing or from the public record. I thank, especially, the magazine's editors Richard Frank, Bill Hogan, Carol Matlack and Michael Wright for helping me to gain a better understanding of my reporting and to communicate it in a lucid fashion to readers. Also at *National Journal,* budget reporter Viveca Novak and health reporter Julie Kosterlitz were unfailing in sharing information with me and patient in trying to help me to navigate significant issues and events. Other colleagues, notably Jim Barnes and Graeme Browning, aided me with their reportorial findings and newsroom bonhomie. Jonathan Rauch and Burt Solomon were especially helpful with their suggestions for improving the manuscript. In addition, the enterprising staff of *National Journal's Congress Daily,* led by editor Lou Peck, has shown that editors and reporters who work under deadlines every day also can produce noteworthy nuggets of information and analysis.

I express special appreciation to the staff and advisers of Macmillan College Publishing Co. and, in particular, Robert Miller, the editor for this book. The following professors provided useful comments after reviewing early drafts: Steven Smith of the University of Minnesota, Cary Covington of the University of Virginia, Eric Uslaner of the University of Maryland at College Park, Stephen Borrelli of the University of Alabama and Timothy Prinz of the University of Virginia. All were unstinting in helping me to develop and improve both the idea and this manuscript. They worked under tight deadlines and editing pressures so that the result could be completed while the subject matter was still relatively fresh to potential readers. I also must note the continuing role in my life provided by my parents, Milton and Charlotte Cohen. Although each of them died from illnesses during the early days of this project, their encouragement always gave me the freedom to pursue my interests and their memory, though sometimes sorrowful, is a source of inspiration. Finally, my wife Lyn Schlitt remains my best editor as well as my constant friend and patient companion. Notwithstanding the constructive advice from these many directions, I take full responsibility for the results in this book.

Endnotes

1. William Greider, *The Education of David Stockman and Other Americans* (New York: E. P. Dutton, 1992).
2. Lawrence J. Haas, *Running on Empty* (Homewood, Illinois: Business One Irwin, 1990).
3. Richard E. Cohen, *Washington at Work: Back Rooms and Clean Air* (New York: Macmillan Publishing Co., 1992).

1

Making a Revolution

☆ ☆ ☆

When President Clinton spoke to Congress on Feb. 17, he unveiled his economic-reform package, which was designed to fulfill his campaign promises. Democrats gave him a rousing ovation as he sought to place their party's stamp on federal policy.

A Transfer of Power and Generations

Washington is filled with majestic buildings and powerful institutions. But the individuals who run the federal government and typically serve in the top positions for only a few years at a time are more mortal. As they exercise the public trust and the burdens of great authority over everyday lives, they often work and live in grand style, but they quickly realize when they depart—if not before—how fleeting that power can be. Never is this sense of power—rising and ebbing—more dramatic than when the nation changes presidents and parties. That transfer involves, in part, the physical trappings: occupancy of the White House, the stroke of a pen that can sign legislation or command executive action, control of the world's strongest military force and other pieces of the vast federal establishment. But also at stake are the less tangible aspects of the presidency, which may be at least as powerful: the symbol of public authority, the opportunity to speak to the nation and to inspire its people in a common mission, and the responsibility for countless formal and informal decisions that ultimately can affect an entire nation.

When the authority passed in January 1993 from George Bush to Bill Clinton, several factors enhanced the dramatic sweep of the change. Clinton's age and cultural background gave the new president a closer connection to much of the public. His broader understanding of the details of government programs and his sympathy with their goals would make him a more absorbed president than was his predecessor. And not least, the disdainful relationship between Bush and the Democratic-controlled Congress during his final two years in office would be replaced by far greater cooperation on both goals and tactics. Among the results would be major shifts in the presidential handling of issues such as tax policy, federal spending priorities and health care. The 1992 election, in short, marked a dramatic shift from a divided government stuck in neutral to one in which a single party was operating the vehicle and had well-defined goals. Granted, hostile back-seat drivers in his own party would occasionally force the president to move off that course. But there was no mistaking the renewed sense of momentum in the nation's policy-making.

Clinton's takeover, combined with the Democrats' continued majorities in Congress, represented a rare moment when the government—and, therefore, the nation—prepared for a potentially sweeping change of course in Washington. Divided government had ended. The new president brought to the office a far more activist view of domestic policy. The agenda was full. And the public was prepared for, and counting on, action. Although his 43 percent share of the vote hardly amounted to a ringing mandate, the outcome left Clinton and his party with little choice but to seek to rekindle the engine of government and a national revival of spirit. "This election is a clarion call for our country to face the challenges of the end of the Cold War and the beginning of the next century," he said on Nov. 3, the night of his victory. "We need more than new laws, new promises or new programs. We need a new spirit of community, a sense that we're all in this together."

Congress was ready to join Clinton. After 12 years of Republican presidents, the majority Democrats were brimming with ideas to fix whatever ailed the nation. And most of them had gained a keen appreciation that they would need to cooperate and follow the lead of the new president. During much of the Reagan and Bush tenures, they had controlled the House and Senate and had sought to place their imprint on federal policy. But those Democrats had come to realize that the U.S. Constitution's system of checks and balances usually demands a presidential initiative to help enact major legislation and that the diverse Congress, which represents the broad array of the nation's factions, is designed to function in a reactive role. In short, only the president can speak with a single voice to the nation. (And speak he would. During his first formal address to Congress, for example, Clinton began by saying, "It's nice to have a fresh excuse for giving a long speech." That State of the Union speech was the longest by any president in recent memory, according to congressional historians.)

Some brief scenes, both public and private, from those early months help to capture the scope of the change resulting from the election. One key to political success is personal contact. The Democratic leaders of Congress, who had become accustomed to talking with presidents mostly from a distance, instead found themselves spending so much time with the president at the White House that they joked that they were too busy to do their own work at the Capitol. "What makes things work is that the president is hands-on and a great communicator," said House Majority Leader Richard Gephardt. Clinton's inexperience in Washington occasionally resulted in painful defeats at the hands of his more savvy foes, such as Senate Minority Leader Robert Dole. Some Democrats engaged in lengthy post-mortems about whether they could have prevented those setbacks if, for example, Clinton had not scheduled a trip to Oregon and Canada at a crucial moment or if he had taken some legislative threats more seriously. Top officials in Congress and at the White House later agreed that some of their work had been done too hurriedly and that a key proposal was a "turkey." But Clinton's enthusiasm would serve him well as he sought to learn the ropes and set up working relationships, as when he called most congressional Democrats to the White House in small groups to get their recommendations before he unveiled his proposed economic plan. Even before he took office, once callous congressional Democrats would bubble like schoolchildren after meeting with him, telling reporters how impressed they were with Clinton's political savvy and his knowledge of details. Members of Congress, like most people, crave attention and reassurances that they have been taken seriously.

The changes in Washington also dealt with the exercise of power. For most of the prior dozen years, Democratic power brokers like House Ways and Means Committee chairman Dan Rostenkowski would offer their own legislative alternatives, sometimes with extensive revisions, to a major presidential initiative. With Clinton's election, they would begin their legislative drafting simply by setting forth his proposals. Often, after consulting with presidential aides, they would make only the modifications required to pass the bill. When these Democrats objected to his proposals, they sometimes would find a way to back down quietly without major concessions by Clinton or the two sides occasionally reached a discreet compromise, rather than run the risk of spreading discord within the party or of creating the public impression that they could not get their act together. Even in the noisy bartering and vote trading that accompanied the narrow victory for Clinton's deficit-reduction plan—the key legislative proposal of his first six months—most Democrats publicly stressed that eventual legislative success was paramount. (See Figure 1.1 for a summary of key events leading to the passage of Clinton's economic package.) The commitment of Democratic congressional leaders was vital to the president's success and represented a striking degree of cooperation. For Republicans, the election of a Democratic president forced them to seek ways to gain attention and to avoid irrelevance. That would prove more difficult in the House, where the

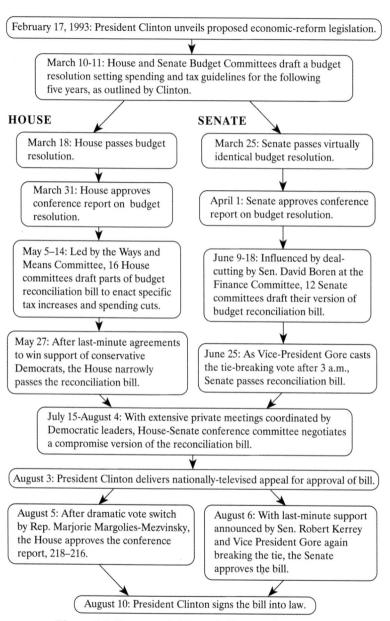

Figure 1.1 Passage of Clinton's Economic Package

majority usually operates as it sees fit, compared with the Senate, where the rules give considerable protection to the minority. With less need for cooperation with Republicans, Democrats often would draft bills in closed-door sessions of their party caucus rather than in open committee meetings.

Clinton was not the only new player in town who sought to change the old ways of doing business. With 110 first-termers in January, the House had its largest freshman class since 1948. Although most of the 63 new Democrats viewed support for the new president as their top priority, many also sought reforms of Congress and the ways that Washington worked. Because the 47 new House Republicans did not have to worry about cooperating with Clinton, of course, they could more freely act as agents of change from their own viewpoint. Not only had that been a theme on which most of the new members had campaigned in 1992, but many of them also understood that they needed to be perceived as outsiders lest the public's continuing discontent with Congress leave them short in an upcoming election.

Even without formal reforms, the election brought major internal shifts to the House's demographics, with a net increase of 13 blacks (to a total of 38 members), six Hispanics (to 17) and 19 women (to 47). Although these new lawmakers often would go separate ways as they sought to make their own mark, their simple presence on the House floor was a significant achievement in redeeming Clinton's campaign promise to make the government "look like America." But these freshmen sometimes made some rookie mistakes or showed indecision that embarrassed themselves and made the job of the senior colleagues more difficult. As for the more tradition-bound Senate, the tripling of the number of women—from two to six in January, then to seven in June—was the most significant internal change, but its impact remained uncertain. Although the Senate, like the House, featured a striking degree of party-line voting and posturing, senators in both parties displayed a continuing penchant for independence that sometimes forced a cumbersome route to reach a final vote.

The institutional changes in Congress and the hostile political environment would have a conspicuous impact on the response to the president's proposals. Clinton often was under siege from factions within his own party. Liberals, conservatives, blacks, women, rural lawmakers, and others had their axes to grind, and many were not shy about seeking public attention and using whatever other leverage they could to achieve their goals. With his relatively narrow majorities in the House and Senate and with a more unified Republican opposition than faced by other recent Democratic presidents, Clinton had little margin for error. His vague promises and distancing from congressional Democrats during the campaign, his own inexperience in Washington, and the fact that most Democrats had never served in Congress with a Democratic president added to the political bumbling during Clinton's early months. In short, the sometimes awkward start of his presidency was a reminder that the conduct of election campaigns can influence the success of governing. Campaigns do matter.

The changes in the players and their roles were not the only factors reshaping the Washington landscape. The new players also brought with them promises to confront two big issues that had deadlocked the Capitol for years—the budget deficit and health care. Dealing with each problem would force the lawmakers to face a potentially lethal set of political land mines plus some complex policy choices. But the earnest Democrats set out to convince the public, and each other, of their serious purpose. By recent Capitol standards, they moved at a rapid pace, suggesting that they understood they had a limited time in which to accomplish their dual goals. As they would sometimes painfully discover, their assessment was an apt one.

A Brief Period of Intense Action

During the past century, the pace in official Washington has been characterized by a few brief bursts of intense legislative action followed by long periods of inactivity or deadlock. An activist president must move quickly to take maximum advantage of these periods. In 1965, for example, Congress passed President Lyndon Johnson's "Great Society." The new laws increased the federal government's role in local activities such as education and housing and, most notably, created the new Medicare program to provide health care for the elderly. By the next year, however, as the nation became bogged down in the Vietnam War, the Democrats' legislative machine ran out of steam and they lost 47 House seats in the election. The bloom was off the rose for Democrats. Then, in 1981, Ronald Reagan and the Republicans marched into Washington to cut taxes and domestic spending. Within seven months, they succeeded in shifting federal policy, at least for the next dozen years. But the active phase of the Reagan revolution expired in the next year—the victim of a weak economy, disputes among Republicans about what to do next and the House Democrats' recovery in the next election. Although Reagan would remain as president for another six years, his dealings with Congress became far more testy and less productive; the few pieces of major legislation typically were initiated by Congress. In 1933, Franklin Roosevelt, aided by the largest one-party majority in Congress during this century, began a long honeymoon, as he won enactment during five years of a vast array of economic and social legislation known as the New Deal. Even his good times had expired by 1938, however, as congressional Democrats grew weary and the world prepared for war. Other recent presidents, including Democrats Kennedy and Carter and Republicans Ford and Bush, have proved less successful with Congress, and their early popularity quickly faded. In Clinton's case, despite the Democrats' enthusiasm, wiser heads knew that the new president's mere 43 percent of the popular vote in 1992 made it difficult for him to claim a strong national mandate. Likewise, since he won a smaller vote percentage in their state than did all Democratic senators elected in 1992 and all but four House Democrats in their districts, it would be difficult for him to contend that he had a better sense of the local pulse than did the lawmakers. Public officials, after all, are solicitous of the opinions of the voters who have the power to elect them or to throw them out of office.

Washington's cyclical pattern featuring brief bursts of activity reflects, in part, that it may require many years for one party or the other to develop a new political consensus and to educate the public about its proposals. The nation's historic tendency to stick with the status quo and its skepticism of magic formulas are part of its conservative character and tradition. But Clinton's 1992 campaign skill in appealing to the public and the deep-seated public unhappiness with how Washington had performed the nation's business in recent years provided what many Democrats hoped would be a rare opportunity for major change, a theme that the candidate himself had repeatedly invoked. "I have news for the forces of greed and the defenders of the status quo," he said when he accepted his party's presidential nomination at its convention in New York City. "Your time has come and gone. It's time for a change in

America." Although that was not his direct intention, this statement also became something of a threat to many members of his own party and its many factions who resisted his call for change.

The election outcome had been one of the most unusual and unpredictable in recent years. It featured an incumbent president, Bush, who suffered a huge drop in popularity in less than a year, his major-party opponent, Clinton, who barely escaped a series of character mishaps, and an independent challenger, Ross Perot, who apparently could not decide whether to run and ultimately staged a very unconventional campaign. But the constant, underlying theme of the election and the events that set its framework was the voters' unhappiness with the mess in Washington, including recent shenanigans that placed public cynicism at record levels. The public distrust and alienation from Washington and virtually all of its leading players—including lobbyists, political consultants and reporters—had reached a dangerous level for a democratic society. That surely was a message that politicians ignored at their peril, either before or after they were elected.

Once Clinton won the election and Democrats found themselves in control of Washington, they faced the virtual requirement that they had to perform. After their 1992 campaign against Washington's gridlock and their own pledge to address the nation's problems, failure to find agreement could be politically devastating for the party and many of its members. As their work began, they voiced confidence that they would meet the test. "We are trying to help the president do what a lot of us have tried to do for a long time," Gephardt said. But Democrats also spoke openly about the adverse political consequences if they failed. "We realize that [Clinton] is our guy and that we have to stick with him when he puts the plan on the table," said Rep. Barbara Kennelly, a member of the Democratic leadership. "There is no alternative." Democrats understood that if either the economy or the president's popularity went downhill, distancing themselves from Clinton might not be a viable or successful political option for many members who are little known or may face a loud chorus of Republican opposition. A complicating factor was that most congressional Democrats would have to face the voters in the 1994 election, while Clinton himself would not be on the line until two years later. Although the Clinton team acknowledged that the fate of the two camps was inextricably linked, the electoral threat was more immediate to members of Congress.

The Democrats agreed that they had to act on issues such as the economy and health care, but it was something else actually to put forward and pass specific proposals. Clinton and his congressional partners readily agreed soon after the election that some of their campaign promises were, in effect, rhetoric that they should quickly jettison. A greater problem was that the Democrats, like other 1992 candidates, had run a national campaign that mostly was long on rhetoric and short on specific proposals. Unlike 1980, when Reagan and the Republicans ran on a commitment—which they kept—to cut income tax rates by 25 percent over three years, the Democrats after the 1992 election would have to start nearly from scratch in crafting their program. And, they quickly learned, it is far easier to cut taxes than to swallow the tough medicine that the Democrats faced. Although Clinton's congressional allies hoped that he would embrace some of their ideas, they had no guarantee. In addition, the distance that the two sides kept from each other during most of the campaign meant that they had spent little time getting comfortable with each other or discussing how they would govern. Rep. Rosa DeLauro of Connecticut, whose husband Stan Greenberg was Clinton's pollster, said before the election that as a result of Clinton's attacks on Congress and its recent pay raise, he "hasn't been the most popular person" on Capitol Hill. Clinton's campaign aides candidly weighed the pros and cons of the candidate's links to Democrats in Congress. "You condemn the sins, the insularity of the institution," said spokesman George Stephanopoulos, who had been a top House aide. "But you praise their strong efforts, like on health care, and talk about how they've been stymied by a do-nothing president."

Achieving Change Is No Simple Task

The Democrats moved quickly to try to exploit their electoral victory. But they would encounter the reality that legislating in a democracy is never a simple task, especially in the face of huge budget deficits and when the results impose burdens—such as new taxes and less generous federal spending—for millions of citizens. The legislative process, even in the best of times, imposes a formidable series of hoops in the House and Senate through which advocates of change must jump. Compounding their challenge was that they were trying to jump start a balky institution—Congress—whose woeful performance in recent years left even some of its own members dubious that they could get the job done. Usually, Clinton had the requisite support from top congressional Democrats as he pressed for legislative action. But, among the initial Democratic corps of 258 House members and 57 senators, there were bound to be objections to the programs as well as efforts to accommodate the objections from party critics. In addition, the sometimes conflicting demands of the House and Senate and the Democrats' narrow majorities posed further obstacles and left little room for error for the success of Clinton's program.

Managing the diverse elements of that team and its response would require careful and continuing coordination between the White House and Congress. Complicating the difficulty of their task was that both sides felt the pressure to move quickly to achieve results at a time when they were still developing their new working relationships. Clinton wanted to make a quick start to prove to the public that he was serious about fostering change and to provide momentum for subsequent actions. In addition, the Democrats could not ignore the views of their political friends among Washington's interest groups. Whether the special pleaders were leaders of organized labor, the black community, women's groups or others, Clinton and the congressional leaders were under constant pressure to fulfill their many commitments, however vague. At times, these obligations, real or implied, created their own conflicts—for example, with the promises by many Democrats to reform how government works. Other elements of the permanent Washington, including lobbyists and the news media, would also engage in efforts to shape or criticize the actions of the new president—steps that often did not fit the game plan of the new political team. These cumulative pressures added to the later second-guessing that Clinton's chief proposals, despite all the controversy that they generated, should have been bolder. If he wanted to change Washington, some critics asked, why was he not more willing to make a cleaner break with the past?

Whatever the outcome of their efforts, Democrats believed that they would offer a major improvement in Washington's performance compared with the way government had functioned in the final two years of the Bush presidency. After the early months of 1991, which featured a dramatic U.S. military victory in the Persian Gulf that gripped the nation's attention and boosted Bush's popularity to record levels, the federal government all but shut down when it came to writing new policy. The president and his advisers made clear that they had few, if any, goals that required congressional action; one exception would be the Supreme Court nomination of Clarence Thomas, which became a spectacle that would prove embarrassing to all participants. As for Congress, Democrats spent most of 1991–92 ridiculing Bush and the Republicans, without showing many serious alternatives of their own. Bush's difficulty in dispatching the primary challenge of Patrick Buchanan and the dominance of ardent conservatives at the GOP's Houston convention raised questions of the president's control of his own party. In addition, the final months of Bush's term—even before the election—were marked by unseemly internal clashes, with various participants trying to establish their credentials for the historical record. Probably the most blatant example was the cooperation of Office of Management and Budget Director Richard Darman in a series that ran in *The Washington Post* in early October. In his unattributed comments to the reporter, Darman criticized various officials, including Bush, and defended his own performance. According to the report, Darman believed that Bush's repudiation of his 1990 budget deal with congressional Democrats, which Darman had been instrumental in crafting, was "sheer idiocy" that could not be justified "intellectually and morally."[1]

Republicans, for their part, agreed that 1991–92 was a dismal period in Washington. But most of them blamed the Democrats and many—especially those who retained fond memories of Reagan and his more aggressive political style—assigned responsibility to Bush and his White House team, rather than to the party as a whole. Many were frustrated by Bush's limited interest in domestic policy and his tendency to cooperate with Democrats when it came time for tough decisions. They had grown weary of publicly defending him while privately urging more aggressive action. House Republicans gained 10 seats in the election and Senate Republicans defied predictions and suffered no net loss of seats in the wake of Bush's dismal performance, leaving many in the party's congressional wing convinced that he had been the political problem. Also, like many Democrats, Republicans had had their fill of divided government. Taking the long view, some welcomed the Democratic takeover on the basis that the resulting accountability ultimately would benefit their own party by allowing them to show that their warnings about the Democrats' inherent shortcomings had been justified. Conservative Republicans, especially, were convinced that Clinton's program would prove an economic and political disaster for Democrats and that this would give a big electoral boost to the GOP.

Some Leading Actors

As with any story about Washington, some of the actors take a particularly prominent role, and they sometimes develop intricate dealings with other players during the several months of this case study. Here are brief sketches—in the order of their most prominent appearance—of some of those who will be highlighted because of either their interesting activities or their leadership.

Leon Panetta: As Clinton's director of the Office of Management and Budget, he played a major part in formulating and selling the economic package that was the first major domestic priority of the new administration. Because of his extensive background on budget issues and the respect that he had gained during 16 years serving in the House from a California district, many of his former colleagues viewed him as a major asset to Clinton's team. But Panetta's demands for strong deficit reduction were often rejected in the White House inner circle. And the horse-trading by various groups in Congress would add to his frustrations and to the difficulty in achieving the goals outlined by Clinton and so avidly advocated by Panetta.

Richard Gephardt: The House majority leader, who represented the St. Louis, Missouri, suburbs, was an invaluable ally in maneuvering Clinton's agenda through the House. With his indefatigable efforts and his ability to reach out to the various wings of the Democratic party, Gephardt helped to overcome many legislative obstacles and keep the program on track. His efforts to help Clinton had to be a source of some ambivalence to Gephardt, a party leader who ran a strong campaign for the Democratic presidential nomination in 1988 but fell short, partly because his chief opponents raised more money. In addition, Clinton's efforts to complete action on economic and health-care issues represented the fulfillment of goals on which Gephardt had worked for years.

Dan Rostenkowski: The House Ways and Means Committee chairman since 1981, the Illinois Democrat styled himself as Clinton's ally in steering the controversial economic and health-care proposals through his key panel, the first to take formal action on the details. A sometimes gruff, old-style Chicago politician, Rostenkowski embraced Clinton's efforts to take serious action on issues that had long been the source of deadlock. But he also knew that some parts of the program were dead ducks politically, and he moved quickly to drop them. Rostenkowski's focus on these issues was complicated by a long-running federal grand jury investigation of his personal finances, which embarrassed and distracted him but did not keep him from doing his job during Clinton's early months.

Mel Reynolds: The only freshman selected for a Ways and Means Committee slot, Reynolds worked hard to master the difficult policy and political challenges required to achieve success on that panel. He shared Rostenkowski's background as a Chicago Democrat, which had helped him to win the committee seat. But Reynolds, who is black, represented a lower-income district, and he sometimes had different priorities than the chairman did for himself and his party. As a leader of the large group of new House members and the expanded number of minority-group members, he also faced the dual tasks of learning the legislative skills in the House while seeking to remain faithful to the winds of change that helped to elect him. And he worked to be an unflagging ally of Clinton.

George Mitchell: As the Senate majority leader, the Maine Democrat faced the difficult task of managing the sometimes arcane rules of the Senate and what he called the "independent contractors" among its Democrats. As he had earlier shown with the 1990 passage of the Clean Air Act, Mitchell has a deep understanding of the major issues that face Congress and an extraordinary patience in achieving results with his hands-on control. Like Gephardt, he had earlier been frustrated in seeking to build Democratic consensus in Congress. But he worked hard to overcome the obstacles on Clinton's behalf. Although he emphasized his support for the new president, Mitchell sometimes was forced to resolve conflicts independently of the White House.

David Boren: A Democratic senator from Oklahoma since 1979, Boren was probably the most dramatic symbol of opposition to the new president from within his own party. He claimed that Clinton was too quick to abandon his background as a moderate "new Democrat," the cornerstone of his election campaign, and to link his fate with that of his party's liberal establishment. Boren's seat on the tax-writing Senate Finance Committee and his frequent efforts to foster bipartisanship made him a force whom Clinton and Democratic congressional leaders had to seek to accommodate. With his penchant for publicity, Boren's critics accused him of placing personal aggrandizement ahead of the interests of his own party.

Patty Murray: A freshman Democratic senator from the state of Washington, her 1992 election symbolized the public's desire for changing the Senate's business as usual. A self-styled "mom in tennis shoes" who had had limited political experience, Murray came to the Capitol intent on shaking up the system. Once she arrived, however, she burrowed herself in her work and studied the complicated procedures for getting things done, while largely avoiding the often distracting publicity. Although Murray backed most of Clinton's program, she voiced unhappiness with the managerial skills of Clinton and congressional leaders.

Howard Paster: A veteran Washington lobbyist, he became Clinton's top assistant for legislative affairs. That post placed Paster at the center of the Democrats' efforts to take quick action on the Clinton program. As a lobbyist who had worked for the United Auto Workers and later represented the Chrysler Corporation, Paster knew how to work both sides of the street in Washington and was adept at building broad coalitions. Under the intense and conflicting demands of his new job, which required him to satisfy both the White House and congressional Democrats, he found that the dynamics sometimes were difficult to manage. But his service as a liaison between the two ends of Pennsylvania Avenue made him a valuable player.

Richard Armey: The chairman of the House Republican Conference, he was one of Clinton's loudest and most persistent critics. A former economics professor from Texas, Armey was convinced that the new policies would fail and that, eventually, Republicans would reap their rewards. In articulating his case, he worked hard to garner public attention for his ideas and himself. As a new member of his party's legislative leadership, he brought a confrontational style that rubbed even some Republicans the wrong way. But he believed that one reason for his party's past failures was its reluctance to present its case aggressively.

Robert Dole: Although it would have been poor form for him to gloat over Bush's defeat, the result left Dole of Kansas—the

Senate minority leader—as the most important Republican in Washington and freed him to be the party's chief spokesman and strategist in confronting Clinton. After 32 years in Congress and two disappointing presidential campaigns, Dole was ready for the challenge. But he faced several dilemmas: How much should Republicans seek to cooperate with Clinton? Did they need to worry about condoning a return to congressional gridlock? Could his own party overcome its own divisions? And, as a veteran Washington insider, could he articulate a message that would respond to the national demand for change?

These 10 players would join many others in Congress and at the White House in drawing the lines for one of the most contentious and active periods in Washington's recent history. The effort by Clinton and the congressional Democrats to change the course of government during the new president's early months in office would be a dramatic saga with broad implications for the nation. But those results in 1993 would be significantly shaped by the dispiriting events of 1991–92, an unusually grim period for the nation's politics. To understand how Clinton fared after the election requires a review of the context in which he campaigned and took office.

Endnote

1. Bob Woodward, "Primary Heat Turned Deal Into a 'Mistake'," *The Washington Post*, Oct. 6, 1992: A1.

2

Demise of the Old Order

Bill Clinton and Albert Gore receive their party's nominations for the presidential ticket, at the July 1992 Democratic National Convention in New York. They launched a campaign keyed to the theme of change.

An End to Complacency

The context of Clinton's election was vital to the start of his presidency. Like other leading elected officials, he would be defined and limited by the nature of his candidacy and by the perceived wishes of the electorate. Although many underlying aspects of the campaign were beyond his control, he appeared to have a much sharper appreciation of the political tides than did President Bush, and he shrewdly manipulated them to advance his cause. In distancing himself from Washington, including the discredited Congress, Clinton also succeeded in reviving the reputation of the Democratic Party, whose legislators had experienced a dismal time during Bush's final two years.

The 1992 election was held in the most negative political environment since 1980, when President Carter's failures enabled Republicans to gain control of the White House and Senate. But there were important differences between the two elections, which would have a major impact on Clinton's presidency. In 1980, which was marked by inflation and interest rates in the double digits, plus the seizing of 52 American hostages in Iran, candidate Ronald Reagan and his party's platform produced a very specific agenda for change in Washington: lower federal taxes and spending, and a more muscular foreign policy. A dozen years later, voters were demanding something new, although they were not sure what and many were unhappy about the choices offered by the two major parties. The politicians' official world in Washington, meanwhile, was collapsing around them in 1992, and they seemed powerless to respond. Even the most entrenched officeholders sought to position themselves as agents of change. But many of them were far from convincing. The 1992 campaign context was set by events—ranging from the embarrassing events surrounding the confirmation of Clarence Thomas as a Supreme Court justice to a fire-ravaged urban riot in Los Angeles—that reinforced the notion that government had become inept and powerless. According to a June 1992 Gallup Poll, 84 percent of the respondents said that they were dissatisfied with the way things were going in the United States at that time. A separate poll by CBS News and *The New York Times* found that 85 percent felt that the political system needed fundamental changes or a complete rebuilding.

In historical terms, the economically bullish and high-flying 1980s had been a political hibernation. After Carter's defeat, the public had shifted its attention from Washington and had closed its eyes to many worsening domestic problems. Exhausted by the internal divisions of the Vietnam War and by the social revolutions of the prior two decades, the nation turned inward. It ignored festering sores, such as the alarming rise in public and private debt, and the signs of a growing chasm between the rich and the poor. Presidential campaigns were run in soft hues that portrayed "morning in America" and gave little attention to serious issues. But the apparent calm was deceptive: The problems were mounting, not disappearing. Many of these issues had been swept under the political carpet as the conflicts had been deadlocked or deemed impossible to resolve. The apparent calm was a depiction not so much of a citizenry that was self-satisfied as of the paralysis between the two parties. Although the nation's history has been marked by relatively few and brief bursts of activist government, the 1980s featured an unusually deep political torpor.

The 1992 campaign would mark a jarring end to that complacency, although agreement on new directions was far from clear. But its "politics of protest" also represented a deep and abiding strain in American history. That spirit of populism dates, at least, to President Andrew Jackson in the early 19th century, and it has endured in important aspects of our political life. As defined by historian Richard Hofstadter, the populist movement is partly "an undercurrent of provincial resentments, popular and 'democratic' rebelliousness and suspiciousness, and nativism." Without this spirit of protest and reform, he added, the American system "would probably have failed to develop into the remarkable system of production and distribution that it is."[1] Various elements of 1992 American politics—from the presidential candidacies of Democrat Jerry Brown, Republican Pat Buchanan and independent Ross Perot to the voters' anger at virtually all exemplars of the public and private "establishment"—suggested that Hofstadter's analysis remains apt.

Yet, as late as the summer of 1991, the political climate was anything but volatile. President Bush, still basking politically in the afterglow of the Persian Gulf War military victory, was secure in his own party. Public-opinion polls showed his national popularity above 70 percent. By year's end, many prospective Democratic candidates (including Rep. Richard Gephardt, Sens. Albert Gore

Jr. and Jay Rockefeller, and Gov. Mario Cuomo) dropped by the wayside, intimidated by the incumbent's likely re-election and by the grueling personal demands of a presidential campaign. The economy appeared to be emerging from an extended recession, and Congress—perhaps mindful of Bush's popularity—was in a languid mood. The incumbent's defeat was about the last thing on anyone's mind. The prospect of a competitive two-candidate— much less a three-candidate—contest for the White House seemed remote.

In retrospect, the campaign's shifting dynamics and demands for change should have been no surprise. The two presidents who were elected before Bush represented facets of the populist tradition. Neither had previously held elected or appointed office in Washington. They were American originals. Carter, who had made a fetish of carrying his own suitcase and of cutting the White House heating bill, sought the office with his message, "I will never lie to you." After Nixon and the corrosive Watergate scandal, Carter promised a return to cleaner, simpler government. Judged by his administration's economic breakdowns and its foreign-policy debacle of the hostage-taking in Iran, however, his idealistic goals perhaps were no longer attainable. The election of Reagan represented a different element of protest politics—a self-styled revolt against high federal taxes and spending. Although the election of the former Hollywood actor produced a peculiar form of American royalty at the White House, Reagan never abandoned his popular anti-government tenor and outsider status, even after eight years in the seat of power. But the success of his efforts was difficult to measure. By the time he left office, taxes and spending, as a percentage of the gross national product, had changed little from when he entered. And the federal debt had tripled.

Bush made no pretense of fitting either the Carter or Reagan presidential mold. As the son of a former senator and as an official who had himself spent the better part of two decades in the corridors of power as both an elected and appointed official, he could not credibly masquerade as a revolutionary. But any president sets the tone of Washington. His four years as president were marked by a downward spiral in the public's self-confidence and in its can-do spirit. Despite greater experience in the ways of Washington than his two predecessors had, Bush as president further displayed the limits of the office's power. He governed on the premise that he could not and should not do much to change policy. The Republican presidents (Reagan, Ford and Nixon) who preceded him were activists in prodding and challenging the Democrats on Capitol Hill to produce legislation or to change their ways. The less combative Bush, on the other hand, often seemed to avoid the fight rather than to risk defeat or compromise. He also was faced with the dilemma that his party had only 175 House seats in 1989, the smallest share for any newly elected president in the 20th century and a level that would require the cooperation of Democratic leaders to act on most issues. Washington in the Bush era was a capital that operated more by gamesmanship than by conviction or by a clash of principles. Because the Democrats' could not override Bush's vetoes and the Republicans could rarely find the votes to pass their own bills, only a handful of significant bills were enacted. By 1991–92, Bush rarely bothered to meet with Democratic congressional leaders.

The White House, of course, was not the only source of public discontent. Congress was beset by its own internal problems: the unprecedented 1989 resignation under fire of House Speaker Jim Wright, the Texas Democrat; the extended investigation of the "Keating Five," five senators accused of influence peddling for Charles Keating, who was later convicted of savings-and-loan felonies; and debates over congressional pay raises, in which the public typically reacted with rage to lawmakers' secretive dealings.

This sense that Washington was fiddling while it failed to address worsening national problems contributed mightily to the raucous political environment of the 1992 campaign. The first sign of that mood came in an unusual special election in November 1991 for the Senate seat that had been vacated when Republican John Heinz of Pennsylvania died the prior April in the crash of his private airplane in a Philadelphia suburb. Even most Democrats predicted that Harris Wofford, their party's nominee, had little chance to defeat Republican Dick Thornburgh, who had served eight years as the state's governor and then became Attorney General under both Reagan and Bush. But Wofford, with the shrewd advice of political consultant James Carville, turned Thornburgh's experience against him and campaigned with an anti-Washington message on the need to shake up the political establishment. "It's time to take care of our own," Wofford told Pennsylvanians. That neo-isolationist message would soon be echoed nationwide by politicians from both parties. In advocating a shift of federal attention and resources from overseas to domestic needs, Wofford focused particularly on the need to overhaul the health-care system. Although his prescriptions for change were vague, they were enough to convince voters that he was ready to fight for them and to get government moving again. In response, Thornburgh campaigned on conventional Republican themes that had often worked during the past decade: he was experienced, tough on criminals, and tight-fisted about federal spending. But that rhetoric had become tired and had lost its punch for many voters, a strong warning to Bush and his team. Adding to the significance of Wofford's unexpected 55 percent to 45 percent victory was that Pennsylvania had elected its first Democratic senator since 1962. Clearly, something was brewing in the political stew.

The Wofford victory was particularly bad news for Bush because it shot holes in the Republicans' aging strategy that they could run as the outsiders against the evils of Washington. Although they had perfected that technique during the past decade, it was growing thin to an electorate aware that the GOP had won the last three presidential elections while the nation's problems deepened. Now, the public was warning both parties that had been responsible for running the show.

Bush's Shortcomings

Because Clinton offered a stark contrast to the incumbent in both style and substance, he gave the voters what seemed to be a real choice in the election. The bumbling Bush of the 1992 campaign was not what he had appeared to be earlier when he was in greater control of events and the political dialogue. In effect, despite some successes while in office, he allowed his opponents to demonize him while he failed to provide an effective rejoinder.

At first, Bush's approach had offered symbolic hope that he would seek cooperation with Congress. During his January 1989 Inaugural address on the west front on the Capitol, he extended his hand to both Speaker Wright and Senate Majority Leader George Mitchell, a Maine Democrat, inviting them to work with him to produce a budget agreement. Congressional Democrats welcomed the conciliatory tone from the White House, if only because of the apparent contrast to Reagan, who had rarely sought to discuss details with them. They viewed Bush as someone who understood government, and they hoped that he would work with them to make it function more effectively. Despite the Democrats' willingness to work with Bush on some issues, however, the two sides were constantly at odds because of their differences on fiscal policy. Many of them begrudged the success of his 1988 campaign, when his most memorable comment came during his acceptance speech at the Republican convention in New Orleans: "Read my lips, no new taxes." Although that line helped to cement support for his November election, it ultimately contributed to the unraveling of his presidency by exposing his own lack of convictions and his weak public support. Even during that campaign, it was already apparent that the annual federal deficit was stuck at about $150 billion, despite several years of robust economic growth. Economic experts and responsible leaders in both parties were demanding credible deficit-reduction efforts.

Those conditions set the background for the most important legislative conflict of the Bush era, when Democrats in 1990 finally found a way to skewer the president on his "no new taxes" pledge. The extended budget "summit" that summer between the White House and Congress, which Bush had requested, initially made many Democrats nervous that Republicans would again set them up as big taxers. But Democrats played their hand skillfully in the early rounds, prompting Bush to issue a statement in late June that "tax revenue increases" would be required as part of a deficit-reduction plan. Bush's move, though it was coupled with his continued insistence on a capital-gains tax cut, also produced an uproar among Republicans. They fumed that he had betrayed his 1988 pledge, jeopardized the limp economy and exposed their party to Democratic charges that the GOP is the party of the rich. Senate Minority Leader Robert Dole initially fumed that Bush's support for tax increases gave him "an Excedrin headache." Once Bush and bipartisan congressional leaders finally unveiled a deal in late September on the White House South Lawn, Republican conservatives rebelled against its modest tax increase; their votes, combined with opposition from liberal Democrats, were enough to scuttle the package. Days later, Bush decided that he had no alternative but to reopen negotiations with Democrats. Now, they had gained the leverage to extract terms more to their liking, including higher taxes on the wealthy. The political tables had turned. The Reagan era was, in effect, over.

Agreeing to the budget deal, a leading conservative commentator later said, was "the greatest mistake of the Bush presidency."

Terry Eastland, a top aide to former Attorney General Edwin Meese, added that the outcome exposed Bush's shortcomings. "Committing himself to what Washington is pleased to call 'process,' Bush failed to clarify the political and economic choices available to the nation . . . Bush thus committed his presidency to a method of seeking legislation that disdains public debate over important policy ends, relying instead on private meetings aimed at producing a Washington consensus."[2] Later, as his Republican primary opponent Patrick Buchanan attacked Bush for flip-flopping on the issue of taxes, the president turned contrite. "Listen, if I had it to do over, I wouldn't do what I did then, for a lot of reasons, including political reasons."[3] Public-opinion polls made clear the damage that Bush incurred after dropping his tax pledge. Only 9 percent of the respondents said that Bush had kept all or most of his 1988 campaign promises, according to a June 1992 *New York Times*/CBS News poll.

The 1990 budget negotiations, in which the president sought to place the national interest over factional pressures, exposed what other critics viewed as Bush's reliance on deal-making over a commitment to substance. "Relations with Congress early in his administration reflect Bush's faith in the process of government for problem resolution," wrote political scientists Kerry Mullins and Aaron Wildavsky. "Rather than charging into the presidency with a policy agenda, Bush stressed cooperation and a division of duties."[4] When combined with the conventional partisan tendencies of Democratic congressional leaders and his own limited vision on and apparent lack of interest in domestic policy, the result reinforced a sense of domestic drift. Despite success on some legislation early in his presidency—chiefly, 1990 laws on clean air, child care and the rights of the disabled—the president's relative passivity would expose him to fierce political buffeting.

Bush fared better, both with Congress and in the larger arena, in his highest-stakes foreign-policy showdown: the military conflict with Iraq. The outcome would raise Bush's international influence and his domestic popularity to record-high levels. In the longer term, however, it would not overcome his political shortcomings. After Iraq's Aug. 1, 1990, invasion of Kuwait, he worked with other foreign leaders, at the United Nations and elsewhere, to pressure Iraqi leader Saddam Hussein to remove his forces. Bush gradually tightened the noose by placing more than 500,000 allied military forces in and around Saudi Arabia and by winning U.N. approval of a series of increasingly firm demands and deadlines. Meanwhile, he sought to move on a parallel track to win domestic support by keeping congressional leaders lined up behind his efforts. At first, he was successful. In the weeks following the Iraqi invasion and Bush's resolve that the conquest of Kuwait "shall not stand," few members of Congress raised questions about the rationale or conduct for the U.S. response, nor did they leave much doubt that they would stand behind his actions. Bush's military and diplomatic steps had presented Congress with a fait accompli.

By the end of 1990, when the prospect of a military showdown grew inevitable, some congressional Democrats became more vocal in their questions and criticism of Bush's pressure tactics, urging that he withhold force pending the continuation of economic sanctions on Iraq. Senate Armed Services Committee chairman Sam Nunn warned that it would be "the wrong strategy" for U.S. forces to get bogged down in a ground war in the Mideast. But both Senate Majority Leader Mitchell and Thomas Foley, who had taken over as House Speaker, were more circumspect, and they resisted pressure to reconvene Congress in November to debate war scenarios. As the final days approached before the Jan. 15 deadline given to Iraq to abandon Kuwait, Bush's international coalition was firmly behind him and the allied forces were prepared to move against Iraq. Congressional opponents of military action, however, decided to make a last-ditch stand by demanding Senate and House votes authorizing the use of force. By narrow votes, the Senate and the House on Jan. 12 sanctioned Bush's authority to take military action. Although more than two-thirds of Democrats voted against the use of force, they took credit for the historic debate and they joined ranks behind Bush once the military conflict began four days later.

After a six-week air war and a 100-hour land war, the U.S.-led forces in Operation Desert Storm drove Iraq out of a devastated Kuwait on Feb. 28, 1991. In political terms, however, the triumph for Bush became bittersweet. The outcome in Iraq was marred by the survival of Saddam Hussein and by the dictator's subsequent attacks against factions inside that nation. Domestically, the military victory dramatized the gulf between Bush's foreign-policy success and his failures at home. When he appeared before a cheering Congress in March 1991, after the war's end, he had a rare political moment to force the nation to turn to its own problems. He failed to seize the opportunity. Instead of calling for action, for example, to address the nation's energy problems, an underlying cause of the war in

Kuwait, he told Congress to get moving on two modest initiatives, crime control and transportation funding. The first legislative goal proved unsuccessful; the second was changed substantially before enactment. For Congress, the Iraq conflict had been an embarrassing interlude: It showed both the institution's inability to be an equal partner with the president in exercising war powers and the serious misjudgment by most Democrats of the likely military scenario. But the good news for them was that the victory allowed them to return to the more comfortable ground of domestic issues. Foley and Mitchell separately predicted, at the war's end, that it would have little long-term political impact. They would be proved correct.

Bush's political malaise steadily deepened throughout 1991, from his failure to take advantage of the Gulf War victory to Wofford's victory in the Pennsylvania Senate race. His war-induced popularity in the public-opinion polls in the first half of the year masked a thinness in his support, which eventually would be eroded by the sputtering economic recovery of 1991. And unlike Reagan, Bush lacked either core convictions or a political base on which to rely during political hard times. As foes in both parties began to attack him, chiefly for his limp response to poor economic conditions, his Gallup approval score dropped from 70 percent to 39 percent in the six months leading to the New Hampshire primary, in February 1992. Faced with that formidable political obstacle, he eventually resorted to attacking a convenient scapegoat: the Democratic-controlled Congress. During a June 1992 speech to the Texas Republican convention, he said that some people had asked him, "Why can't you bring the same kind of purpose and success to the domestic scene as you did in Desert Shield and Desert Storm?" The answer, Bush told his receptive audience, was, "I didn't have to get permission from some old goat in the United States Congress to kick Saddam Hussein out of Kuwait. That's the reason." Republicans believed that he had selected a very vulnerable target to campaign against as he sought to rehabilitate his own weak standing.

Anti-incumbency Strikes Capitol Hill

Whatever Bush's political problems as the 1992 election approached, they paled by comparison with the woes facing Congress. In April 1992, a Gallup Poll found that only 17 percent

approved the way Congress was doing its job, a drop from 49 percent in June 1991. Such disdain was nothing new. Congress has
long been the nation's whipping boy, a target for comedians and
other social commentators. Typically, however, its members could
distance themselves from the fallout by pointing to their own
deeds, especially those that benefit their constituents, and by attacking the problems in Washington. In this case, however, the
self-inflicted wounds were harder to ignore. Facing this hostile
mood, many lawmakers simply decided to walk away rather than
defend the congressional misdeeds. The 1992 campaign would take
place in a different political climate.

Two disparate events served to focus public attention and to
galvanize the anti-Congress sentiment. The first came in October
1991, when the nation became transfixed and divided by the Senate
Judiciary Committee's hearings on the Supreme Court nomination
of Clarence Thomas. The televised airing of the charges by law
professor Anita Hill that Thomas sexually harassed her launched
an unprecedented national soap opera that ultimately resulted in
an adverse judgment on the Senate more than on the two protago-
nists. In the midst of that conflict, reports emerged that House
members had been abusing privileges at their private House bank.
After an extensive internal investigation, it was revealed that more
than 300 current and former members had written overdrafts on
their personal accounts. The "check-bouncing" allegations, on the
heels of earlier public outrage over congressional pay raises, would
become the final straw for a public convinced that Congress had
become a pampered institution whose members had lost touch
with the real world. Unlike more complex scandals, such as the loss
of tens of billions of taxpayer dollars in the savings-and-loan industry, anyone who kept a checkbook could understand the apparent
abuses at the House bank. And the lawmakers were not very convincing as they sought to defend their actions. Voters would soon
gain their revenge.

The first victim of the House bank scandal was Rep. Charles
Hayes, a Chicago Democrat, whose inclusion on the initial list of
24 members was revealed by reporters three days before his March
17 primary. He had written 716 bad checks in the 39-month period
reviewed by the Ethics Committee. The 74-year-old Hayes, an obscure former labor-union official, found himself the victim of a
whirlwind of bad publicity that he could not control. He lost his
contest to Bobby Rush, a Chicago alderman who campaigned on

the need for change and criticized Hayes for being out of touch with his low-income district. In the following weeks, dozens of other members who had each written hundreds of bad checks either announced their retirement or prepared for a difficult campaign. But many lawmakers would not be spared. Typical was Democrat Beryl Anthony of Arkansas, who wrote 109 overdrafts. Despite his friendship with Bill Clinton and his seat on the influential House Ways and Means Committee, he unexpectedly lost his primary in June to Arkansas Secretary of State Bill McCuen, whose chief theme was the need to clean up Congress. To a public increasingly disenchanted by their elected officials, the bad checks had become a convenient symbol for the anti-incumbency fever.

Congress and campaigns for congressional offices usually play second fiddle in a presidential-election year. Occasionally in recent elections, such as in 1980, there have been "coattail" elections, in which a landslide presidential victory helps to increase the number of seats for the winner's party. More typically, voters have been content to ratify the performance of their local lawmaker, regardless of party. On occasion, Senate contests have provided real competition; but even those races have mostly been driven by personalities or local conditions rather than by ideology or the national context of congressional goals and achievements. In 1992, however, many members in the Senate and House found to their discomfort that they were being judged on the basis of the public's hostility toward Congress. For many of them, that was a jarring and profound shift for which they saw little immediate recourse. "We, as a nation and in Congress, don't want to face the real challenges," said Rep. Charles E. Schumer, a New York Democrat, at the time. "We tend to find scapegoats." Changes in the media, especially television, have accentuated the focus on "blame and trivialization," he added.

Outside of Washington, voters were saying that it was time for change. In 1990 the popular movement to impose term limits for legislators in many states, including California, had revealed a reversal of the entrenched power of incumbency. These proposals had special appeal to many voters who felt disgusted with government but were unable to affect the performance of any legislators except their own. Although the national proponents of the idea were chiefly conservatives who were venting their ire on Democratic-controlled legislatures, some liberal advocates joined the cause because they, too, were tiring of business as usual. The success of the referenda was also a warning to aging lawmakers and their aides who had become permanent fixtures in the halls of government. Although most of the ballot referenda were directed at state lawmakers, Speaker Foley successfully mounted the barricades in 1991 to defeat a limitation on service by members of Congress from his home state of Washington.

Another reason for the unusually intense public focus on its internal operations was the failure of Congress to address the many issues facing the nation during the Bush presidency. Democratic leaders responded that they were blocked and frustrated by Bush's effective use of his veto pen; during his four years in office, he vetoed 46 bills and Congress overrode only one of them—a bill reimposing regulation of cable television. But the Democrats compounded their problems by failing to agree internally on their own agenda and by failing to take advantage of their legislative majorities to press persistently for new proposals. On many issues, they were slow to act. When they did move, often they were divided or they took the course of least resistance.

Perhaps the most stark example of the Democrats' missed opportunities came on health-care policy. The rising cost and declining availability of quality care were growing social problems for tens of millions of Americans during the early 1990s. Despite Bush's occasional rhetoric about the need for action, he did not send a comprehensive proposal to Congress in his four years. The Democrats did not fare much better, although their failure to pass a new health-care program did not result from a lack of trying by their congressional leaders. Despite extensive meetings, Senate Majority Leader Mitchell and House Speaker Foley met similar problems when they separately assembled the major Democratic players, including the chief committee and subcommittee chairmen with jurisdiction over health care. In each case, the Democrats could not even agree internally on a bill to bring before their chamber for a vote. Further action would have to wait until after the presidential election. This failure to meet public demand for a revised health-care system was further evidence of the difficulty of enacting major legislation without presidential leadership.

These and other failures to agree on policies contributed to what became widely known by 1992 as the Washington "gridlock." Disagreements on other issues ranging from taxes to crime to bank regulation left Congress spinning in circles with little to show other than more rhetoric and suspicion. Lawmakers could not do much more than wring their hands about their institutional distress. "Things are much more complicated in the society, not just in Congress," Speaker Foley told reporters at a breakfast in late 1991. "We are in a more participatory society. . . . The acceptance of hierarchy and authority is much less clear."

Walking Away from Congress

As the 1992 congressional campaign began, it was unclear whether the combination of the many internal problems had reached the critical mass required for election-day combustibility. But the national cynicism toward Congress obviously had soured both the voters and their elected officials. "There's a veritable feeding frenzy out there," said Rep. Dennis Eckart, an Ohio Democrat, in late 1991, "and the Congress is the first entree on the menu." The anger about Congress was just as strong inside the Capitol as it was at the grass-roots level. "Most people come here highly motivated to do good," said Rep. Vin Weber, a Minnesota Republican. "But divided government forces lowest-common-denominator solutions and drains the energy out of people. You are forced into a defensive mechanism to avoid making things worse." The decisions by Eckart and Weber to retire in 1992 were dramatic evidence that profound change was in the air; each was little more than 40 years old, had served 12 years and had already embarked on a promising congressional career.

Eckart and Weber were among the 67 House members who voluntarily gave up their office in 1992, the highest total since the House increased to 435 members in 1912. Also fueling the high turnover was the once-a-decade national reapportionment of the House resulting from the 1990 Census; those shifts, in turn, caused major redistricting shifts in many states, which opened the door to a considerable change in partisan balance. By the time that the voters had selected their party nominees for House seats in the 50 states, another 19 members had lost their primary campaigns for renomination. That left 57 Democrats and 29 Republicans who had become lame ducks who would not return after the election. (By contrast, an average of 36 House members had declined to seek or failed to win renomination in each election between 1982 and 1990.) There were many causes for the high turnover. Because of the unusually light retirement rate between 1984 and 1990, the average length of service for House members in 1991 exceeded six terms, the highest in the nation's history.[5] For the increased number of lawmakers over 70 years of age, the grueling pace and the frustrations of the job were reasons not to face the added rigors of redistricting. A related factor for some of these members was the enticement provided by the "grandfather clause." That law, originally enacted in January 1980, barred House members first elected after that date from pocketing the surplus in their campaign funds and also set a departure deadline for members who had been elected before that date and wanted to keep their surplus campaign funds. That final deadline, which had previously been extended, was the 1992 election; it forced dozens of lawmakers to choose between staying in office or keeping the hundreds of thousands of dollars in contributions that many had legally accumulated.

As members lined up to retire, they offered a variety of reasons. Rep. Raymond McGrath, a New York Republican, said that he wanted to spend time at the Little League games of his son rather than of his constituents. Rep. Ed Feighan, an Ohio Democrat, departed with some bitterness over the political climate and the feeling that the job was no longer worth the effort. "I have never had to endure such a mean-spirited, ugly and dehumanizing atmosphere as the one which now prevails in Washington," Feighan said in announcing his retirement. It was probably no coincidence that he was among the members with the most overdrafts (397 checks) at the House bank. But, ironically, New York Democrat Matthew McHugh, who had chaired the Ethics Committee investigation of the bank, offered a similar rationale for his unexpected retirement; "I will admit to some pain and frustration when I find myself frequently put in the position of defending my character simply for being a member of Congress," McHugh said in his retirement statement. Some, like Dante Fascell of Florida and William Broomfield of Michigan (respectively the chairman and ranking Republican on the Foreign Affairs Committee) had passed age 70; each said that he wanted to enjoy his retirement years. Still others, like Pennsylvania Republican Richard Schulze and Michigan Democrat Howard Wolpe, found that their seats had been largely eviscerated because of redistricting and that they lacked either the desire to seek a new constituency or the prospect of emerging a winner.

Similar patterns prevailed in the Senate. Of the 35 senators facing re-election, seven retired and one other lost his primary campaign. Republicans Jake Garn of Utah and Warren Rudman of New Hampshire had had enough of the job, and they saw the opportunity to retire and make more money in the private sector. Others, like Democrats Kent Conrad of North Dakota and Timothy Wirth of Colorado, were relatively young, but they indicated that they suffered from a similar form of professional burn-out that led many House members to retire. After he announced his retirement, Conrad said, envious senators approached him and said "they wished that their [own state's election] filing deadline had not passed. . . . They're angry." (Ironically, Conrad changed his mind later in 1992 and decided to stay in the Senate, successfully seeking the seat of fellow North Dakota Democrat Quentin Burdick after he died in September.) For Alan Cranston of California, there were the combined effects of advanced age, ill health and the severe embarrassment that resulted after the Senate Ethics Committee voted in 1991 to reprimand him following its lengthy investigation of influence peddling by Charles Keating, the savings-and-loan executive who was later imprisoned for his swindling that cost the federal Treasury more than two billion dollars.

These departures and the infusion of new members in 1993 would generate a changed climate inside Congress and subsequent efforts to fix its ailments. Reformers hoped that the huge turnover also would become an effective, self-correcting alternative to more structured term limits, which Congress would not vote for itself.

The Voters Speak

If the record number of retirees was a congressional confession that something was amiss, many voters added their own unhappy testimony. The victims came from both parties and across the ideological spectrum. What most of the defeated lawmakers had in common was the sense by the public that they had been in Washington too long and had lost touch back home. This second round of departures, which was anything but voluntary, hit Washington even harder because re-election rates had been so high in recent elections. In the House, the 19 members who lost in their party primary and 24 more who were defeated in November were a

larger total than in any election since 1974. The five defeated senators were not so high in historical terms. But the total of 14 newly
elected senators was the highest since 1980.

An early warning came when Sen. Alan Dixon, an Illinois
Democrat who had become a political fixture in his home state,
was ousted in a three-way primary in March. He was the victim of
at least three major factors—his 1991 vote for Clarence Thomas to
the Supreme Court, which provoked unusually intense opposition
from local women; the challenge of wealthy Chicago lawyer Albert
Hofeld, a political novice, who spent millions of his own dollars in
an advertising campaign to exploit Dixon's weaknesses; and the
underdog candidacy of Carol Moseley-Braun, an underfinanced
black woman, who was the first major 1992 candidate to exploit the
public demand for change. Braun's victory and her subsequent success in November, the first ever by a black woman seeking a Senate
seat, were dramatic evidence of the winds of change. Another notable result in the Illinois Democratic primary came when Mel
Reynolds defeated Rep. Gus Savage in his third challenge to the
incumbent. Reynolds campaigned against Savage's ineffectiveness
in Washington and his failure to address the serious problems in
his low-income district on Chicago's South Side, where two-thirds
of the voters were black. "This was a classic case that the incumbent wasn't doing his job and doesn't deserve to be there,"
Reynolds said after his victory.

Another four House members suffered a pre-election ouster
when they lost renomination battles against another incumbent in
a redistricting-forced contest. Because these campaigns matched
lawmakers who had long worked closely with each other, they often were unusually bitter contests that typically showed local connections were more useful than Washington effectiveness. In
Illinois, for example, their state's loss of two House seats merged
Democrats Bill Lipinski and Marty Russo into a new district in
Chicago's white ethnic communities. Although Russo's membership on the Ways and Means Committee made him far better
known in the Capitol, Lipinski had worked effectively during his
decade in the House to bring federal grants to his district. Lipinski
effectively used that neighborhood appeal and the old-style political machine that he headed as a Democratic ward committee
chairman to portray Russo as an interloper with an expensive
home in the suburbs. Russo responded by pointing to his role as a
leading advocate for health-care reform and by attacking his oppo-

nent for driving a foreign-made car. But Lipinski won 58 percent of the vote.

Incumbent match-ups were just the tip of the iceberg of the traumatic change resulting from the redistricting process. With its impact compounded by the other forces at play in 1992, the once-a-decade cycle of events became more turbulent and painful for more House members than had typically been the case. Literally dozens of incumbents found themselves at serious risk as many states underwent radical changes in their district lines, especially in the largest states. Among the major factors that shaped redistricting results were broader public participation, more sophisticated use of computer and map-drawing technology, heightened partisanship, the increased importance of the Voting Rights Act as enforced by the Department of Justice, and finally, the assertive role of federal and state courts abetted by private attorneys.

Take California, for example, the largest state and one with a history of bitter redistricting battles. After the 1990 Census found that its population had grown from 23.7 million in 1980 to 29.8 million, the national reapportionment increased the Golden State's House members from 45 to 52, the largest delegation in the nation's history. The 1982 Democratic-controlled redistricting, which had left deep partisan scars, gave California Democrats between 26 and 28 seats from 1982 to 1992; few seats in either party were more than slightly vulnerable at any time during the decade. When Republican Pete Wilson was elected governor in 1990, he set a fair redistricting as one of his top priorities. When the Democratic-controlled legislature sent him three separate redistricting maps in October 1991, he vetoed each of them because they favored the Democrats and they did not produce enough competitive seats. When the legislature failed to override his veto, the state Supreme Court took control and appointed an academic expert as "special master." The impact of the map that he drew and the Court subsequently ratified was widely expected to be a Republican bonanza. California Democrats such as Rep. Howard Berman conceded, after the ruling, that the GOP probably would increase from 19 seats to at least 26. But, as throughout the nation, the November election in California produced surprising twists and turns. Democrats ran unexpectedly well in new suburban districts and added five new women to their House ranks; they ended with a 30–22 majority in that delegation. Regardless, the more competitive seats drawn by the 1991–92 redistricting were likely to make members of both parties more vulnerable and to produce changes in the partisan mix for California's House delegation throughout the remainder of the decade.

Another significant change in the 1992 redistricting, which would have a big impact on the distribution of power in the House and the way that business gets done, was the increase in the number of seats won by blacks and Hispanics. This development was abetted by a little-noted 1982 change in the federal Voting Rights Act of 1965, as subsequently interpreted by the Justice Department and the federal courts. Wherever possible and however oddly shaped, states were required to draw a new district with a sizable minority-group population that could elect its own House member. Support for this view came from a coalition with odd political parentage: Black and Hispanic groups that have long complained about a lack of political power combined forces in many states with Republican redistricting experts who saw the opportunity to deprive white Democrats of a major share of their base vote and to make many suburban districts more definitively Republican. With added pressure from federal judges, virtually all of the new "minority-majority" seats that could have been drawn in 1992 were, in fact, drawn. The result increased the number of House seats with a black voting plurality from 22 in 1990 to 36, many of them in the rural South, where black political power had been slower to mature; the number of seats with a Hispanic population majority rose from 10 to 19. (Hispanic voting registration figures are much smaller than the population in many areas and are more difficult to calculate.)

Candidates as Agents of Congressional Change

These extraordinary changes resulting from the anti-incumbent climate and the new redistricting landscape helped to produce many more competitive contenders than usual for House and Senate seats in 1992. Individuals without political experience or skills enthusiastically lined up to seek offices. Candidates who would have been dismissed as political jokes in other years suddenly seemed credible. As skilled politicians—both incumbents and challengers—examined the hostile environment to prepare for the 1992 campaign, they concluded that the two parties had broken down at the highest levels. Republicans, disillusioned with their president's ambivalent and spiritless style, worried that their failure to accomplish much or to even agree on a prescription for the nation's ills jeopardized the continuation of their reign. Congressional Democrats, in disarray after 12 years out of the White House and with their discredited leaders working ineffectively to set the agenda, struggled to offer new messages while preserving their shrinking base. The public understandably was turned off by the shenanigans in Washington. Candidates had to present themselves as agents of change who would offer a new approach, either in substance or in style.

In distancing themselves from the status quo, candidates recognized the need to reinforce their grass-roots connections. "People get fed up with politicians who have lost touch with reality," said Bob Filner, a history professor at San Diego State University who had entered local Democratic politics as a civic activist. He won a new California seat in the House by emphasizing his plan for active constituent service. In the state of Washington, Democrat Patty Murray, who had served less than a term as a state representative, appeared to have no chance of winning when she launched her candidacy against Democratic Sen. Brock Adams. But her own determination plus a startling series of events—starting with the unexpected retirement by Adams after a lengthy newspaper story with sexual-harassment allegations from local women—finally turned the contest her way. Murray emphasized that she wanted to change the Senate's elitist character. When the public watched the Senate Judiciary Committee hearings on Clarence Thomas, she said, "they didn't feel that these people are tangible and understand public problems."

The political map appeared tailor-made for innovative approaches by candidates and voters as they tried to define and send their messages. But cutting through the cynicism and anger would be no easy task. In contrast to recent contests in which political professionals had driven the process, the 1992 campaign was one in which the voters were saying that they were ready to take back their government. The following prototypical candidate helps to illustrate the new political breezes.

In Pennsylvania, 40-year-old Ron Klink was well known in the Pittsburgh area as a weekend anchorman on KDKA, the most-watched television station in that region. He had spent much of his life talking to politicians as part of his work, but he had never been active in party organizations. Nor did he consider running for office until early 1992, when his unhappiness about the quality of the local public officials started to boil over. "I had an intense personal dissatisfaction with what was happening to this region—politically and economically—and an intense anger with the caliber of leadership that I have seen in Congress," he recounted. Armed with two aides and a budget of less than $100,000, he challenged in the April primary Rep. Joe Kolter, who was little known nationally but seemed to be entrenched locally. Klink's job became easier after a disgruntled Kolter aide released a recording in which Kolter cynically called himself a "political whore" who would do anything to get re-elected. "Just walk in [to a funeral home]," Kolter said, "and, if I faintly remember who these people are, just walk in and shed a little tear and sign my name and take off." With such help, it was no wonder that Klink won with 45 percent of the vote in the four-candidate Democratic primary and Kolter finished third with 19 percent.

But Klink's success depended on being more than an alternative to Kolter. A high school graduate, Klink said that he gained the voters' support because they were "comfortable" with him after his 14 years on local television and because he released a 37-page document outlining his agenda for restoring the economic vitality of the Pittsburgh area. "Let's start to work," he told the voters. His success was based on vigor and a promise of change. Klink was not troubled that his lack of political experience might make it difficult for him if he were elected to Congress. "You carry on the battle day in and day out," he said. "It's salesmanship. Ron Klink can do that better than can Joe Kolter."

Some incumbents proved far more skillful than the hapless Kolter in countering the unhappy public mood. Elsewhere in Pennsylvania, for example, Republican Arlen Specter sought re-election to his Senate seat by aggressively selling his accomplishments for his state during the previous dozen years. Facing Democrat Lynn Yeakel, a well-financed activist for women's causes who emphasized her opposition to Specter's harsh cross-examination of Anita Hill during the Clarence Thomas hearings, Specter turned the campaign focus to what he had done for countless local governments and business and labor groups across Pennsylvania. "I have been responsible for more change in Pennsylvania," said Specter, as he sought to turn his opponent's message to his favor. "When I talk about what I can do in the future, it's more than a political cliche."

Yeakel also suffered because of her political inexperience in dealing with the array of campaign issues and the state's diverse interest groups. Her 51 percent to 49 percent defeat, especially disappointing to national women's groups, was a testament to Specter's survival skills and to the superior fundraising of GOP incumbents, who carefully kept their distance from the failing Bush. Specter's tactics and the outcome also represented a striking Republican turnaround from the Wofford–Thornburgh contest a year earlier. Other Republican senators who barely retained their seats in the face of stiff November 1992 challenges were Alfonse D'Amato of New York and Bob Packwood of Oregon. As it turned out, if Democrats had won these three elections, all of which were in states won handily by Clinton, they would have initially gained the 60 Senate seats that would have permitted a unified party control of the Senate agenda by shutting off Republican filibusters.

The final results featured fewer Election Day defeats for senators and House members than had been predicted by campaign experts in both parties—two for each party in the Senate (including Democrat Wyche Fowler of Georgia, who lost a disputed runoff to Republican Paul Coverdell three weeks after the election) and 16 Democrats and eight Republicans in the House. Of the House members who lost seats, many were victims of their own complicity in the anti-incumbency mood. Veteran Democrats Tom Downey of New York and Mary Rose Oakar of Ohio, for example, had many overdrafts at the House bank; Nicholas Mavroules of Massachusetts, an active lawmaker on defense issues, suffered from his pre-election indictment on bribery charges. Others faced uphill battles because of redistricting, including veteran Republican Bill Green of New York City, who had many new voters in his heavily Democratic Manhattan district.

The 110 new House members (63 Democrats and 47 Republicans) were the highest freshmen total since 1948. Many of them immediately proclaimed themselves as agents of change. But the Democrats' net loss of 10 House seats would mean that their party's new president would not have much breathing room. Even in the Senate, where there would be 14 new faces (following the resignations of Vice President Gore and Treasury Secretary Lloyd Bentsen), Democrats were disappointed by their failure to change the partisan balance. One major effect would be that Republicans would have considerable parliamentary leverage to use a filibuster threat to thwart some of the Democrats' goals.

As they endured the months of campaign combat, insiders and outsiders alike understood that they were on the threshold of major change in politics and Congress. The large numbers of new players and the public demand for action would force a move beyond the status quo and toward political accountability. But not all incumbents had a hard time winning re-election in 1992. Despite the jarring changes surrounding them, the unremarkable facts were that most Senate and House members decided to seek another term and most of them proved to be successful. "I feel somewhat apologetic about what I am going to tell you," Rep. Barney Frank, a Massachusetts Democrat, wrote to his supporters during the campaign. "I do not plan to quit Congress. . . . I understand the frustration that many members feel at their inability to bring about social and economic changes. I share that frustration, but I do not understand how quitting would make it easier for me to accomplish them." Frank won re-election with 72 percent of the vote. But, with his active support for causes such as gays in the military, he was anything but a proponent of the status quo.

The Presidential Campaign

The presidential campaign, as usual, captured far more public attention than did the congressional contests. In many respects, it was a strange contest. Clinton kept bouncing back from repeated assaults on his character by reporters and his political opponents. After fits and starts, Ross Perot spent more than $60 million of his own money to finance his unconventional independent campaign, according to his reports to the Federal Election Commission. And once he finally rolled up his sleeves, President Bush said little about what he had accomplished in his first term. Each of the three struggled to promise change, without directly providing much detail, and to identify himself most firmly in opposition to the status quo in Washington.

The work product and the political environment of the newly elected Congress would be significantly influenced, of course, by the voters' selection of a new president. Changes in the rules for presidential primaries and the selection of convention delegates during the past two decades and the diminishing of the power of party barons have reduced the role played by most members of

Congress. Although few would say so publicly, many Democratic lawmakers were ambivalent about the presidential election. True, they had grown frustrated by dealing with Republican presidents for 12 years. But some Democrats had grown comfortable with the fruits of divided government. Not only could they stage press conferences and hearings to assail the other party for whatever ailed the nation, but they also could depict themselves in Washington as the chiefs within their own party; the private sector and other political leaders would have to pay proper homage to them and to their views. That influence would be diminished if a Democrat won the White House and became the leader of their party.

From a Capitol Hill view, Clinton's early success in the primaries fueled additional doubts. Although the Arkansas governor had dabbled in national politics, he was little known by most members of Congress. What they knew left many of them unenthusiastic. He had been a founder of the Democratic Leadership Council, the centrist group that sought to recast the party's liberal image. As the primaries began, Clinton went out of his way to separate himself from the mess in Washington and to blame both parties for the problems. "Back in 1990, I was attacking the way Congress was doing its business," he said during an ABC-TV interview in March 1992. "I ran the first ads against the congressional pay raise in this campaign. I have been for change." When he joined the national bandwagon criticizing Congress, a few congressional Democrats who viewed his actions as gratuitous posturing privately made known their displeasure. But they had little muscle to bring Clinton into line, and most Democrats decided not to rock the boat. "Clinton's criticism of Congress doesn't bother us," said Sen. David Pryor of Arkansas, his long-time friend. "From one politician to another, we understand the environment in which he is working."

While Clinton methodically wrapped up the nomination in the spring—as two Senate Democrats, Tom Harkin and Bob Kerrey, made unimpressive showings—he made only limited efforts to reach out to his would-be allies in Washington. Unlike leading Democratic candidates in recent years, he did not spend much time pursuing endorsements on Capitol Hill. Encouraged by campaign aide Carville, who had helped to elect Wofford in Pennsylvania, Clinton decided to keep his headquarters in Little Rock for the remainder of the campaign and to keep congressional leaders away from attention at the party's July convention in New York

City. These were signals to both the voters and the party pros that Clinton wanted to be a "new Democrat," both in his philosophy and style. Although they welcomed some of his message, including his call to lower taxes for the middle class, and they mostly approved his choice of Tennessee Sen. Gore as his running mate, many congressional Democrats worried that he was not sufficiently attuned to their political needs. A Texas Democrat in Congress complained about the absence of "a comfort level" with Clinton. An aide to a top House Democrat referred during the party's convention to "a culture gap" between the Clinton–Gore ticket and Democrats who subscribe to the need to bolster the nation's manufacturing base. "Gore is animated on global warming but not on issues that interest people in places like Chicago and Parma, Ohio," the Democrat said. But Clinton backers responded at the time that they were not worried about the doubters. "Clinton has said that Congress would turn this country on a dime if it had someone to lead it," said George Stephanopoulos, one of his top aides.

In politics, nothing succeeds like success. When Democrats saw the glowing public reaction to the masterfully staged convention and to the subsequent Clinton–Gore bus caravan from New York to the nation's heartland, the doubts on Capitol Hill began to subside. Their sense of optimism grew further as they observed the Republican convention in Houston during August, where conservatives dominated the party's message and paid little attention to the concerns of swing voters who had become alienated by the GOP's record on the economy. Although Bush leveled harsh attacks on the inexperience and personal credentials of his 46-year-old opponent, he did not give the national audience enough reason to believe that conditions would change measurably in a second term. Clinton also received a major boost during the summer when Perot unexpectedly announced that he would abandon his independent candidacy for president. That decision, which Perot declared on the final day of the Democratic convention, was a double dose of positive news for Clinton: It meant that the anti-Bush vote would not be split. In addition, Perot's dramatic statement included positive comments about Clinton's promises of change.

Clinton also ingratiated himself with Democrats in Congress because his campaign message in the closing weeks was one with which many of them agreed. His support for a middle-class tax cut and his call for combining government activism with individual responsibility provided common political ground with many of them.

In fact, they had worked for months and years to develop that partisan appeal as they sought to respond to Bush. And some powerful Capitol Hill Democrats developed amicable personal ties with Clinton during the fall campaign. House Ways and Means Committee chairman Dan Rostenkowski regularly sent briefing papers to Clinton about the complex tax, trade and health issues that his committee handles, while House Energy and Commerce Committee chairman John Dingell worked actively with the candidate to assure that his vital home state of Michigan voted for Clinton. Other congressional Democrats, likewise, became more eager to appear with Clinton in their home towns during the fall campaign as polls showed that he was maintaining a comfortable lead over Bush. Even Perot's belated Oct. 1 announcement that he had changed his mind—and became a formal candidate—did not diminish the Democrats' growing enthusiasm. They were impressed with Clinton's mastery of the domestic policy agenda and with his gritty campaign style that allowed him to rebound from potentially damaging incidents. Democratic senators, worn out by dealing with two Republican presidents, nearly bubbled with enthusiasm as they discussed the prospects of Clinton's election. "I have a sense of excitement," said Sen. Paul Sarbanes of Maryland in mid-October. "We have been through 12 years of sheer torture. . . . Now, I think that we can show the country that we can govern."

But the campaign also sent clear warning signals to Congress. With his drumbeat attack on how Washington works, Perot sought to exploit public disgust with congressional malfeasance and the bipartisan gridlock that had prevented the nation from addressing its problems. "The American people are good, but they have a government that is a mess," he said when he launched his candidacy. Although his level of support in the polls, which earlier exceeded 30 percent, declined as the election neared, his final 19 percent share was the highest by any candidate outside the two major parties since former President Theodore Roosevelt won 27 percent of the vote as the Progressive Party candidate in 1912.

When Election Day ultimately gave Clinton his impressive victory, with 370 electoral votes to Bush's 168, congressional Democrats were delighted, but many of them were numb. The prospect of a Bush defeat had been so unlikely to them a few months earlier that they had made little preparation—either legislatively or psychologically—for their party's return to the White House. As these lawmakers would soon learn, their role would significantly shift and they could look to the Clinton team to take the initiative on legislative proposals. But it surely would take time for them to adjust to their new partnership status with the president and to the prospect that they could pass legislation with an expectation that it could soon become law, rather than face a presidential veto.

The lessons of 1992 are important for political participants and observers alike. For the presidency, the election was a compelling national call for leadership and courage; the public had tired of its leader, who was afraid to lead and would not keep an important promise. In Congress, the smugness that can result when lawmakers do not have to worry about competitive elections back home can be an institutional hazard that the voters ultimately will cure. And, for the voters, the verdict was clear: it was time to end the stalemate in Washington and to address the nation's problems with some new approaches. Divided government, as it had become known, was not a practical long-term method of governing for either the president or Congress. Now, Democrats had a mandate to show that they could perform.

Endnotes

1. Richard Hofstadter, *The Age of Reform* (New York: Vintage Books, 1955), 5, 18.
2. Terry Eastland, "Bush's Fatal Attraction" in *Policy Review* (Washington: The Heritage Foundation) Spring 1992, pp. 20–24.
3. Ann Devroy, "Breaking Tax Pledge a Mistake, Bush Says," *The Washington Post,* March 4, 1992: A1.
4. Kerry Mullins and Aaron Wildavsky, "The Procedural Presidency of George Bush," in *Political Science Quarterly* (New York: Academy of Political Science) Spring 1992, pp. 31, 49.
5. Norman J. Ornstein, Thomas E. Mann and Michael J. Malbin, *Vital Statistics on Congress, 1991–92* (Washington: Congressional Quarterly Inc., 1992), 19–20.

3

The New Order and Its Mandate

During their first post-election visit to Washington, Clinton and Gore visited the Capitol and were greeted by House Speaker Thomas Foley. Although the president-elect was short on the details of his new program, Democrats warmly received him.

The Transition Grows in Size

The 11 weeks between a presidential election and the Inauguration have gained greater importance in recent decades and a political rhythm all their own. For the intellectually probing Clinton, the transition period was like an advanced academic seminar. He used the time and his staff to conduct an intensive review of federal operations and his possible options for addressing major problems. But he did not have to make any decisions other than to choose personnel. As later became apparent, this pattern of extensive review before he takes an action probably ill-served Clinton's early months in office. Although he made a faster start in defining his top priorities than have many other presidents, the results of his preparation fell short of the expectations for when he took office that he himself had set with the public.

Any presidential transition is, in effect, a tale of two presidents. Despite the sparse contact between the Bush and Clinton camps between November and January, the reins of government were transferred in the smooth fashion that has marked the nation's history. After his victory, the ebullient Clinton went to work with his congressional allies on the formidable task of creating a new government. He shared with them a genuine enthusiasm for tackling what lay ahead. But several factors compounded his challenge: his limited and not especially warm pre-election dealings with Congress and its folkways, the ambiguity of important facets of his campaign agenda, and the inexperience of most Democrats in managing the vast federal apparatus. In addition, the Democrats' weak results in the congressional elections would make it difficult for them to claim that the vote represented a national mandate for their party as a whole. As Jan. 20 arrived and much of the new administration's direction remained uncharted, the president-elect and his top aides complained that they lacked enough time to complete all the preparations that they had wanted to make. President Bush, meanwhile, had a much different view of the interregnum. He languished as a lame duck during the period while his successor prepared for the Inauguration. As his top aides sought new jobs and his successor prepared plans for major change, Bush surely felt the pain of public rejection and of his own authority slipping away. He left no doubt that he viewed the transition as too long and that he would have preferred to leave office much sooner. "Bush is finding the 11-week hiatus between his defeat and Bill Clinton's inauguration stripped of splendor, but still plenty isolated," wrote *The New York Times*. "Moody, fidgety, maybe a little bitter, he has fallen out of the hyperactive, quirky character that even critics found endearing."[1]

Like other aspects of the federal government, the activities and complexity of the transition have grown sizably in recent decades. Aided by a grant of $3.5 million from the federal Treasury (plus an estimated $28 million from the private sector to subsidize his inauguration), Clinton established large office staffs for the two months in both Little Rock and Washington. By contrast, when John Kennedy prepared to take over the presidency in 1961, he had no taxpayer money and only a handful of advisers. (In 1963, Congress passed the Presidential Transition Act, providing funds to help both the incoming and outgoing teams.) Regardless of how it functions, the essential purpose of a presidential transition is to allow the new president to define his goals and to hit the ground running when he takes office. The transfer of power is filled with both peril and opportunity, according to scholar Carl Brauer: "It is a brief and unique period, one in which those who are about to take over the largest, most complex, and important institution in the world must consider in much more concrete and specific terms than is possible in a campaign what they want to accomplish and how, when, and with whom they hope to accomplish it."[2] The fruits of those efforts typically become apparent both in the activities of the first few days in office and in the White House's priorities for, at least, the next several months. Indeed, the management of the pre-Inaugural period often determines the initiatives and success of a presidency.

Like his predecessors, Clinton had several basic priorities. They included the selection of his Cabinet officials and White House staff, preparation of an agenda for his initial months in office, and a switch in the political emphasis from his campaign to his hopes for governing. In addition, because Clinton had promised change in Washington and a new momentum in addressing the nation's needs, he faced the added burdens of providing direction to the nation and of bolstering public confidence. That shift would require both real and symbolic steps by the newly elected president, as he sought to rally the public—including the 57 percent of the voters who had voted for another candidate. Adding to the burden of those tasks was the personal toll that the campaign and its outcome had taken on Clinton and his advisers: the physical exhaustion and emotional strain, the uprooting of lives and families in Arkansas and elsewhere, and the need to prepare for their new homes in Washington. But the demand for change that Clinton had set in motion would give him little time to relax and recuperate. Indeed, he may have created undue expectations by the press and others. Only a week after his election, *The New York Times* ran a front-page article spotlighting Clinton's retreat to a "conspicuously deliberate" pace and his tight control of information.[3]

For Congress, the transition period also allows a period for rest and renewal, and it provides the new members an orientation period for their new lives. But they played a more passive role than did Clinton during the initial phase of reshaping government. While some would recommend new policies to him, the lawmakers would mostly react to the new president and, for the Democrats, support his goals. Although they were inclined to be supportive, most of them had revealed little commitment to his views. The chief exceptions would be the Democratic congressional leaders— House Speaker Foley, Majority Leader Gephardt and Senate Majority Leader Mitchell. They met and spoke regularly with Clinton, mostly to advise on specific plans and to offer a public display of unity within their party and the new government. But there would be no question about who was in charge. Even on a simple matter of body language, such as his positioning next to the legislators-in-chief on a podium, Clinton showed at an early point that he was the team leader. Although he would welcome recommendations from knowledgeable allies, he would make decisions on his own terms. His congressional allies provided their views, but they left with no sense of shared decision-making. "I feel comfortable that the president consulted me extensively before he made his decisions," Mitchell said after the Inauguration. "But he didn't accept every bit of advice that I gave him."

As they prepared for their own swearing in on Jan. 5, 1993, the members also sought to get the House and Senate in order with the usually routine, but vital, steps required to make their chambers operate: election of party leaders, some rewriting of internal rules and committee assignments. As the majority party in Congress, Democrats wanted to show that they were responding to voter discontent over their internal miseries of the previous two years. But they also took internal actions to encourage party discipline and to increase the prospects for quick approval of Clinton's program;

some of those steps would prompt an angry reaction from Republicans, who complained about heavy-handed tactics. Alas, it would not take much time for a return to business as usual in the sparring between the two parties on Capitol Hill. In contrast to four years earlier, however, the end of divided government meant there was little pretense that the parties would have to accommodate each other. Democrats were under pressure to produce on their own. And even many Republicans had a hard time contesting the notion that they would be mostly irrelevant on legislation, at least for the next two years.

Clinton Prepares for a Quick Start

Clinton's efforts to place an early imprint on Washington took several forms, but the goals were consistent. Whether the activities featured private sessions with members of Congress, his well-organized and highly publicized conference on the economy in Little Rock, or the glittery events during the Inaugural festivities, Clinton sought after the election to rally the public behind him and to create the framework for his early actions as president. The transition became an extension of his election campaign, but its sophisticated political tactics were modified to advance his policy goals.

Some of his plans were no surprise to anyone familiar with his campaign rhetoric. In meetings with members of Congress soon after the election, he listed health-care reform and a package of economic changes as his chief legislative priorities. Separately, Clinton aides began work on other initiatives that he could take unilaterally, such as allowing gays to serve in the military and rescinding the Reagan- and Bush-era prohibitions on government-backed steps to encourage abortion. They also prepared to abolish the White House competitiveness council, which Vice President Quayle, as chairman, had used to review enforcement of environmental laws. Clinton would soon learn that it could be one thing to make the promise and something else actually to change the way Washington works. But he and his allies wanted to prove that they could turn their rhetoric into reality. "The sense I get from the American people," he told reporters on Nov. 19 during his first post-election visit to Washington, "is they don't expect miracles of us, but they do expect progress and they do want us to work. They want the finger-pointing and the blame-placing to stop."

But deciding on the specific details of his program would become a complicated task, not least because of divisions within his own camp. What resulted, in some cases, was a conflict for control of Clinton's mind among various factions of the Democratic party. The testing took several forms. On one level, staff aides battled over ideology. On Nov. 12, Clinton appointed a 48-member transition staff with diverse demographic backgrounds. Most, though not all, of them would join the White House staff or gain another top post two months later. Al From, who had been close to Clinton for several years, was placed in charge of domestic policy for the transition staff; as president of the Democratic Leadership Council, which Clinton had chaired, From had backed a diminished federal role in domestic programs and sought to move the Democratic Party away from its most liberal views. Reaching to another perspective, Clinton named Harvard University government lecturer Robert Reich to direct economic policy during the transition. Reich, who had been a Clinton friend since they were Rhodes scholars more than two decades earlier, took a more activist view of Washington's role in encouraging economic development and help for the poor. Within weeks, Clinton named Reich as his Labor Secretary. But From—and his ideas—returned to the private sector. Although From insisted that he had not wanted a government post and that some of his ideas would gain currency in the new team, it appeared that Clinton was content not to bring his former ally into the top ranks of his administration. Another revealing example of where power would lie in the new administration came when Clinton decided to pick Donna Shalala, chancellor of the University of Wisconsin, as his Secretary of Health and Human Services; Shalala also had chaired the Children's Defense Fund, a liberal public interest group with which Clinton's wife Hillary had long been associated. Marian Wright Edelman, the founder and president of the fund, would have a major voice in shaping policies and selecting officials on the domestic side of the new administration. That became apparent when she successfully opposed the selection of former Democratic Rep. Tom Downey for a top administration position, despite support for Downey from Vice President–elect Gore. Downey had had an angry battle with Edelman on child-care legislation in 1990.

The battle for Clinton's mind also took place among outsiders not part of the Washington scene. After the chiefs of the three largest domestic automobile manufacturers and the president of the United Auto Workers visited Clinton in Little Rock on Jan. 6, they told reporters that they were pleased with the discussion of federal issues that were of special concern to their industry. Although Clinton said that he wanted cars to be more environmentally efficient, "he did not want to do anything detrimental to the auto industry," said Harold Poling, the chairman of the Ford Motor Company. Clinton—who had placed special emphasis on his election-day victory in Michigan—issued a statement the same day that lauded the meeting as a "fresh start on how business, government and labor can work together." Private-sector leaders had a more elaborate opportunity to press their views when Clinton hosted in mid-December a two-day conference. More than 300 business executives, economists and heads of interest groups joined him in what became a national seminar on the economic problems facing the nation. Although the televised meeting did little to develop a consensus on solutions, it did help to polish Clinton's reputation for policy expertise and for skillful use of the bully pulpit. The power elite gained another useful opportunity to socialize with Clinton and, in some cases, to advance private concerns when he and his family vacationed with hundreds of other politically prominent guests at an annual Christmas-week conclave at Hilton Head, South Carolina.

Clinton's chiseling of his own persona may have been the most interesting example of how the transition period served to frame the presidential portrait. As candidate, he had campaigned as an outsider who kept his distance from the old ways of Washington and of his party. Mindful of the appeal of Ross Perot, he had sought to identify himself with the middle class and to criticize special-interest groups and big companies that hired slick lobbyists. But once he was elected, Clinton's actions refuted that rhetoric. To supervise his transition, he named two wealthy lawyers, Vernon Jordan and Warren Christopher, to the top posts of chairman and director of his transition team. Both were senior partners in large law firms whose powerful corporate clients had a major stake in the plans of the new president. The potential for ethical conflicts reached deep into the transition team. After lawyers prepared rules to prevent conflicts of interest by its staff, they had to make exceptions for many Clinton advisers moving through the "revolving door." During the transition, Clinton also sought to cultivate the often self-important leaders of Washington's political and press establishments by attending fancy dinners hosted by fashionable doyennes such as Pamela Harriman, a socialite and major Democratic donor (who was later named ambassador to France), and Katharine Graham, chairman of *The Washington Post.* But Clinton also sought to instill the notion that his presidency would be connected to the grass roots by taking actions that were plainly symbolic. During his first visit to Washington, for example, he walked through a commercial district of mostly black-owned businesses, ostensibly to hear what the people had to say; his aides worked to ensure that the visit would receive extensive broadcast coverage. Later, on his entry to Washington for the Inauguration, he would take a bus ride that started at President Jefferson's home in Monticello and stopped in several rural Virginia towns. To critics who contended that Clinton was trying to have it both ways, aides said that he was seeking change without unnerving the political bigwigs. But consumer advocate Ralph Nader, for one, was not impressed. "He'll have a populist [public] relations strategy to project a good ol' boy, down home, one of the people [style]. . . . [But] he's bending over backward to constantly reassure the corporate power structure that he is not going to destabilize their entrenched power."[4]

In his many public appearances during the transition, Clinton showed that he would actively take his case to the public in order to bolster prospects that his presidency would have a successful start. While vacationing in California in November, he met former President Reagan and voiced admiration for his communications skills with the American public. Clinton said that he also hoped to replicate Reagan's record of achieving major legislative accomplishments during his early months in office. No one needed to point out the contrasts to Bush's lower-key start and style.

Even before he took office, however, Clinton suffered from his habit of waiting a long time, sometimes until the final moment, to make decisions. The starkest case was the slow pace and complexity that surrounded his selection of Cabinet members. In announcing his choices during seven Little Rock press conferences between Dec. 10 and 24, he conceded that his quest for diversity—especially racial and gender—had slowed the process. Clinton also showed a tendency to respond, sometimes querulously, to pressure from his nominal allies who sought to influence his choices. When leaders of national women's groups sent him a letter criticizing his failure to choose more women for top posts, for example, he responded with a testy admonition against "these bean counters" who were more concerned about numbers than with the "substantive impact" of the choices. In the end, his initial 18-member Cabinet included five women, four blacks and two Hispanics. In other respects, however, the Cabinet choices were anything but revolutionary and seemed to contradict his earlier promise to select a group of advisers who "look like America." Of the 18 with Cabinet-level status, 13 were lawyers; several of his top economic advisers had been wealthy businessmen. Clinton later conceded that the rush to meet his self-imposed Christmas deadline resulted in a major headache. Zoe Baird—the general counsel for Aetna Life and Casualty Co. and his first choice for Attorney General—was forced to withdraw in the midst of her confirmation hearings before the Senate Judiciary Committee because she and her husband had hired a "nanny" who did not file proper documentation with the federal government. The next day, Clinton took the blame for his failure to review her background more closely before deciding to nominate her. "I'm sorry about this," he said. "I feel very bad for [Baird's withdrawal,] but I'm responsible for it."

Clinton Meets Congress

In at least one transition focus, Clinton showed his commitment to firm and quick action. When it came to consulting the members of Congress, especially Democrats, Clinton was thorough in taking the steps required to build a cooperative working relationship. His two visits to Washington before the Inauguration—in contrast to his pre-election distance from Washington—were prompted chiefly by his scheduled meetings with an array of lawmakers, both senior power brokers and the rank and file. He also made many telephone calls to supplement those meetings. The frequent contact, similar to the way that Clinton dealt with the Arkansas legislature, had several objectives. First, it encouraged the members of Congress to view their dealings with the new administration as a team effort. After a dozen years struggling with Republican presidents, most lawmakers welcomed the notion of the open door, even if they did not always agree with Clinton's policies. If he could bring them under the same tent, Clinton believed that they would be less likely to criticize him from the outside. Second, the meetings became a forum where Clinton impressed the lawmakers with his knowledge of both the issues and the internal politics of Capitol Hill. "I have never been so impressed as with the amazing competence and self-confidence of Bill and Hillary," said Rep. Louise Slaughter, a New York Democrat. Clinton and his allies also viewed praise from Congress as a welcome signal to the public that the Washington gridlock had been broken and that Democrats could create a spirit of positive action.

The liaison started with a Nov. 15–16 meeting in Little Rock, in which Clinton, his wife—Hillary Rodham Clinton—and Vice President–elect Gore hosted the three top congressional Democratic leaders—Foley, Gephardt and Mitchell. The group, who had had no extended discussions about legislative plans during the campaign, agreed that they needed to consult regularly among themselves. When Clinton asked how often President Carter had met with Democratic congressional leaders during his presidency, Foley later recounted that he had answered that the White House hosted breakfasts every other Tuesday. Clinton responded, somewhat incredulously, "Every other Tuesday?" Then, implying that he planned more frequent regular meetings with Congress, he added that he had met every day with legislative leaders in Arkansas. What turned out to be another positive signal from the meeting came when Clinton asked the leaders for recommendations on new Cabinet members. Foley and Gephardt suggested that Clinton pick Rep. Leon Panetta of California, the chairman of the House Budget Committee, as the new director of the Office of Management and Budget. A few weeks later, Clinton announced that he had taken their advice. Although Clinton had promised just before his July nomination "an explosive 100-day action period" once he took office, both sides tried to dampen expectations of quick and dramatic action. "I will be in a hurry," Clinton said at a press conference following his initial meetings with the congressional leaders, "but I don't have an agenda which says we're going to do this in 100 days." They also voiced some differences over how to handle ethics and abortion legislation, for example, and on the need to cut the congressional payroll. But they emphasized that they planned to work together closely. "The message of this meeting is simple and clear," Gephardt said. "Gridlock is over, and cooperation and teamwork have begun."

Three days later, Clinton expanded those discussions by meeting with broader groups of congressional leaders and committee chairmen in Washington. Trailed by a large group of reporters at the Capitol, he moved easily from sessions in the Senate to the House. He had gotten to know some members—such as powerful House committee chairmen Dingell and Rostenkowski—during the campaign. For some others, he did not know much beyond their name. Among the latter was Senate Appropriations Committee chairman Robert Byrd of West Virginia, who sought to smooth over their reported differences on budget procedures. To all of them, Clinton said that he promised "an open door," a pledge that presidents sometimes find easier to embrace in theory than in fact. In a press conference whose tone was similar to the one that he and the congressional leaders had held in Little Rock (except that it also included the two top Republican congressional leaders, Sen. Dole and Rep. Michel), Clinton pledged to seek a "consensus" behind the economic program that he said he would introduce soon after he took office. Still in the early phase of forming his agenda, he offered few specifics to the lawmakers, who obviously were seeking some signals of what they faced. Instead, Clinton typically asked them at each session for their views on what they regarded as the most important issues.

Despite the lack of details, the congressional leaders had been highly impressed with Clinton's skills as a fellow politician. Members of Congress accustomed to being ignored by presidents enthusiastically welcomed his high-level "stroking." "He is a very warm, engaging and connecting person," Rep. Steny Hoyer of Maryland commented after the get-acquainted meetings. Hoyer, whose tenure as Speaker of the Maryland House had educated him about the importance of executive-branch leadership, called Clinton "a good pol, a very quick study"—an expression of admiration from a fellow practitioner. He added that Clinton probably already knew more about how the House Appropriations Committee decides to spend money than did either Presidents Reagan or Bush at the end of their terms. Hoyer, who chairs the House Democratic Caucus and who would become an important player in the handling of Clinton's economic package, also said that Clinton obviously had "a very good sense of what the American public will accept as the lowest common denominator." Reports on some of these meetings, no doubt, encouraged an artificial sense of camaraderie. But the sessions were important, if only because they served to set up the start of a professional relationship among individuals who would be dealing with each other frequently and in high-pressure forums. Although some remained troubled that Clinton had campaigned as a self-styled Washington outsider and that he had kept an arms-length distance from congressional leaders at the summer convention, senior members later said that they were optimistic about their prospects for success in dealing with him at the White House. Their chief worry, said an aide to the House Democratic leaders, was a problem over which they had little control: During the past decade, the huge increase in the federal deficit had made the choices they faced vastly more complex and difficult.

During a second set of Washington meetings with a still broader group of members of Congress on Dec. 8, the positive response grew. "It was mostly a love-in that this place hasn't seen in a very long time," said Rep. Charlie Rose of North Carolina, a senior lawmaker. Rep. Barney Frank of Massachusetts, normally an iconoclast, praised Clinton's knowledge of how Washington works: "He knows everything."[5] By this time, however, Clinton's intensive study of the federal budget led him to alert members that they faced painful choices on reducing the federal deficit. He told reporters that he needed to propose a multiyear plan to address that problem. Two days later, when Clinton announced that he had chosen Sen. Lloyd Bentsen as his Treasury Secretary and Rep. Panetta to run the budget office, both of whom had consistently urged tough congressional action on the budget, his message became more ominous. He planned to "shoot straight" on the deficit and was preparing to offer "tough choices" to Congress. Although few members were focusing on the implications of that pledge, Clinton's warning put them on notice that they would face several difficult months of work.

As the transition period reached its conclusion, Clinton lost some of his luster. His once-fawning press coverage became more skeptical when reporters began to focus on an array of problems. Some of his top appointees such as Commerce Secretary Ron Brown, for example, were questioned for their past dealings as Washington lobbyists. His apparent retreat from key campaign promises revived earlier "Slick Willie" accusations. And the slowness in organizing his new team raised doubts about whether he would be ready to take charge quickly in Washington. "Maybe all of us were a little bit surprised by how quickly this all comes upon you," Clinton spokesman George Stephanopoulos conceded on Jan. 15 at his final pre-Inaugural briefing for reporters. "Obviously, there are some changes between campaigning and governing, as you face new circumstances, as you face new complications."[6]

Questions about Clinton's economic plans were probably the biggest problem that he faced as he prepared to take office. In early January, when Bush released his formal projections for the economy, Clinton and his advisers professed shock over the projected increase in the federal deficit. Although the figures were similar to publicly released congressional forecasts that Clinton had cited in the summer of 1992, Clinton said that the new numbers might force him to reassess his own plans. The first major victim of the budget recalculations was Clinton's campaign pledge of a tax cut for the middle class. But Democratic congressional leaders noted, with some relief, there was little adverse public reaction when they suggested their change of course.

Clinton also became the target of criticism for his micro-managing style, which delayed the appointment of top officials throughout his new government. Stephen Hess, a presidential scholar at the Brookings Institution, said that the slow pace on staffing and decision-making had produced "the least successful transition I've seen since 1960. . . . He seems to want to make every decision and hold on to every bit of data."[7] Although that judgment may have been a bit harsh, the bloom had dropped from the rose just when Clinton faced his toughest test in asking the nation for sacrifice.

Congress Gets Set

Democrats also moved quickly to organize Congress for the transition to a new federal regime. Once the election results were in, House and Senate leaders sought to prepare themselves and their members for the arrival of the new president and to generate momentum for the new mission that they all faced. After 12 years of working with, and against, a Republican president, that would be no simple task. But they understood that they had no alternative. "Democratic leaders will have to work closely with the Clinton administration to assure cooperation," Sen. Charles Robb, a Virginia Democrat, said on election night. "No senators will cede their independence. But . . . the expectations of the American people are very high." It remained to be seen, of course, how well Clinton and the Democrats in Congress would cooperate. But their party's lackluster congressional election results meant that they had little margin for political error. In addition, it quickly became apparent that the Democrats' relatively slender majorities in the House and Senate gave their various factions virtual veto power over a controversial presidential action.

Building the relationship with the new president would require major changes on Capitol Hill. Even with their congressional majorities during most of the Reagan and Bush years, many Democrats had fallen into the habit of acting as the opposition party. The use of the presidential veto and the Democrats' own difficulty in building consensus had discouraged serious legislative efforts. Instead, they often would stage press conferences, hold hearings or move bills chiefly to gain publicity to make themselves look good or the Republicans look bad. As a result, they functioned chiefly as advocates who grew less interested in negotiating legislative nuances with the White House or with Washington's array of interest groups. On campaign-reform proposals, for example, Democrats were confident that Reagan and Bush would veto virtually any bill. So, they faced little risk in passing sweeping legislation though many of their members, who feared the political consequences, privately opposed enactment. Now that they would be shooting with real bullets, however, many Democrats grew far more wary of the details of campaign-finance bills. The arrival of a new administration from their own party also presumably would require Democrats in Congress to play a subservient role in responding to proposals crafted by the president rather than seeking to deal with the White House on an equal basis. The demand for discipline within Democratic ranks would become a new priority. While preparing for these broad changes in 1993, Democrats also would set aside potential conflicts inside Congress that might distract attention from the prime goal of shepherding the new president's agenda.

Speaker Foley and the other House Democratic leaders took the first step to rally their troops. Less than one week after the election, they hosted three unprecedented get-acquainted meetings across the nation with the 63 newly elected House Democrats. Their stated purpose was to listen to the concerns of the new lawmakers and to give the freshmen a forum to speak to the nation and to their party. But the meetings served another vitally important goal. The leaders wanted to send an early message to the freshmen that they were part of a new team; although their views would be given suitable attention, the first-termers would be expected to show party loyalty. Senior members lectured their new colleagues about the need to avoid a repetition of the Democrats' disarray during the Carter presidency. Most of the participants responded by pledging their allegiance to the House leaders and, especially, to Clinton. Few of them showed much interest in organizing themselves as a separate force for policy changes or for procedural reforms in the House. And those who did, according to later accounts, may have paid a price. After one self-styled activist, Luis Gutierrez of Illinois, urged his freshmen colleagues to work together to reform the House and to prepare their own agenda, party leaders viewed him as too rambunctious. "I might as well have said something terrible about their mothers," he recalled.[8] Later, Democratic leaders abandoned plans to consider Gutierrez seriously for an opening on the tax-writing Ways and Means Committee, chaired by Dan Rostenkowski, his fellow Chicagoan. Instead, the only freshmen to win a prestigious Ways and Means seat was Mel Reynolds, also from Chicago, who had pledged to be a team player.

The would-be reformers among the first-termers caught another glimpse of the obstacles facing them when some tried to organize themselves as a force for changing the House. Before the election, several House candidates had decided to convene in Omaha a bipartisan affair to harness pressure for reform. "For decades, Congress has been dominated by 'To get along, go along' types," said Tom Huening, a California Republican who became the chief organizer. "But we're not going to let the 'inside-the-Beltway' gang set the agenda." Huening announced in late September that 94 Republicans and 28 Democratic candidates had pledged to attend the event in late November. Among their plans, Huening said, would be big cuts in the congressional operating budget, abolition of the seniority system, term limits and reducing pork barrel projects. Unfortunately for Huening and his friends, however, several other events intervened. To start, few of them accomplished their first priority of winning election. Among the losers was Huening, who ran in a competitive district south of San Francisco that had usually elected Republicans to the House. Without Huening as organizer, the meeting lost much of its organizational focus. In addition, House Democratic leaders discouraged their party's freshmen from participating in the Omaha conference. In the end, only 14 freshmen, all of them Republicans, attended the

Omaha meeting. They completed their agenda several hours early, after taking no significant actions. This deflating of Huening's earlier hopes was another strong signal back to Washington that the 1992 freshman class would not become a new version of the 1974 "Watergate" freshman class, which had helped to bring sweeping reforms to the House.

Undoubtedly relieved by the failure of the freshmen to organize major changes, House leaders welcomed their new troops to Washington in early December for the customary several days of official orientation. By the time those briefings were concluded, the freshmen were on their way to being woven into the political fabric of the House and of Washington, as well. That was good news for both Foley and Clinton. Despite their potential to demand sweeping change, a majority of the huge class of 110 freshmen had previously served as legislators. They understood the complexities of a legislative body, including the scorn that was often heaped on troublemakers, and most initially were not inclined to stir the waters. Instead, they wanted to focus on the nation's agenda and to develop legislative solutions to the major problems of the economy and health care, which Clinton had already identified as priorities.

A similar desire to get down to business prevailed among more senior members of the House, most of whom wanted to move beyond the petty infighting and paralysis that had recently surrounded their work. When all House Democrats convened in Washington on Dec. 7 for their caucus to organize for the new Congress, they moved with unusual speed and harmony in the next three days to select committee chairmen and to assign the new members to House committees. These more senior Democrats also paid little attention to reform proposals, largely because they did not want to cause further disruptions in the House. So, when a plan to grant a vote on the House floor to the delegates from the District of Columbia, Guam, Puerto Rico, American Samoa and the Virgin Islands caused many Republicans and some Democrats to object, Democratic leaders retreated to a backup plan. Their alternative allowed the delegates to vote only on amendments and not on the final passage of bills. That, along with other procedural changes, made the delegates' votes all but meaningless legislatively, Democrats later conceded. They also backed away from another proposal to limit "special-order" speeches after Republicans complained that they were being muzzled. Some Democrats had wanted to limit these speeches, which follow the conclusion of the

House's daily legislative business, because they contended that many Republicans had turned them into an excessively partisan exercise. Despite the widely held view that other reforms were needed in House operations, Democratic leaders feared that such a discussion in the early months of the new administration would distract them from carrying out the new president's agenda.

In the Senate, meanwhile, the post-election period brought little attention to reform proposals or to efforts at Democratic party discipline. Historically, the Senate has disdained reforms designed to encourage efficiency because of its more free-wheeling and less disciplined style. Senators from both parties generally have opposed reform because so many of them welcome the individual freedom that the current rules give them. Majority Leader Mitchell, who has frequently wrung his hands about the limits of his authority, used the start of the new Congress as an opportunity to unveil proposals designed to increase his authority to manage the Senate. But he appropriately acknowledged that the proposals faced a dim future, and he exerted little effort to force a Senate discussion. In contrast to the House, the Senate waited until January to assign members to committees. The unusual delay resulted, in part, because two states had not completed their Senate elections on Nov. 3. In North Dakota, the result was routine, with a strange twist. Democrat Kent Conrad was re-elected after having decided earlier in the year not to seek another term; instead, he won a special election in December to fill the seat of Quentin Burdick, who had died in September. But Democrats suffered a serious setback in Georgia, where a peculiar state law forced Democratic Sen. Wyche Fowler and Republican challenger Paul Coverdell into a runoff because neither had received 50 percent of the vote on election day. Coverdell's Nov. 24 victory in their second contest meant that Democrats failed to increase their 57 Senate seats; it also was at least a small repudiation of Clinton and Gore, fellow Southerners who campaigned for Fowler and were hoping to show their political appeal.

The post-election focus on the Senate was primarily on the four new women who had been elected, all of them Democrats— Barbara Boxer and Dianne Feinstein, both of California, Carol Moseley-Braun of Illinois, and Patty Murray of Washington. Leaders of national women's groups hoped that the increase from two to six would make the Senate more sensitive to their issues and that the change also would lessen the male clubbishness that has historically pervaded the chamber. But another event dramatized the pressures for change. *The Washington Post,* in a lengthy story on Nov. 22, reported that Sen. Bob Packwood of Oregon allegedly had harassed 10 women during the previous two decades. The news was a political bombshell in Washington and in Oregon, where Packwood had just been narrowly re-elected and where there were demands for his resignation. At the very least, the Senate Ethics Committee would be forced to investigate Packwood, the senior Republican on the tax-writing Finance Committee. The inquiry would give the Senate's new women a chance to show that the old rules of senatorial behavior were no longer acceptable. And it could leave new blemishes on the chamber's character.

Congress as Stimulator

Despite the post-election skirmishing between the two parties and the political sideshows on Capitol Hill, the main focus was preparing for the new president's economic agenda. Perhaps the most critical facet of this transition was the attempt to develop a relationship and sense of trust between Clinton and key congressional Democrats. This liaison, which grew largely during private meetings and telephone calls, gave both sides a needed sense of increased confidence to face the difficult decisions that lay ahead of them. Speaker Foley, Majority Leader Mitchell and many congressional chairmen represented an older political generation; they needed time and some discussions to grow comfortable with the new kid on the block. They also had to reach an understanding with Clinton about his self-styled outsider status and his campaign attacks on Congress before they determined how they could work with him. As for Clinton, he wanted proof that Congress was equipped to deal seriously with his proposals to make sweeping policy changes. By the time of the Inauguration, the major players were comfortable with each other's rhetoric and approach. Clinton had satisfied the leaders, as one top congressional aide said at the time, that "they not only will be consulted but that he will work hand-in-hand with them in fashioning legislation." And the key players in Congress came to realize that, while Clinton had his own ideas, he also would be willing to play the vital role of breaking the deadlocks that had forced prolonged stalemate among Democrats on key issues, including taxes and health care.

What he heard during his meetings with the more experienced Democrats reinforced Clinton's instinct to present an activist agenda. Partly because he was new to Washington, Clinton looked to senior congressional barons for advice on the shaping of his new administration. House Ways and Means chairman Rostenkowski repeatedly urged him to be "bold," according to an ally of the chairman. After a dozen years of what he considered bad ideas or merely incremental change in Washington, he was ready to defer to a president who would advocate big steps in fixing the federal deficit and health care. Based on the positive response, Rostenkowski told his friends that he saw echoes of Lyndon Johnson in the younger Democrat, someone who loved politics and believed that government could play a positive role in public life.

But it takes more than good ideas to carry the day on Capitol Hill. By the younger congressional Democrats, such as Gephardt, Clinton was repeatedly told that legislative success also required the effective shaping and communication of a compelling message. After the years of gridlock, the public needed reassurance that government could be a positive force and that it could act sensibly to affect their daily lives. With regular coordination between the White House and Congress, Democrats saw the opportunity to restore public confidence that they could govern on the major issues. But making a quick start would be no easy task. Despite the mythology surrounding newly elected presidents, many—including Kennedy and Nixon—have had relatively slow starts in seeking to change course in Washington. Although congressional Democrats realized that it would take both a new mindset and effort in 1993 to reverse their pattern of attacks on the president, they also welcomed the opportunity to regain the bully pulpit and its powerful capacity to reach the American public. "We will emulate the Reagan model," a leading Democratic message-crafter said during the transition period. "Don't mess with success."

Clinton and the Democrats were impressed with Reagan's 1981 achievements because of the Republicans' ability to move quickly on major economic issues and their success in convincing Congress to go along without an elaborate rewriting of the president's original plan. The Democrats recognized, of course, that it always is easier to pass a big tax cut—as Reagan proposed in 1981—than to swallow the more painful medication of tax increases and benefit cuts that would be required for deficit reduction and health-care reform in 1993. Reagan, unlike Clinton, also had the advantage of a defined agenda from his election. But Clinton had a major asset that Reagan had lacked: a majority for his own party in the House.

If Congress could stimulate a new president's agenda, it also could act as a brake. Although Clinton had four years until his next election, all members of the House and one-third of the Senate would face the voters in 1994. As politicians, they knew that the new team in Washington would have to show results, and they also were mindful of the need to avoid political land mines. Recalling the Reagan model, Democrats were well aware that a deep recession in 1981–82 led to the Republicans' loss of working control in the House after they dropped 26 seats in the 1982 election; the Reagan era, in effect, ended in 1986, when the GOP also lost its Senate majority. Given the limited voter mandate of the 1992 election, including the Democrats' loss of 10 House seats, Clinton and his team faced all the more pressure to make their mark quickly and convincingly. Congressional Democrats understood that they had little alternative and that Republicans would be ready to pounce if they did not produce or if conditions worsened. "Every member will find it hard to vote for some things," said Rep. Kennelly of Connecticut. "But it will also be hard to go home after having done nothing."

Endnotes

1. Michael Wines, "Hi. Goodbye. This Takes 11 Weeks and $3.5 Million," *The New York Times,* Nov. 22, 1992: Sect. 4, p. 1.
2. Carl M. Brauer, *Presidential Transitions: Eisenhower Through Reagan* (New York: Oxford University Press, 1986), 256.
3. Thomas L. Friedman, "Change of Tone for Clinton: High Energy to Low Profile," *The New York Times,* Nov. 11, 1992: A1.
4. Kirk Victor, "Asleep at the Switch?" *National Journal,* Jan. 16, 1993: 131.
5. "The Final Word," *Congress Daily,* Dec. 8, 1992: 5.
6. Richard L. Berke, "Clinton Aides Wonder, 'Where's Our Honeymoon?'" *The New York Times,* Jan. 16, 1993: 7.
7. Jeffrey H. Birnbaum and Michael K. Frisby, "Clinton's Slow Start Picking a Team and Policies Dooms His Hope of Hitting the Ground Running," *The Wall Street Journal,* Jan. 13, 1993: A16.
8. Dick Kirschten, "Gutierrez: Out and In," *National Journal,* Jan. 30, 1993: 256.

4

Setting the New Agenda

☆ ☆ ☆

Clinton met with congressional Democrats as he prepared his economic plan. In the photo are House Majority Whip David Bonior, Senate Appropriations Committee chairman Robert Byrd, House Speaker Thomas Foley and Senate Majority Leader George Mitchell.

The Brief Honeymoon

Presidents typically have their most power to influence national policy on the day that they are sworn into office. Then, they must decide how to spend their limited political capital to accomplish their own goals and to address the nation's problems. Bill Clinton decided to focus his attention initially on strengthening the economy and reducing the federal deficit. With the agreement of Democratic congressional leaders, his first legislative priority would be a plan to redirect federal spending and tax priorities while also cutting the deficit. Enacting the proposal would be a major achievement, given Washington's constant budget wars of the Reagan–Bush years. But the Democrats, now that they controlled both the White House and Congress, were confident that they could succeed. And they believed that they could not afford to fail—politically or financially—if they hoped to find the money to address other national problems later during Clinton's presidency. Getting a quick start was also important because the skeptical and impatient public was expecting change and an end to stalemate, as Clinton had often promised during the campaign. Like any new president, he entered office with a reservoir of public good will and a widespread national hope that he would help to correct the nation's problems. A January 1993 poll conducted jointly by Democratic and Republican pollsters found that 71 percent of the respondents had a favorable impression of Clinton and 84 percent believed that he was off to a good start. But he knew that the positive feelings could dissipate quickly as the Democrats forced the nation to swallow bitter medicine. And other domestic and international events could intervene at any moment, forcing him to move in new directions. He would have little time to spare. "The early actions of a new administration are crucial to its legislative success," said presidential scholar James P. Pfiffner. "This is so both because the main legislative accomplishments of an administration are often achieved early in its first year, and also because early success or failures can set the tone for the rest of the administration in its relations with Congress."[1]

Reducing the federal deficit and stimulating the economy would require Clinton to educate the public so his goals and programs would gain broad national support. That, in turn, would force him to abandon some of his prominent campaign promises, such as a tax cut for the middle class, and to develop and sell painful medicine—tax increases and cuts in federal spending—that he had barely discussed before the election. Even after he selected his Cabinet officials and White House staff, it would take several more weeks for him to review his economic options, organize a legislative strategy and prepare the proper political climate. As the Washington community awaited his proposals, he had the time and discretion that are provided by what is sometimes called the new leader's honeymoon period. Clinton would discover, however, the vast differences between campaigning and governing. Some of the same skills are required, including the ability to communicate a compelling message to the public and the need to act as the party leader. But presidents quickly learn that they often cannot control the actions of other political players, not even their supposed allies. "Early successes will not be handed to a new president on a silver platter," Pfiffner wrote. "The idea that a 'honeymoon' with Congress naturally follows the election of a new President is greatly exaggerated."[2] And the unyielding public spotlight on the White House allows little room for hesitation or error.

Most congressional Democrats would give him the time and an extended leash to maneuver once he took office. They recognized, as Senate Majority Leader Mitchell often repeated, that they needed to stop acting as the "guardians of gridlock," who had brought so much public scorn on government. Clinton also encouraged their cooperation by holding many private meetings where Democrats offered their views on what actions he should take. The president, in turn, sought to develop a team spirit in support of their common agenda. For some Democrats on Capitol Hill, however, the start of the Clinton presidency also would be a learning period of a different type. Especially in the Senate, senior Democrats chafed at their new subservient role. Even Clinton's supposed allies could not resist the temptation to lecture their new president—at the risk of publicly embarrassing him—on subjects where they believed that they were more expert and where they were unaccustomed to a challenge from within their own party. At a time when Clinton was trying to establish his credentials, some of his worst enemies were Democratic committee chairmen from the Senate who dispensed advice as though Bush were still president. "All Democrats face a deep psychological adjustment from being in the opposition, where you can take shots at the president," said a senior House aide after a few embarrassing incidents. "For some, it will take time to recognize that it is in their interest to support a Democratic president." At least initially, most House Democrats gave Clinton a more friendly reception than did their Senate colleagues, and they encouraged him to show leadership on both the economy and health care.

Clinton needed their morale boost. No sooner had he completed the often-glitzy Inaugural festivities and taken office, with a Kennedy-style pledge that a new generation of Americans was prepared to "define what it means to be an American," than he ran into a buzz saw of criticism. In what may have been a case of early-season nervousness, his initial days in office were marked by errors, misjudgments and lapses that placed him on the defensive. Although the incidents would soon fade in public importance, their memory would leave questions on Capitol Hill about the competence of Clinton and the advisers surrounding him. Instead of developing teamwork and a positive spirit, the new president found himself clashing publicly with Democratic senators on three separate issues during his first two weeks in office. After complaining that they had not been adequately consulted, the senators forced a retreat in each case from a position that Clinton or one of his top officials had publicly advocated. At the time, the events distracted the White House from its efforts to focus the nation's attention chiefly on addressing the economic problems. In doing so, the conflicts also short-circuited Clinton's effort to gain public attention for efforts to show that he would be the instrument of change on other issues, such as his Jan. 22 announcement of executive actions to reverse Reagan–Bush era restrictions on federal support for abortions.

First, he was forced to withdraw his support for his nominee for Attorney General, Zoe Baird, after she told the Senate Judiciary Committee that she had hired a "nanny" who was an illegal alien and had failed to make proper payment of federal taxes for child-care services. Although Clinton aides had been aware of Baird's plight, they did not believe that she should be disqualified. But after hostile reactions by radio talk-show callers and some Democratic senators' unhappiness with her explanation, the Senate Judiciary Committee, led by its chairman Joseph Biden, second-guessed the White House's handling of the nomination; in effect, the senators left Clinton with little choice but to abandon her. She announced her withdrawal on Jan. 22, two days after his inauguration. Biden complained to reporters after the incident about Clinton's failure to consult him on the Baird nomination, noting that the new team was "behind the curve in getting started." The next mini-crisis came the following week, when Senate Armed Services chairman Sam Nunn had a protracted and public conflict over Clinton's campaign promise to order the Pentagon to drop its policy of prohibiting gays to serve in the military. "If there's a strategy here, it hasn't been explained to me," said Nunn, with an air of condescension. Clinton agreed to delay the implementation of his pledge pending six months of study by the Pentagon and Congress and a political "cooling-off" period and eventually agreed to a less sweeping change in Pentagon policy toward gays, known as, "Don't ask, don't tell." Hardly had that problem been muffled when the new Senate Finance chairman Daniel Patrick Moynihan voiced his unhappiness over White House suggestions to limit the annual cost-of-living increase for Social Security beneficiaries and over Clinton's failure to consult him on other revenue-raising options. The proposal, which Office of Management and Budget director Leon Panetta had advocated, was "a death wish," Moynihan told reporters, and he vowed to block it. Senate Budget Committee chairman Jim Sasser quickly echoed Moynihan's view. On yet another conflict—his campaign advocacy of a line-item veto designed to cut "pork" from congressional spending bills—Clinton demurred from promoting the issue and seeking congressional action, rather than stir the ire of Senate Appropriations Committee chairman Robert Byrd, an avowed opponent of the line-item veto.

Clinton and his staff were taken aback by the zest with which the Senate barons moved to protect their turf and to warn the new team in town that it should tread carefully. Although they had a logical explanation that sought to downplay each conflict, top White House aides acknowledged that they had received a political warning shot and that they faced a test of power. The mutual pledges of cooperation, which top Democrats made during the transition period, were abandoned once Clinton decided to act. "It's possible to make too much of early stumbles, but it is also true that the early weeks of a presidency are important in defining what it hopes to accomplish and what it represents," *The Wall Street Journal* editorialized.[3] It was no wonder that, by early February, Clinton and congressional Democratic leaders sought to emphasize their areas of cooperation. Both the House and Senate, for example, passed a Bush-vetoed bill to allow employees in the private sector to take unpaid leave in the event of a family or medical emergency. Clinton spent even more time consulting with members of Congress on his economic program. And, as if to distance himself from his Washington problems, he went back on the road with a town-hall meeting from a Detroit television studio to exchange thoughts with citizens in four cities about his plans.

Confronting the Deficit

The focus on Clinton's early mishaps was soon overtaken by the Democrats' decision to repair the nation's economy. That effort, which would dominate the national debate during the next several months, would be central to their party's attempt to reshape federal priorities and to recast how government operates. Because of the pervasive impact that the huge budget deficit had assumed over federal policy during the past decade, the White House and Congress had become preoccupied by their annual budget fights. Those exercises, which rarely produced credible results, had come to symbolize what ailed Washington to an unhappy public.

Some statistics starkly dramatize the bleak dimensions of the budget picture. During Jimmy Carter's last full year as president in fiscal 1980, when federal expenditures were $591 billion, the deficit reached a record total of $74 billion. Limiting it to that amount required Carter and congressional Democrats to struggle in 1980 to produce a deficit-reduction package of $16 billion. During the Reagan and Bush presidencies, however, the annual deficit never fell below $128 billion. By fiscal 1993, when George Bush left office, the roughly $266 billion deficit represented 19 percent of total expenditures. Worse yet, the federal government's annual interest payments to service the debt increased from $53 billion in 1980 to $198 billion in 1993, making debt service 14 percent of federal spending, compared with 9 percent in 1980. Finally, the national debt increased from a total of slightly less than $1 trillion when Carter left office to more than $4.1 trillion at the end of Bush's presidency. What made these numbers even more appalling and frustrating to many members of Congress from both parties is that they had spent so much time during those years working on widely heralded plans to cut the deficit by combinations of tax increases and spending cuts. In 1985, 1987 and 1990, Congress passed laws that were designed to set the deficit on a fixed downward path over a multiyear period and that also provided enforcement procedures to achieve those goals. But with the deficits steadily increasing instead, those laws obviously did not achieve their goals.

It was far more difficult for the two parties to agree on who or what was responsible for those huge deficits, which came during a decade of steady economic growth. Democrats, not surprisingly, pointed their finger at the two Republican presidents and their budget directors, who often set rosy scenarios that Democrats said were based on little more than sleight of hand. Congressional spending committees regularly pointed out that they spent less money than the presidents had proposed in their budgets but, the Democrats said, their party could only make modest modifications of those plans. According to the Democrats' platform approved at their 1992 national convention, "In 12 Republican years a national debt that took 200 years to accumulate has been *quadrupled.*" In the Republicans' view, their presidents' attempts at fiscal responsibility and an overhaul of outdated federal programs were continually stymied by the big-spending Democrats who controlled the House throughout that period and who held a majority in the Senate during the last half-dozen years. Not only did these Democrats treat the White House budgets as "dead on arrival" during most of that time, they also repeatedly made spending and tax-policy changes that, according to the Republicans, blocked steps to spur the economy and to reduce the deficit. "For 12 years, Republicans in the White House and Congress have battled a Democrat system corrupt and contemptuous of the American taxpayer," stated the 1992 Republican national platform. "Deficits have grown as Democrat Congresses have converted government assistance programs into entitlements and allowed spending to become uncontrolled."

The conflict over the causes and impact of the deficits during the 1980s and early 1990s would continue and remain unresolved. But the end of divided government in 1993 would banish questions of political accountability for federal actions. Now that Democrats controlled the White House and had majorities in both the House and Senate, they could not escape responsibility for future deficits. That shift had an immediate sobering impact on their party and its leaders. Throughout 1992, for example, most Democrats had voiced their support for cutting taxes on the middle class. That was the centerpiece of a tax bill that Congress sent to Bush in March, which he promptly vetoed. Clinton also made a middle-class tax cut a major tenet of his campaign, both in the Democratic primaries and in the general election. And, in a more modest version, it was promised in the party's national platform. Leading Democrats repeatedly lambasted Bush and the Republicans for allegedly seeking to tilt the tax code to favor the wealthy. But once Clinton was elected, it did not take long for Democrats to throw overboard the vaunted middle-class tax cut—one of his first campaign promises. In early January, Speaker Foley said that earlier support for the tax cut should be "rethought" and that Democrats "have to be realistic about the problems that are facing the country." Sen. Mitchell, for his part, acknowledged that "because of the [budget] deficit" in 1993, it might not be possible to pass the tax cut, of which he had been a prime supporter. Both leaders cited the outgoing Bush administration's forecast that the projected fiscal year 1997 deficit would be about $300 billion, not the $237 billion that it had predicted six months earlier. But critics of the Democrats' change in plans noted that the widely reported congressional study in August 1992 had provided gloomy estimates that were similar to the January 1993 Bush numbers. Although incoming budget director Panetta had certainly been aware for many months of the more negative numbers, Clinton advisers in Little Rock claimed in early January that they were surprised. Despite their insistence that the comments from Capitol Hill had not been coordinated with the new president, they did not reject the leaders' assessment of the dim prospects for a tax cut.

They did not stop there. Soon after they ditched the tax cut, Democrats began to talk up a new tax on all forms of energy, which would unavoidably trigger a tax *increase* for the middle class. On Jan. 24, Treasury Secretary Lloyd Bentsen—from Texas, no less—launched that debate during his first television appearance after he took office, when he said on NBC News's "Meet the Press" that a consumption tax, probably on energy, "is going to take place." Advocates of that proposal, which was not the subject of serious public discussion during the 1992 campaign, contended that it would encourage energy conservation and reduce imports of energy resources in addition to raising revenues. Although most congressional Democrats, at first, kept silent on Bentsen's idea and Clinton said that he had made no decision, Republicans were not so shy. "It took less than one week in office for the Democrats to abandon a middle-class tax cut and replace their campaign pledge with a tax increase on everyone, from poor to middle class to wealthy," Minority Whip Newt Gingrich told the House. Voicing a response that many voters would find disingenuous, at best, a Clinton adviser said that a careful reading showed that the president was not breaking his campaign pledge. "Every time Clinton said 'I'm not going to raise taxes on the middle class,' he always added the phrase 'to pay for my programs.' He never, never said just, 'I will not raise taxes on the middle class,'" the aide told a reporter, who characterized that response as "politics by loophole."[4]

In these cases and others, Clinton and his congressional allies were willing to go out on a political limb. They believed that the nation was ready for Washington to make tough choices and to stop pandering to the public. "If we talk common sense, the public will respond," said Rep. Robert Matsui, a California Democrat who serves on the tax-writing Ways and Means Committee. When he discussed his support for a higher gas tax and new taxes on employee health benefits with his Sacramento-area constituents, Matsui said, "you hear the groans but not the anger about politicians." The Democrats also believed that they faced significant pressure and a narrow time period in which to act on a legislative package that would address the nation's economic problems. Speaker Foley described "a sense of great enthusiasm" in Congress after Clinton took office. But he warned at the time that the euphoria must be tempered by the reality of the problems and that "there is a great likelihood that, if we don't succeed, there will be harsh criticism" by the public.

For the Democrats to succeed with their economic programs would be a difficult challenge. As the budget debates of recent years had shown, the "easy" political steps had been taken. And certain basic realities had to be faced. For example, most Democrats said that they supported cuts in defense spending. But the fact was that national spending for the military already had been on a steady downward slope. In the seven years since fiscal 1986, annual inflation-adjusted spending had been reduced by 27 percent to $273 billion. In addition, the budget outline submitted by President Bush a few days before he left office assumed billions more in cuts. For Clinton and the Democrats to seek additional defense retrenchment, therefore, would raise questions about what role the nation should play in a post–Cold War world. And the cuts would jeopardize spending and jobs for politically sensitive defense facilities and military contracts, which already had been feeling the pain of recent cutbacks across the nation. On the domestic side of the budget, the biggest costs, by far, were for two "entitle-ment" programs—Social Security and Medicare. Together, they would account for an estimated $439 billion of federal spending in fiscal 1993—nearly one-third of all federal expenditures. But be-cause of the proven political clout of senior citizens, the beneficia-ries of most of this money, members of Congress from both parties feared making any changes. Another major share of the federal budget that was truly untouchable was the estimated $210 billion in 1994 interest payments that were due to bondholders who were fi-nancing the federal debt. Altogether, these three large compo-nents—defense, Social Security and Medicare, and interest payments—accounted for about 64 percent of all federal spending in the projected fiscal 1994 "baseline," which referred to the total of federal spending if no changes were made. The remainder of the federal budget comprised chiefly aid to low-income groups and "discretionary" domestic spending. But these areas already had suffered sizable reductions in recent years at the behest of Presi-dents Reagan and Bush. And the Democrats were not inclined to take new whacks at these programs, many of which were vital to their party's political constituencies.

The outlook was hardly any brighter for cutting the federal deficit by raising revenues. Increasing taxes is never an easy politi-cal matter. Now that they controlled Washington's policy-making machine, Democrats were especially wary of fueling the Republi-cans' repeated charge that they are the "tax and spend" party. Al-though polls showed there was broad public support for increasing taxes on the wealthy, who were viewed as big winners from the Re-publican tax policies of the 1980s, the reality was that socking the millionaires would only raise a few billion dollars annually for the Treasury. And Democrats were reluctant to impose much of a bite on the new middle class, in which a working husband and wife of-ten make between $50,000 and $75,000. For a party whose presi-dential candidate had not received more than 50 percent of the popular vote since 1964, Democratic strategists saw the need to at-tract those taxpayers as a vital building block of their new electoral majority.

Ironically, Bush complicated his successor's dilemma by be-queathing him what appeared to be an improving economy. Al-though the result came too late to rescue Bush, the nearly 5 percent spurt in economic growth during the last quarter of 1992 was the most robust rate of his presidency. In theory, Democrats could have cited that performance as a rationale to abandon or reduce the scale of their campaign promises to stimulate the economy. But Clinton and his top allies determined that they had to press that goal, and, at the same time, they could not ignore the deficit. After a campaign in which the new president had harshly attacked Bush's management of the economy and after 12 years in which congressional Democrats had repeatedly lamented the Republicans' failure to cooperate with them in reducing the deficit, they concluded that they had no choice. Also, Clinton left no doubt that he believed that the economy needed a further jolt, both to assure that the growth and new jobs would continue and to maintain public and business confidence. That led him to support additional spending in certain sectors of the economy that needed the stimulus, according to his advisers. Regardless of arguments over the economic variables, in the end Democrats concluded that their own political credibility was on the line. Enacting Clinton's economic program, Majority Leader Mitchell often told other Democratic senators, would be "a metaphor for whether government works."

Clinton's Package

Like a splash of icy water, the preparation and unveiling of Clinton's economic package to reduce the deficit and recharge the economy marked the end of the Democrats' post-election celebration and the start of their painful decision-making. The president extensively consulted both his own advisers and congressional Democrats to craft the plan. In addition to reviewing specific items, they made calculated economic and political assessments of the overall prospects. Although many lawmakers focused on the parochial local impact of the specific changes, the participants also recognized that they had to consider the effect on the larger national picture. "We all know that there will be things that we don't like but that we need to do this for America," said House Democratic Caucus chairman Steny Hoyer of Maryland. It did not take long for the pain to hit home, even for influential lawmakers. Clinton's proposal to freeze the salaries of federal employees would prove especially troublesome for Hoyer, whose suburban Washington district includes tens of thousands of federal employees. To compound his political dilemma, Hoyer did not learn of the pay freeze until a Clinton aide privately disclosed the final decision to him when it was too late to force a review. That was one of many examples in which administration officials kept tight control over the details of their budget drafting. Nor would the Democratic lawmakers accept all the president's advice. Hoyer, for example, later led a successful effort to soften the proposed pay freeze for most federal workers.

Clinton was the central player in preparing his new administration's program. Shortly after the inauguration, the president and his economic advisers convened meetings nearly every day; during these sessions, which often extended for many hours, they conducted detailed reviews of budget options. With the plan scheduled to be unveiled in a speech to Congress on Feb. 17, he had less than four weeks to prepare the outlines of a budget, which normally requires several months of White House planning. That accelerated schedule had been prompted, in part, by the promise Clinton had made for one of the most "productive" early starts of any president. His task was further complicated because he was preparing such sweeping changes in federal policy and because, with many of his administration's top policy-making slots vacant, the circle of expertise was limited. Nor, it became clear, had Clinton and his advisers spent much time or made many choices on budget issues during the transition period after the election.

All of these factors would have seemed to work to the advantage of Leon Panetta, Clinton's director of the Office of Management and Budget. He had gained broad knowledge as a leading player on budget policies and procedures during 16 years in the House, including four years as House Budget Committee chairman. Panetta's deputy, Alice Rivlin, also had gained considerable budget expertise during her eight years as director of the Congressional Budget Office. But many details of the White House plan were anything but Panetta-driven. Clinton rejected Panetta's call for a preponderance of spending cuts over tax increases plus significant cuts in all major areas of federal spending—a goal that Panetta stated in January during his confirmation hearings, when he called for two dollars of spending cuts for each dollar of additional taxes. The president also took issue with his budget director on many specifics. Panetta, for example, wanted to impose a one-year freeze on many cost-of-living adjustments in the budget, including for Social Security beneficiaries. When that suggestion became public and drew intense criticism, Clinton quickly shot it down. Nor did Panetta have much more success when he tried to end what he viewed as many pork-barrel spending projects benefiting certain regions of the nation.

Although Clinton committed himself to a large deficit-reduction plan, he was especially sensitive to the political implications of proposed spending cuts. For example, many Democrats—led by Clinton's friend, Sen. Dale Bumpers of Arkansas—had fought for years to eliminate two multibillion dollar federal projects that President Bush had supported for his home state of Texas: the National Aeronautics and Space Administration's space station and the superconducting supercollider, a huge advanced physics project. Although well-placed Democrats said that Clinton sympathized with opponents, including Panetta, who wanted to scrap the two projects, he came down, instead, on the side of relatively modest budgetary tinkering: a delay in the supercollider's completion date and a redesign of the space station. A major factor that drove his initial decision was an effort to protect the political interests of appointed Sen. Bob Krueger, who faced a May 1 special election in Texas to keep the seat that Treasury Secretary Bentsen had held. In the view of many Texans and others, Clinton's caution on the Texas projects was prompted by well-founded fears that if Krueger lost his seat, the result would adversely affect the popularity of the president and his program. Once the special election was completed, Clinton might be able to take a more skeptical view of that spending.

In extensive consultations with congressional Democrats about his budget package, Clinton sought to promote the members' comfort level with his plan by focusing on its broad features, but he steered clear of many details. At the suggestion of House leaders Foley and Gephardt, Clinton met with groups of about 30 House Democrats in the several days before he unveiled his plan. At those White House sessions, Clinton typically gave lawmakers a minute or two each to comment on budget issues that were especially important to them. But the members of Congress hardly had a chance for a dialogue on the vitally important details of Clinton's program. In fact, some of those specifics would not be resolved until months after Clinton unveiled his budget plan in February. On the proposed "restructuring" of the space station, for example, Democratic Rep. Mike Andrews of Texas was miffed when Clinton and Gore gave him only vague details of NASA's plans, which might cause the loss of thousands of jobs among his Houston-area constituents. But Andrews decided that he had little choice but to be a good political soldier, while continuing to press for his local interests. Although the space station was "different" from other federal programs because it was "a national project . . . that is a platform for the next century," Andrews added, all Americans must share Clinton's goal of "shared sacrifice." Clinton also heard many of these parochial concerns during his frequent telephone conversations with rank-and-file lawmakers. These contacts, which often ran late into the evening, quickly became a matter of Capitol Hill lore as members sought to impress each other and outsiders with their White House calls.

Selling the Plan to the Public

But gaining sufficient political support would require Clinton to do more than convince the legislators. To sell the package to the public, the White House launched an election-style promotional campaign across the nation, both before and after his Feb. 17 speech to Congress. "Like the marketing division of a corporation launching a product whose success is crucial to the company's future, the group had mapped out a political and communications strategy long before the final shape of the product itself was known," according to one news report after the plan was unveiled.[5] With the help of advisers from his political campaign, Clinton and top administration officials returned to the grass roots to convince the public that the nation faced serious problems and that bolstering the economy would require "shared sacrifice," a politically hazardous term that he had not invoked before Nov. 3. In his Feb. 10 town-hall meeting in the suburban Detroit television studio, for example, he listened to the views of Americans worried about their nation's future as well as their own. He referred euphemistically to the likely new taxes as the public's "contribution to the changes we have to make." Then, he traveled to Missouri, Ohio, New York, California and Washington state in the five days after his speech. As when he met earlier with members of Congress, he focused more on the general goals than on the specifics of his economic package. His constant refrain was an appeal to patriotism: "You can't just say what's in it for me. You have to ask what's in it for us."

The most important speech of Clinton's early months in the White House was the formal presentation of his domestic program. When he entered the House chamber on Feb. 17 shortly after 9 p.m. (a few minutes late for the nationally broadcast address), the new president was greeted by the most enthusiastic Democratic welcome since the heyday of President Lyndon Johnson's Great Society. The sustained cheering that accompanied Clinton's arrival and repeatedly interrupted his lengthy speech was like an emotional release for a party that had suffered through a long period of dormancy and self-doubts. The chamber was packed with the usual dignitaries—members of Clinton's Cabinet, Supreme Court justices, ambassadors from nations around the world and the like. But it also had the cozy feeling of a college reunion, as House members warmly greeted their former colleagues—including budget director Leon Panetta and Defense Secretary Les Aspin—who had left to join Clinton's Cabinet, and House aides welcomed several pals who had become senior aides to the president. But the most remarkable aspect of the evening's performance was that it soon became apparent that Clinton was reading perhaps only one sentence in three from his prepared text and that he was ad libbing a large and fact-filled share of his speech. For both lawmakers and spectators in the gallery, who were accustomed to presidents who read their addresses to Congress with few diversions that appeared spontaneous, Clinton's performance had the aura of a sincere and personal pleading to both Congress and the nation. Although the speech was not filled with memorable lines, it allowed the new president to show his well-informed efforts to change the direction of the ship of state. On issues from health care to early childhood education to his national service program, his easy grasp of detail allowed him to speak directly to his audience. But in the end, the new president focused on his opportunity to show leadership. "After so many years of gridlock and indecision, after so many hopeful beginnings and so few promising results, the American people are going to be harsh in their judgments of all of us if we fail to seize this moment."

In their post-mortem assessments of how Clinton assembled the economic package, administration officials emphasized his intense personal involvement. "Participants in the long, grueling sessions say there was scarcely a detail of the plan that wasn't reviewed and questioned by the president himself," concluded one news report.[6] Unlike Reagan and Bush, Clinton was a policy "wonk" who knew how domestic programs operated; as a former governor, he also had seen their strengths and weaknesses. But his commitment to an activist role for government in domestic affairs became something of a political down side when it came time to add up the bottom line. The "deficit-reduction" exercise had gained a sizable chunk of new spending. Included was his call for a $100 billion spending increase in the next four years to promote some of his favored domestic programs, including health services, job training and highway building plus a major expansion of the earned income tax credit, an income supplement for low-income working families. And, partly to appeal to liberals worried about spending cuts elsewhere in the budget, he proposed a separate package of economic "stimulus" proposals ($19 billion in spending and loans, $6 billion in tax incentives), which he wanted Congress to approve mostly for 1993. One major consequence of these additions was that Clinton was forced to abandon yet another campaign pledge: a 50 percent cut in the federal deficit during his first term. Making things worse, a top White House aide later conceded, was that the details of the stimulus plan were prepared "hurriedly" and late and without much consultation with potential Democratic allies in Congress. As would later become evident, this part of his economic plan did not inspire much enthusiasm, even among its intended beneficiaries. Even with his hefty new taxes and the abandonment of his heralded middle-class tax cut, the budget he submitted called for only a one-third decrease to a $206 billion deficit by fiscal 1997. Clinton defended the more modest goal by invoking the earlier claim of Democratic congressional leaders—that Bush's final deficit forecast had unexpectedly grown higher. When he was reminded that the estimates had been publicly revised months earlier, Clinton responded that it was enough for him simply to start the deficit on a downward path.

During the subsequent days and weeks, Congress and the public would gradually learn more details, and their reaction was not always positive. Often, opposition to the proposals was slow to form, if only because lobbying groups often spent many weeks scurrying to find the details or waiting for Cabinet agencies to provide the specifics. On the tax program, for example, few public tears were shed for the increased taxes on the wealthy. But quite another matter politically was the proposed new tax on all forms of energy use, which was the plan's second biggest revenue raiser. Because of the wide discrepancies in energy use and cost across the nation, this proposal would have varied regional effects. There-fore, it would provide an opportunity for aggressive lobbying and claims of unfairness by groups ranging from hydroelectric-power users in the Northwest to ethanol producers in the Midwest's corn-producing region to heavy users of home-heating oil in the North-east. Further complicating the proposed energy tax was that Clinton sought to soften its impact on low-income groups by giving them billions of dollars in food stamps or home energy assistance to offset the additional costs. Another part of Clinton's budget that made many Democrats nervous was the proposal to increase the taxes on Social Security income for relatively well-to-do retirees. For Clinton, who wanted to direct more federal resources to needy children, the proposal seemed equitable; after all, the tax rate that these individuals were being asked to pay would be increased only from 50 to 85 percent of the rate paid by working people, and many analyses showed that retirees were receiving far more in benefits than they had paid into the Social Security system. But Social Secu-rity was widely known as the "third rail" of politics, which meant that anyone who touched the issue risked the equivalent of a polit-ical electrocution. And the Democrats themselves could recall how successfully they had used the issue against Reagan and his con-gressional allies during the 1980s, when Republicans proposed modest changes.

Another big political problem in Clinton's package was its re-liance on tax increases ($337 billion over the next five years, ac-cording to CBO, the non-partisan Congressional Budget Office) over domestic spending cuts. Because of his proposals for addi-tional spending in selected programs, net domestic discretionary spending would increase from $209 billion to $262 billion annually by 1998, a projected increase of 7 percent over inflation; mean-while, so-called "mandatory" spending such as Medicare, student loans and retirement benefits would decrease only slightly less than budget expectations. Most spending cuts came from defense programs, where the after-inflation reduction would total 21 per-cent in 1997. The net effect for the federal deficit was less dramatic than budget "hawks" like Panetta had initially hoped. Clinton's proposals "would make a substantial contribution to reducing the deficit, but they are not sufficient to solving the long-run problem," concluded the CBO. "The deficit would decline only through 1997 and then resume its rise." Clinton's hopes for making further deficit cuts with his forthcoming health-care reforms may not be realistic, the report added, because of the additional costs that likely would be generated.

Drawing the Lines

Despite some of these ominous factors, Democrats were not inclined to focus on the details in the immediate aftermath of Clinton's unveiling of the plan. Instead, most of them closed ranks and said that it was important to rally behind Clinton. "We should recognize that it is in our self-interest to support the president," Senate Majority Leader Mitchell often said. He and other congressional leaders constantly urged colleagues to show discipline and to "keep our disagreements internal," a House leadership aide said. Heeding the White House's message of previous weeks, most Democratic lawmakers already were inclined to be good soldiers, in any case. They helped to spread the message that they would sink or swim as a party. "The public wants us to get moving again and not be distracted," said Rep. Slaughter of New York. Rep. Reynolds, the Illinois Democrat and the only freshman named to the House Ways and Means Committee, said, "Let's give the president and his people an opportunity to try to change America."

But it would not be that easy. In the days immediately following Clinton's speech to Congress, some veteran Democrats said, with only a trace of humor, that they wished that they could vote without delay on Clinton's program. On one hand, with the public's initial support, they knew that they were on a political roll and they wanted to exploit the opportunity this presented. On the other hand, with their political experience, they knew that the good times could not last for long and that legislative problems inevitably would arise. For them and for Clinton's program, the reality was that legislating in a democracy is a deliberative process. In almost every case, the advocates must allow time for adversaries and the public to explore the consequences of new proposals. Though Congress would start to debate Clinton's economic agenda after a delay of only a few weeks, the interval allowed opponents to raise questions that pointed out potential problems with the plan. Those doubts occasionally were voiced, often quietly, by Democrats themselves. These lawmakers had many concerns, some of them conflicting: Some of the more conservative members felt that Clinton's attack on the deficit was too weak; others felt that the spending cuts and tax increases were too sweeping. Some worried about how the program changes would affect their constituents. And others from political swing seats feared the electoral consequences for the party and, especially, for themselves. Adding to the fear factor was the Democrats' small majorities in both the House and Senate, which meant that party leaders were forced to walk a fine line to accommodate a wide variety of ideological views. If they granted the requests for more domestic spending that many black, urban lawmakers made, suburban and rural groups might object; and when the conservatives demanded more spending cuts, the liberals would say no. Success required a delicate balance. So long as Clinton remained popular, most Democrats kept their disagreements private and closed ranks publicly. But the sense of unease was palpable. "The public needs to see decisive action," said Rep. Timothy Penny of Minnesota, who worried about a tendency to return to business as usual.

Congressional Republicans, of course, were the most obvious stumbling block for the Democrats. As the so-called loyal opposition, Republicans had several options, each of which they would use at various points. They could offer alternatives, where feasible, to present their own viewpoint. They could try to force votes on politically risky pieces of Clinton's program, to make the Democrats squirm over the partisan consequences; after all, there would be an election in November 1994 that might serve as a referendum on the Democrats' economic plan, especially if it was not working well. Or they could make use of parliamentary barriers such as the filibuster in an attempt to force delay, especially in the Senate, and to increase the public's focus on the weaknesses in Clinton's program. But whether they could effectively use the limited time to prepare a strategy highlighting problems with Clinton's program was uncertain. And Republicans conceded that, after 12 years during which they could look to the White House to take the initiative, they lacked confidence in their own ability to unify their often-disparate forces around a common set of principles and to challenge the new president. Further complicating their task were the internal recriminations and second-guessing among party factions after Bush's devastating loss. And the posturing began early among prospective presidential candidates for the 1996 campaign—not the least of whom was Senate Minority Leader Dole. Most Republicans also were under no illusion that Democrats would seriously consider their views or solicit their support for key parts of Clinton's agenda. But the GOP leaders hoped to create a scenario in which Clinton and his allies could not ignore them.

The business and economic communities also were filled with doubters. Although Clinton successfully sought support from the computer and high-tech industries, some of whose leaders had backed his election, the corporate sector generally was Republican and wary of the new president. Journalists reporting on economics soon wrote articles lamenting that the package was too limited. "We in the press helped foster a massive public deception," wrote columnist Robert J. Samuelson. "President Clinton calls his program for tax and spending changes an 'economic plan,' and we duly adopt his phrase. Yet, it isn't an economic plan—at least not as it's advertised. Its immediate effect on the economy would be, at most, modest."[7] The non-partisan Congressional Budget Office, while welcoming the budget changes, projected that Clinton's proposals would have "little net effect on the economy" or on job creation in the next few years. Surprisingly, perhaps, the plan's principal incentive for business—a partial restoration of the investment tax credit, which Congress had dropped in 1986—generated little support from that community, which was more focused on opposing another section of the plan, which would increase the tax rate for corporations. As for the plan's economic impact, initial projections of a lower deficit produced lower interest rates from Wall Street that helped to spur public confidence. But because the plan relied so heavily on higher taxes on the wealthy and on business, it could eventually slow economic growth, according to a Congressional Budget Office analysis of the proposal (see Table 4.1).

Finally, the legislative process itself was another potential bottleneck facing the Democrats. Because of the complexities of the 1974 Congressional Budget Act, the House and Senate would have to consider Clinton's program in at least three distinct segments, each of which would have its own complications. First, Congress debates early each year a budget plan that outlines federal spending and taxes for the government's next fiscal year, which begins on Oct. 1. Although that exercise does not focus on specific programs and changes, it commits Congress to a broad policy framework that it must meet in subsequent legislation. In 1993, that $1.5 trillion budget plan would be virtually identical to Clinton's Feb. 17 proposal. In the second step, Congress considers legislation to revise existing laws to implement the changes in both tax laws and spend-

Table 4.1 Projected Impact on the Federal Deficit of Clinton's Economic Package, According to Congressional Budget Office, March 1993 (Figures in Billions of Dollars)

	1993	1994	1995	1996	1997	1998
			Fiscal Years			
Original deficit estimate	$302	$287	$284	$290	$322	$360
Spending Cuts	—	9	20	57	102	126
Tax Increases	—	46	52	68	85	86
Total Deficit Reductions	—	-55	-72	-125	-187	-212
Spending Increases	7	18	32	45	57	67
Tax Cuts	—	18	13	12	13	14
Total Deficit Increases	+7	+36	+45	+57	+70	+81
Revised deficit estimate	308	268	257	222	205	229

ing for "mandatory" programs that have been broadly required by the earlier budget plan. This budget "reconciliation" bill would be more sweeping than usual because of the vast and costly changes proposed by Clinton. Finally, Congress must pass by October of each year the 13 annual appropriations bills that finance the routine operations of the government bureaucracy and the programs that it funds. In addition, Clinton's package envisioned the passage by early April of a separate appropriations bill for the $19 billion "stimulus" package of new spending, much of which he wanted to spend immediately. Supporters hoped that they could turn the complex process to their favor. But they agreed that they faced an ambitious schedule that allowed little room for slippage or error in any one area, which could result in an unraveling elsewhere.

Clinton and his Democratic allies dismissed critics who said that his program was not bold enough. They already faced a perilous few months as they worked to enact the new policies. Given the frustrations of the prior 12 years, however, it was a challenge that most of them welcomed. The election of a Democratic president creates some problems, Speaker Foley observed. "But they are different problems and they are welcome problems."

Endnotes

1. James P. Pfiffner, *The Strategic Presidency* (Chicago: The Dorsey Press, 1988), 137.
2. Ibid.
3. "Bring Back Ham Jordan," *The Wall Street Journal,* Jan. 27, 1993: A16.
4. Michael Kelly, "Read the Fine Print to Know if a Promise Really Counts," *The New York Times,* Jan. 26, 1993: A1.
5. Dan Balz and Ruth Marcus, "The Windup for the Pitch," *The Washington Post,* March 7, 1993: A1.
6. Alan Murray and Gerald F. Seib, "Clinton's Attention to Even Tiny Details Shaped His Budget," *The Wall Street Journal,* Feb. 19, 1993: A1.
7. Robert J. Samuelson, "Plan? What Plan?" *The Washington Post,* April 14, 1993: A17.

5

The House: The Old Guard and the New

When it came time for Congress to start working on Clinton's plan, the first major stop was the House Ways and Means Committee. Here, chairman Dan Rostenkowski (center) discusses strategy with Rep. Pete Stark.

America in All Its Glories and Imperfections

As the first legislative stop for most of President Clinton's agenda, the House of Representatives proved to be a relatively cooperative forum. Success on his economic plan was not achieved without considerable sweat and some accommodations. And the margins of victory sometimes were excruciatingly tight. But Clinton benefitted from the strong support of House Democratic leaders and the large freshman class, many of whose members had run on a similar message, to change the way that Washington works.

When the House is producing results, it can be an impressive legislative machine. Those moments are few and brief, as had been clear during most of the Reagan and Bush years. The initial months of the Clinton White House, however, had the markings of an interval in which the House cooperated with the president in churning out the Democratic agenda. Most lawmakers voting for those changes understood the potential economic and political consequences—both positive and negative—of their actions, and some were more than a little anxious on the key votes. Most, however, believed that they had little choice except to line up behind Clinton, rather than invite a return of the dreaded gridlock. Even the Republicans, who were virtually unanimous in their sustained opposition, usually understood the futility of their own immediate efforts. Instead, they focused more on the long term when, perhaps, they could take control of the House and show how a new majority produces very different results. For now, however, House Democrats were ready to move.

To watch the House from its galleries is to observe America in all its glories and imperfections, its grandeur, and its trivialities. It can be a chamber where the rhetorical combat is direct, the personality clashes are raw and the results are clear-cut. It is a place where widely varying factions of America—urban and rural, rich and poor, North and South—can produce a consensus that, they hope, will serve the national interest. Or on its less productive days, it can resemble an embarrassing street brawl between well-armed gangs. Although the development of C-SPAN on cable television has greatly expanded the opportunity to observe the House, it is far more instructive to view the scene in person from the galleries. To glimpse who is talking to whom and to speculate about what they might be discussing—outside the television cameras' range—offers a fuller appreciation of the richness of the legislative process. The Senate, by contrast, still has the feel of a stately club, where the results are more difficult to decipher. Its 100 potentates spend less time talking to each other one on one and typically speak publicly in indirect and nuanced tones. The contrast between the two ends of the Capitol was more striking than ever after the 1992 election, which produced major increases in the number of women and racial minorities serving in the House, many of whom were eager to speak their mind. The House's huge freshman class also would increase the pressure to get things done and to cleanse the embarrassing stain of the previous year's House bank fiasco and other institutional blemishes.

With its 435 members, gaining a majority in the House can be both easier and more difficult than in the smaller Senate. For those who seek to lead, the tough task is to balance and keep track of the views and needs of the many diverse lawmakers. Legislative victory requires the reconciling of these disparate, and sometimes conflicting, personal interests to gain the necessary 218 votes. Dialogue, more of it in private than in public, is the necessary tool for achieving agreement. But other factors expedite the task of consensus building in the House. The rules of the House are designed to allow a majority to work its will. Its members tend to function in groups or coalitions, whose patterns are predictable and easy to monitor. And they have fashioned a hierarchical system in which deference is paid to committees, especially those with effective chairmen. That is the case, at least, when the House is working smoothly. Because all of its members must stand for re-election every two years, they are keenly attuned to the public mood and responsive to its pressures. That electoral connection also gives them a bond with a newly elected president and tends to make the House more willing than is the Senate to support his agenda, with less quibbling over details or posturing for public attention. But if the public turns sour on a new president, the House can be quick to sound the warning.

Clinton's election received an especially enthusiastic reception among House Democrats because many see themselves, foremost, as legislators. For most of the prior dozen years, they had been stymied in their ability to affect many of the problems that they believed were harming the nation. The federal debt had quadrupled. Health-care costs had spiraled. Urban life had become more desolate. Family structures were eroding across America. And House members had felt helpless to address these issues, largely because they were receiving so little cooperation from the presidency. But that would change overnight. "The most important ingredient in passing a [health] bill is that we will have a president who makes health care a priority," Rep. Henry Waxman, a California Democrat and a leading player on health issues, said a few days before Clinton took office. Compared with their colleagues in the Senate, many of whom have a greater proclivity to giving speeches that merely talk about problems, House members are more action oriented. Another reason they needed to have a leader in the White House was because, as they had learned, they suffered from an inability to break their own internal deadlocks. With the new president's command of the bully pulpit to gain public backing, House Democrats like Rep. Ron Wyden of Oregon voiced confidence that Clinton would "neutralize all those interest groups" that have blocked health reform, for example. Even the committee chairmen, the barons of the House, celebrated Clinton's election with a letter to him on Nov. 4 in which they declared, "One of the lessons of recent years is that it is difficult, if not impossible, to resolve tough issues without strong presidential leadership."

For all the Democrats' optimism about their ability to act, however, they began the year with deep doubts about how well the House would perform. It was one thing to act as the opposition party, taking frequent pot shots at the other party and occasionally working with the president. But they had done little in recent years to act as true lawmakers. And in this case, they would be responding to the lengthy agenda of a new, largely untested, leader. As for the 72 Democrats who had served in the House with the most recent Democrat in the White House, working under President Carter—who often did not grasp the legislative arts—was hardly an instructive or enjoyable experience that many of them wished to recall or emulate. Gephardt, for example, who entered the House the same year that Carter became president, wanted to avoid a repetition of his principal 1979 feat: He teamed then with a junior Republican, Rep. David Stockman (who would soon become Reagan's chief budget adviser), to defeat the president's proposal to control health-care cost increases. Having spent the next decade trying to build a Democratic consensus on health-care issues, he knew the difficulty of the challenges ahead. "None of this is going to be easy," Gephardt told his fellow House Democrats at the start of the session. "We have to demonstrate to the American people that this great institution can work—promptly, creatively and responsively—in the national interest and in the people's interest."

While preparing to take office, one freshman Democrat voiced some trepidation about the challenge that he and his colleagues faced. "Congress has to have the guts, the discipline and the leadership to do the right thing," said Bob Filner of California. In many respects, fulfilling Filner's prescription would require major internal changes for the House. But most Democrats believed that they had little choice.

Using the Rules to Bolster a Majority

On most of the major congressional actions on Clinton's economic plan, the House acted before the Senate. In part, that was because the Constitution requires that tax measures originate in the House. And, by tradition, the House also has acted first on spending bills. Even on issues where the Senate could have moved first, Democratic leaders usually looked to the House to take the initial action, chiefly because its rules and traditions give the majority party greater control of the proceedings. Clinton and his top legislative and political aides, most of whom had greater experience in the House than in the Senate, assiduously took advantage of their procedural edge in that chamber. And with a 258–176 majority in the House (plus one independent, socialist Bernie Sanders of Vermont), Democrats held nearly 60 percent of its seats. In the Senate, they had a smaller share of seats—only a 57–43 majority, which dipped to 56–44 after a June special election in Texas to fill Treasury Secretary Bentsen's seat—and the conservative Democrats had greater influence in their party. (In 1981, by contrast, the Senate acted first on Reagan's budget plan. But that was chiefly because the Republicans had taken control of the Senate and wanted to set the pace, while Democrats still held at least a nominal majority in the House.)

Not much is achieved in the contemporary House unless some force, either internal or external, asserts strong political leadership. But would-be House leaders have available in their arsenal plenty of parliamentary opportunities and mechanisms to seize the initiative. Although the leaders do not always take advantage of them, these tools offer several sources of power that are key to legislative success: control of the schedule, the public and private ability to make the arguments that frame the debate, rewards such as favorable committee assignments for supporters, and comparable disincentives for those inclined to go their own way. Whether most lawmakers prove responsive may be determined by other factors. But, in seeking quick action on the new president's economic agenda, he and his House Democratic allies knew that they could use the rules to good effect, especially on legislation dealing with the budget. For Speaker Foley, the challenge to assist the new president was an especially welcome opportunity, following the body blows that he had sustained during the House's crises of the previous two years. Even many of his critics conceded that his legislative knowledge and his consensus-building skills could provide an important boost to a Democratic White House. And Foley, who was often uncomfortable with the partisan demands placed on his office under a president of the opposite party, was rejuvenated by the task of showing that he could help to break the gridlock and make government work. "This Congress will have a great challenge and a great opportunity in seeking to restore the confidence of the American people in the legislative branch," he told the House at the start of the session.

An especially effective leadership device is the 1974 Congressional Budget Act. Despite its complexities and detailed rules, the law has been used creatively in ways that its authors never intended. In passing that law, Congress had sought to prevent a repetition of President Nixon's 1973 refusal to spend money that Congress had appropriated for domestic programs. By formalizing the annual budget schedule and seeking to provide a more coherent outcome, the law's advocates also sought to make sense of the often balky congressional spending procedures.

But as the law has evolved through its annual applications, experts have deftly improvised many ways to accomplish other budget goals. In 1981, for example, Office of Management and Budget director David Stockman worked with congressional allies to use Budget Act procedures to allow passage of President Reagan's spending and tax-reduction plans despite opposition from hostile Democratic-controlled committees. That plan envisioned a balanced budget within three years. Four years later, Congress passed the inelegantly named Consolidated Omnibus Budget Reconciliation Act (COBRA) of 1985. Better known as Gramm-Rudman-Hollings, in honor of its three chief Senate authors, the law set steadily declining annual deficit ceilings for the next five years, with the intention of a balanced budget in 1991. Although it failed spectacularly in meeting that schedule, the 1985 law also introduced a budget concept called *sequestration,* designed to force automatic spending cuts if the targets were not met. Then, in 1990, the Budget Act became the foundation for bipartisan agreement on a more specific deficit-reduction law, which included actual ceilings for domestic and defense spending for the next five years. That deal also included the modest tax increases, mostly on the wealthy, that violated President Bush's 1988 campaign promise, "Read my lips. No new taxes," and so contributed to his undoing. With each of these three laws, failure to achieve the stated budget objectives was not necessarily inevitable. But the results showed that, even with good intentions or politically motivated goals, the Budget Act alone—or, for that matter, a constitutional amendment—will not balance the budget. Instead, Congress and the president must make the painful choices on both spending and taxes to attain sensible economic policy.

For Clinton and his congressional allies, the Budget Act would become an instrument for legislative speed and efficiency. As in the past, one of its major attributes was that it allowed them to present the budget as a package. That strategy allowed them to circumvent opponents' schemes for sabotaging the overall plan by forcing tough votes on its most controversial parts. By preventing these so-called single-shot amendments, at least in the House, Democrats voting for the package were spared politically painful votes on such pieces as the higher tax on Social Security recipients and the new energy tax. In addition, Speaker Foley and other party leaders were able to stack the membership of the House Budget Committee, which takes the first legislative step in the annual budget cycle, mostly with Democratic loyalists who could be counted on to approve the outlines of Clinton's budget. Despite comments by observers noting the political similarities to the quick start on Reagan's 1981 plan, there were key differences. Unlike that exercise, Clinton's party maintained control of the House and its committees; that gave the Democrats more flexibility to use the Budget Act and House rules to conform with their own timing. But, not insignificantly, the keystone of the 1981 plan was a huge tax cut, while the new deficit-reduction package required a big and politically painful tax increase.

In moving quickly on Clinton's economic program, the Democrats were aided by additional House procedures and traditions that benefit the majority. Another tool that allowed them to limit votes on contentious issues was the House Rules Committee, the House's traffic cop. Virtually all bills that are debated on the House floor require the initial passage by the House of a "rule" that sets the terms of debate, including which amendments may be offered and in what order. Increasingly in recent years, Democrats have used the Rules Committee to their advantage by organizing House debate and votes in a way that stacks the deck in their favor. When the House initially debated the broad outlines of the budget plan in March, for example, the only amendments that could be considered were those that dealt with the entire budget, not simply one section. Consequently, a Democrat who was willing to vote for most parts of the plan but opposed the defense spending cuts or the tax increases faced an all or nothing choice. Also, conservative Democrat Charles Stenholm of Texas was not permitted to offer his amendment that would have increased the total amount of Clinton's deficit-reduction plan. Despite angry objections by Republicans that they should be allowed to force votes on additional options, the Rules Committee and House Democrats allowed them to offer only two alternative plans. As with their other procedural advantages, the result was that Democrats could use the rules to help their cause.

Leadership and Followership

But these parliamentary tools offer little help unless a House majority also has the will to act. On the first big test for Clinton, House Democratic leaders succeeded by making a political plea for party unity to advance their cause. The two-day debate on the budget resolution, which took place in mid-March, only four weeks after Clinton's speech to Congress, was long on appeals to support his program but short on details. Even the Democrats on the House Budget Committee—who were responsible for drafting the legislation that both set the framework for the fiscal 1994 budget and took the initial step for putting into place Clinton's five-year plan for permanent tax and spending changes—kept their budget assumptions intentionally vague. Although these Democrats knew that they later would have to prepare more detailed legislation to implement the major parts of Clinton's program, the Budget Committee proposal permitted lawmakers to take a more general focus. As the following comments from the House debate indicate, the initial budget votes were mostly a partisan exercise designed to show that the Democrats wanted to work with Clinton and his economic agenda. On Election Day, said Majority Leader Gephardt, the American people had voted for change and for action. "They wanted an end to the argument, the gridlock," he said. "The one thing we need to do tonight to save the United States is to stand behind this young man [Clinton]. We want to give him a chance. We want our people to succeed. We want a new day for this country." The Republicans, for their part, posed the choice of what House Republican Conference chairman Dick Armey described as "two contesting visions of public policy." The Democratic plan, he said, would "move the American economy forward with one foot on the accelerator of growing government spending and the other foot on the brake of increased taxation of the American people." The Republican alternative, he summarized, tackles the deficit by relying on private enterprise and freedom.

The Democrats passed their plan, 243–183, on March 18 with only 11 members from their side defecting. Many Democrats decided to ignore, at least for the time being, their personal doubts and their differences with each other on Clinton's plan. This was the time for House Democrats to show that they could govern and act as a party. The conservatives, for example, put aside their well-publicized unhappiness about the additional spending proposed by Clinton and decided to endorse his overall plan. "The blame game is over," said Stenholm of Texas, a leader of conservative Democrats. "Every Democrat that I know wants to help shape the package so that we all get credit." From the liberal end of the party, 85 Democrats voted for a separate budget plan crafted by the Congressional Black Caucus, which would have required additional tax increases on the wealthy, increased domestic spending and mandated further cuts for the military. After their impassioned calls for stronger changes in the nation's economic direction, however, all of the 85 also voted for Clinton's program. With all the party's factions, Democratic leaders consistently pleaded for solidarity behind their new president. "We have an obligation to move the program," Foley said. Almost as an afterthought, the House also passed later the same night the $19.5 billion economic stimulus bill for additional spending in 1993; the vote was 235 to 190, with 22 Democrats opposed. Democratic leaders prevented any amendments from being offered, partly to thwart conservative Democrats who were unhappy with the additional spending.

As for the House Republicans, they were united in voting against the budget resolution in March, and only three Republicans voted for the stimulus plan. But they derived some satisfaction from the unexpected praise for their chief alternative to the budget plan: dropping the Democrats' proposed tax increases and substituting more spending cuts. Even *The New York Times,* which disagreed with its details, commended the proposal, prepared by Rep. John Kasich, the senior Republican on the Budget Committee, as "a good-faith effort" that was far more specific than the Democrats' proposal.[1] But the GOP solidarity did little to take away the luster of Clinton's first big success. At a jubilant White House breakfast on the morning after the House vote, Clinton told Democratic lawmakers that their success showed, "we don't have to spend all of our time posturing and dividing and running for cover instead of moving into the future." Then, he aptly cautioned, "It's a wonderful beginning. But it is just the beginning."

But House Democrats already knew that they faced more heavy lifting following the March vote. Some members who were willing to support the broad framework of the budget resolution would want to take a closer look and, in many cases, seek changes in the specific legislative language that would follow in the coming months. On these narrow issues, the House members would have special expertise, either because the issue affected their local constituency or because they had worked intensively on the matter in the House, often for many years. In these cases, the lawmakers and their aides might very well be more knowledgeable than the White House aides or Cabinet officials who were pushing for the change. For example, Ways and Means Committee chairman Dan Rostenkowski was leery of Clinton's proposals to introduce several new tax breaks for business into the Internal Revenue Code. Rostenkowski had played a vital role in cooperating with Reagan on the 1986 enactment of tax reform, which eliminated an earlier series of tax breaks in exchange for lower tax rates, and he was reluctant to jeopardize those reforms. Likewise, many lawmakers had spent countless hours in previous years fighting such spending as NASA's proposed space station or the Pentagon's "star wars" plans, and they were skeptical of Clinton's attempt to promote yet another overhaul of those programs. So, the first budget vote showed how much the election had changed the House. But much more had to be done to achieve the president's goals.

Rosty's Ways and Means

Because most of the House's nitty-gritty legislative work is done in its committees, the burden for reviewing the details of Clinton's economic plan fell chiefly on its Ways and Means Committee. With its members' intensive experience with the broad issues under the committee's control and their more parochial interest on selected narrow issues, the president's proposal would receive a thorough airing. Once the committee had approved it, with few major changes, the bill had achieved a major political push.

The House historically has set the framework for congressional debate on spending and tax measures. This has been the case not only because of the Constitutional requirement that tax legislation originates in the House, but also because its members have gained more expertise than have senators in dealing with many of these issues. Not only do House members who deal with these issues typically have fewer committee assignments to occupy their attention than do their Senate counterparts, but they also have gained greater influence because their initial handling of a legislative proposal often defines the debate. At both the Appropriations and the Ways and Means Committees, the pivotal House panels for spending and tax bills, Democrats typically have constructed a consensus approach to assure that most members of their party are comfortable with the bill. In addition, Democratic leaders usually have sought to assign members to those panels who have shown that they are team players or skillful legislators.

The Ways and Means Committee would be drafting real changes in the tax code, health programs and other federal laws, unlike the Budget Committee's earlier general language, which did not address specific provisions in federal statutes. As his committee worked on the massive measure implementing its portions of Clinton's budget, Ways and Means chairman Rostenkowski took an approach that was designed to encourage full participation and, ultimately, the support from all of his committee Democrats. Widely known as "Rosty," the chairman had long been proud of his committee's ability to deal responsibly with the complex issues over which it had control, including taxes, Social Security, health care and international trade. He also believed that the panel was a microcosm of the House and mirrored its many diverse interests. "Members outside think that I have an iron fist," Rostenkowski said of the Ways and Means panel. "Members on the inside know that I work with consensus. . . . My committee becomes as active as the individual members want." In one key aspect, the committee's membership in 1993 reflected the massive turnover of the 1992 election. Of its 36 members from the previous Congress, 14 either retired, sought other office or were not re-elected. With the increase in the committee's size to 38 members (24 Democrats, 14 Republicans), that meant that 10 Democrats and 6 Republicans were new to the committee.

Joining the Ways and Means panel is a daunting task at any time because the many complex issues and the intricate internal politics take a steep learning curve. That was especially so in 1993, as the committee prepared to handle major tax and health-care legislation. For Rostenkowski, the turnover was potentially a double-edged sword. For a dozen years, he had chaired the committee with a strong gavel and had suffered few defeats. The new members were even less likely than were their predecessors to pose effective challenges to the chairman, at least in their early months. Even as the congressional reforms since 1974 have spread power more widely, Rostenkowski—like a few other chairmen—has shown the experience, knowledge and parliamentary resources that give him extra ammunition during legislative dealings. "New members need at least one major bill before they understand the intricacies of tax bills," said a former Ways and Means member. "The highly technical aspects of the committee's work mean that members need to take time to understand it." But the jeopardy was that committee newcomers also might be less effective allies in securing the support of lawmakers not on Ways and Means when the committee's legislation reached the House floor.

The Ways and Means Committee had the main job of handling Clinton's "budget reconciliation" bill, designed to implement the details of the budget plan that the House passed in March. It was responsible for achieving more than 70 percent of the total deficit cuts that Clinton had proposed, chiefly the tax increases and most of the spending cuts for federal "entitlement" programs, which ordinarily do not require annual funding by Congress. In addition, 12 other committees prepared at the same time the other parts of the bill that eventually would be combined into a single package that the House would debate in late May. For example, the Post Office and Civil Service Committee worked on a plan to lower the pension costs of retired federal workers. And the Education and Labor Committee was faced with writing language to implement Clinton's changes in the college student loan program. (Clinton's proposed cuts in "discretionary" federal spending programs, which require annual funding, would be handled later by the Appropriations Committee.) But, with most of the action at his committee, Rostenkowski sought to move quickly. First, as was his custom, the chairman organized extensive public hearings to familiarize committee members with the key issues in Clinton's proposal and to permit interest groups to offer their views. Then, the members had several weeks to explore the controversial matters and to talk informally with each other about whether they wished to seek changes in the legislation. Gradually, the 24 committee Democrats prepared to act on the bill by meeting privately as a group for many days until they became more comfortable with the details of the bill and they gained a sense of which sections caused the most problems with other committee Democrats. Rostenkowski usually opposed changes that were not acceptable to Clinton and his advisers, with whom he kept in close contact. "Who am I to say that I won't support the president?" Rostenkowski asked, rhetorically. "We will pass his legislation. But it won't be exact." By early May, the Democrats were ready to vote.

Where were the Republicans during all of these discussions? In theory, at least, each House committee had to "mark up" its legislation in an open session, where all of their Democratic and Republican members could participate. Although Rostenkowski and some Ways and Means Democrats said that they welcomed their help, they determined that their Republican colleagues had little desire to participate constructively in their committee's work. A few of the GOP members said that they might be willing to work on parts of the legislation. "In general, Republicans believe that [the economic package poses] far too heavy a burden on a fragile economy," said Rep. Nancy Johnson of Connecticut. "But Rostenkowski might need us on some issues." That would not be the case, however. Instead, the Democrats formally drafted their version of the reconciliation bill during three days of private meetings in the Ways and Means Committee's library next to the main committee room.

When they completed their work, the Democrats returned to the full committee and kept to their back-room agreement to oppose all Republican efforts to amend their package. They held firm in the face of potentially embarrassing GOP amendments that spotlighted politically risky parts of Clinton's package, such as an increase in the tax liability of Social Security benefits, the broad new tax on energy and reductions in Medicare benefits.

The handling of the budget reconciliation bill was dramatic evidence of the power and effectiveness of Rostenkowski, a 35-year House veteran. An old-style politician from the remnants of Chicago's Democratic organization who believed in the values of political apprenticeship and loyalty, the chairman kept tighter control of the committee's work than did most other House chairmen. He maintained regular contact and closely monitored the views of the other 23 Democrats and agreed to concessions from Clinton's plan only when it was necessary to retain majority support in the whole committee. Despite his sometimes gruff demeanor and tendency to speak publicly about the issues only in general terms, he had a good sense of the substantive implications of legislation. "He comes across as a lumbering politician from Chicago," said Rep. Mike Kopetski of Oregon, a committee newcomer. "But he is a policy-maker who cares about doing something because it is good policy." His task of managing the complex bill was made all the more difficult because, for more than a year, he had been under investigation by an extensive federal grand-jury review of illegal activities at the House post office. If he had been indicted before the bill was completed, House Democratic rules would have automatically forced him to relinquish his chairmanship, thus dealing a grave blow to Clinton's agenda. His committee's success in the face of those pressures was testimony to the Democrats' loyalty. "Members are protective of the chairman," said Rep. Robert Matsui of California. "We are like mother bears when it comes to attacks on him."

Challenging the Status Quo for Doing Business

Although Clinton's deficit-reduction plan was the chief legislative business during the early months of 1993, the other leading issue preoccupying House members was a significant but less visible struggle to change how Congress operates. The two efforts showed two very different sides of the same institution: The handling of the economic package was an attempt to show that the old ways could still produce responsible legislation. But the reformers, especially in the House, believed that Congress also needed to change the federal election laws and the working conditions for its members so that they could spend less time on fundraising and more time legislating. Even if the economic package were approved, the reformers said, Congress had become too balky and balkanized and it needed a periodic overhaul. The reform efforts proceeded mostly in separate forums from the economic agenda, and they achieved little significant change in the early months. But they spawned tensions that had some impact on the concurrent legislative dealings and might have longer-term ramifications on how Congress does its business. The reformers moved on three separate fronts: The large freshman class sought to make the House a more open and democratic (with a small "d") institution; although many of the first-term Democrats and Republicans voiced similar rhetoric, they mostly operated separately because of the continuing partisan pressures in the House. In addition, a group of more senior members from both the House and Senate worked on a joint committee that was created in 1992 to examine the organization of Congress and to make recommendations by the end of 1993. The third and most controversial area was an attempt to overhaul the law for federal election campaigns, which critics have said are too costly, give too much control to special-interest groups and favor incumbents over challengers.

Efforts to reform the House are hardly new. Like most large institutions, the House becomes encrusted by its sometimes age-old ways of operating. And there usually are bands of lawmakers, in both parties, eager to point out the problems. But the forces of the status quo have considerable muscle to discourage what they fear will become menacing or destabilizing change. Consequently, it requires deep-seated unhappiness—either inside or outside the House—to create the critical mass needed to make changes. Such a period was at hand after the 1992 election. The legislative gridlock of the past two years, the House bank fiasco and other well-publicized problems certainly had soured much of the public—plus many lawmakers themselves—on the internal shortcomings. Bill Clinton rode to town on the message of change. And the November election of 110 House freshmen meant that more than one-fourth of the whole House had little stake in the old system;

indeed, many were under considerable pressure from their constituents to make the place work better.

The most recent significant reform effort in the House had accompanied the entry of what had been the largest freshman class since the 1940s—the 93 new members, including 75 Democrats, who were elected in 1974 in the wake of the Watergate scandal and the resignation of President Nixon. Through a variety of actions soon after they were elected, they moved quickly to reduce the power of the seniority system in selecting committee chairmen, enhance the power of subcommittees and their chairmen, and open up the often secretive processes to force more accountability. Among the most dramatic moves backed by these "Watergate babies" was the ouster of three veteran committee chairmen, Armed Services chairman Edward Hebert of Louisiana, Banking chairman Wright Patman of Texas and Agriculture chairman William Poage of Texas. Each had run his panel in what was considered an autocratic fashion and refused to recognize the rights of junior committee members. The demise of these chairmen served notice to other chairmen, present and future, that if they wish to keep their positions, they must pay heed to the majority of their party. In addition, the 1974 freshman Democrats felt free to criticize their party's power structure in the House, and they often did. And they got involved in legislation far earlier than had typically been the case for freshmen members. Those freshmen had received invaluable assistance from some senior House Democrats, who had been advocating these reforms for several years, with limited progress. As time passed, however, the long-term changes in the House that were achieved by the Watergate reformers became less dramatic and were diluted once many of them tasted the fruits of the system that they had earlier criticized.

Some of the freshmen from the Class of 1992 cited the earlier precedent in trying to make their own mark on the House. But there were important differences. The new first-term Democrats faced the additional challenge of enacting the ambitious agenda urged by the new president of their own party. In 1975, in the face of a Congress dominated by the opposition party, President Gerald Ford had a limited program of his own; that meant that the Watergate babies had fewer outside constraints on their activities. Besides, many more of the 1992 freshmen had experience serving in government and the new class had a more bipartisan mix of members than did the 1974 group, which dimmed the prospect of class-wide coopera-

tion. And it had the major disadvantage of no readily available reform agenda. In the view of most Democratic leaders in 1993, including one-time reform supporter Speaker Foley, the House
already had undergone significant reform and it faced the risk of becoming unmanageable if authority was decentralized much further.
That helps to explain why Democratic leaders moved so quickly after the November election to encourage their freshmen to join
forces with their party's team. Those internal changes that Democrats initially made were narrow and, if anything, were designed to
increase their leaders' authority to remove potential obstacles to
House approval of Clinton's agenda. For example, the Democrats
created a leadership working group under Foley's control that was
designed to coordinate policy decisions and to discourage committees and their chairmen from pursuing their own course.

Still, some first-term Democrats believed that the post-election reforms were not enough. With Foley's agreement, they
agreed to work among themselves and to submit to the Democratic
Caucus by the end of March their own reform proposals. The discussions among the 63 Democrats revealed a variety of concerns.
Some of the freshmen wanted to abolish their most heavily criticized and visible office perquisites, such as the House's cut-rate
barber shops and free parking at Washington's airports. The public
perception of Congress as a privileged class, which former presidential candidate Ross Perot was fueling, worried this group. Another group wanted to make additional reductions in the power of
seniority with proposals, for example, to limit the number of years
that a member could serve on a committee or as its chairman. But
other freshmen opposed that kind of change. Members of the Congressional Black Caucus, for example, traditionally have benefitted
from seniority because they represent districts without much electoral competition once they have won office. And some freshmen
had other priorities. Jane Harman of California, for example, declined an opportunity to lead a freshman task force on reform because she wanted to focus her efforts on her Los Angeles district's
need for economic aid. These and other positions were thoroughly
aired during several well-attended meetings of the freshman Democrats. "I have learned that there obviously is a lot of agreement on
the need for change but disagreement on what that entails," Rep.
Eric Fingerhut of Ohio, who co-chaired the reform task force for
the freshmen, said following those discussions.

Freshman Democrats drafted plans to reform House operations. Although their immediate efforts achieved few significant changes, the presence of 110 new members made for a
new mood in the House. In the photo are (left to right):
Reps. Carolyn Maloney of New York, Eric Fingerhut of Ohio,
Ron Klink of Pennsylvania, Maria Cantwell of Washington,
and Lynn Schenk of California.

That ambivalence characterized the newcomers' reform
plans. In the end, the Democrats' package focused on general
points, such as a 25 percent cut in the budget for congressional operations, reforms to subject Congress to the same laws that it
passes for the nation, and the need to reduce the role of special-
interest money and lobbyists in politics. Proposals to change how
the House operates were scant, with a focus on making the daily
congressional schedule better coordinated to reduce meeting conflicts and more "family-friendly" to allow members time in the

evening with family members who had accompanied them to Washington. The proposed reforms received a tepid response from House critics who said that most either were "toothless" or dealt with relatively small potatoes. "It always happens," said a veteran House Democrat. "I watched the 1974 class come in saying that they were really going to change things. After about six months, they forgot all about that. These people will too."[2] Eventually, the House Democratic Caucus considered a modified version of some of the freshmen rules changes designed to improve internal efficiency. Meanwhile, the freshman Republicans produced a more far-ranging package of reforms, including term limits for members in their service as committee chairmen, elimination of the congressional Appropriations committees, and approval of several budget reforms. Since they were the minority party, however, their views on congressional reform would have little impact. Even the activities of their Democratic counterparts, however, also proved to be short-lived as reformers moved to more specific forums.

The prospects for significant internal reforms in the new Congress lay largely in the hands of a joint House-Senate committee of mostly senior members, which had been given a year to study and make recommendations on congressional organization. The committee was co-chaired by experienced Democratic lawmakers: Rep. Lee Hamilton of Indiana and Sen. David Boren of Oklahoma. They supervised extensive hearings in the early months of 1993, during which other members gave testimony on what ails Congress and suggested their prescriptions for change. Some of the proposals were modest, such as restricting the numbers of members on existing committees and subcommittees or limiting the number of such assignments that each senator and House member could hold. Other ideas, if accepted, would have a major impact on the institution. For example, some lawmakers echoed the freshman Republican call to eliminate the congressional Appropriations committees, which are responsible for funding most federal agencies. In its place, they wanted to change the budget process so the so-called authorizing committees would have the power to allocate money according to the budget plan agreed to early each year. Not surprisingly, that proposal generated hostility from the influential leaders of the Appropriations committees.

The joint committee faced other problems as well. As they received the array of proposals, its members did not appear to be developing internal consensus for any particular plan. Nor were they building support for action from congressional leaders or other key lawmakers, many of whom were preoccupied with Clinton's economic plan and other more pressing issues. Indeed, their group "grope" won its greatest public attention when Ross Perot, the 1992 independent presidential candidate, was invited to present his ideas on what is wrong with Congress. "Fairly or unfairly, the people feel that our government is for sale," he testified. After Perot's litany of criticisms, Democratic Sen. Harry Reid of Nevada lectured him to "start checking your facts a little more and stop listening to the applause so much." The exchange won extensive television coverage, but the lambasting did little to help the joint committee with its defined mandate. In that sense, Perot's testimony was a good illustration of a major problem with Congress: extensive publicity-seeking is no substitute for the hard work of building internal agreements. That failure became all the more apparent in June, when the joint committee members informally assembled in quest of a proposal. Instead, they found that they were badly divided, and they were forced to delay several deadlines for their planned preparation of a package.

Congressional action on campaign-finance legislation had somewhat deeper support and, consequently, moved more quickly to the legislative center stage. When Clinton decided to join with Speaker Foley, Sen. Mitchell and other congressional Democratic leaders in support of a reform plan similar to a proposal that Bush had vetoed in 1992, it sent somewhat conflicting signals. On one hand, the Democrats agreed with would-be reformers who contended that the existing system for financing campaigns was too costly and that it chiefly benefitted incumbents from both parties. These Democrats also believed that the solution lay in the direction of spending limits on candidates and in a system of partial government subsidies for campaigns. "This plan will change the way Washington works, the way campaigns are financed, the way that politics is played," Clinton said when he announced the plan. On the other hand, Republicans continued to criticize the Democratic plan for taking what they termed a partisan approach that was to the advantage of Democratic candidates because it preserved political action committees (PACs); most of them have been heavily financed by Washington-based special interest groups that direct their money overwhelmingly to incumbents. Sen. Mitch McConnell of Kentucky, a leading Republican opponent of the proposal, called the plan "food stamps for politicians" and he objected to retention of the PACs. But, on specific provisions of the reform package, the partisan divisions were not so straightforward. In the House, many Southern Democrats objected to the publicly financed vouchers that congressional candidates would be able to use to lower the cost of their advertising. Other Democrats privately worried that any change could have adverse consequences for their own political prospects. They hoped that Republicans would help to kill the bill in the Senate and take them off the hook. But no such luck. After Senate Democrats made enough concessions to pick up a few Republican votes required to break a three-week Republican filibuster and pass the bill in early June, House Democrats began to prepare for what they feared would be a nightmarish debate and outcome. Although Foley initially said that the House would consider the bill in July, later he cited the busy legislative demands as explanation for postponing action until the fall.

These exercises of congressional business as usual and the initially modest action on reforms proved frustrating to many of the House freshmen who wanted to show the voters before the 1994 election that they could change how Washington works. When told that a senior member had said that the freshmen were planning "to use a machine gun on Congress," freshman reform advocate Fingerhut lamented, "If the things in our package are really viewed as machine-gunning the institution, then we all have a long way to go."[3] Although the House Democratic Caucus accepted a few operational changes proposed by the freshmen, the limited impact of their reform initiatives reinforced the need for more effective organization for a definitive agenda. Nevertheless, despite the lack of specific reforms, the very presence of so many new members had a cathartic effect on the House by bringing in fresh blood that challenged the old ways of thinking and of doing business. Even such a small change as the House's decision in early 1993 to eliminate four unimportant "select" committees, each of which had been temporarily created to study problems more than a decade ago and had no legislative power, signaled a change in the status quo. Likewise, many of the newcomers were more willing than were their predecessors to take a fresh look at questionable spending programs. But the House's resistance to change was a hard lesson for the new members who had come to Washington excited about their prospects.

Women and Minorities

If their initial reform efforts proved disappointing, there was no mistaking the freshmen impact in making the House more demographically diverse. With 24 new women, 16 new blacks and seven new Hispanics among its 435 members (making totals of 47, 38 and 17, respectively, including some overlap), the House began to lose its stereotype as a bunch of overweight white men in smoke-filled rooms. Although most of the women and racial-minority members were Democrats, there were a handful of Republicans among the newcomers. No doubt, all of these changes created cultural shock; for some House old-timers, it took time to grow accustomed. Early in 1993, *The New York Times* reported, a "young black woman with the gold sneakers, braided hair and Mickey Mouse watch stepped into the elevator in the Capitol." After the woman elevator operator three times told the attractive black woman that the elevator was for "members only," the attendant finally saw the blue pin with the congressional seal hanging on a gold chain around the neck of Rep. Cynthia McKinney, a freshman Democrat from Georgia. "The elevator lady was very apologetic and I told her that it's wonderful now that members of Congress come in all shapes and hues," McKinney said.[4]

The changes generated by new members such as McKinney were more than visual. (She was one of five new black women, all Southerners with prior experience as state or county legislators, raising the total to eight among House Democrats.) In the often detached world of the House, they could become symbols of a part of America that received sparse attention in the House. By their very presence, the newly elected blacks, Hispanics and women would change the congressional debate. As lawmakers who were especially concerned about the problem of poor young welfare mothers, for example, they could be a voice inside the House pressing for more federal funds for pregnant and working women. "We have to force people, if they're not willing to come along on their own, to accept that black folks have dignity," McKinney said.[5] Other first-term black members wanted to refocus the civil rights debate from its early emphasis on political power to a greater consciousness of economic power. Rep. Mel Reynolds of Illinois, who focused on the need to reduce the high unemployment in his district on Chicago's South Side, described himself as among "post–World War II blacks who look at the civil rights revolution as something that we have won. . . . We also want economic rights."

Diversity became something of a rule inside influential sectors of the House. Of the Democrats' four chief deputy whips, there was one woman, one black and one Hispanic. The Ways and Means Committee increased from two to five blacks among its 24 Democrats. At the Appropriations Committee, there was also an increase from two to five women among the 37 Democrats. For some old-timers who had been trailblazers, the change was a welcome symbol. Reps. Ronald Dellums of California and Patricia Schroeder of Colorado, who were scorned as anti-war activists when they joined the Armed Services Committee two decades earlier, in 1993 started to chair that committee and its two most important subcommittees. Rep. Charles Rangel, who represents Harlem in New York City, talked about turning the five blacks on Ways and Means into a potential swing bloc that would use its muscle on behalf of America's inner cities. For other junior members, the move up the congressional ladder was more routine. Democratic Rep. Rosa DeLauro of Connecticut sought to downplay her gender as a factor in winning a seat on the Appropriations Committee and becoming a part of the House's power structure. "We need to all work with men and women here and not to marginalize ourselves" by focusing solely on women's issues, she said. And Reynolds, the first freshman to gain a seat on the Ways and Means Committee during Rostenkowski's 12-year chairmanship, acknowledged that he benefitted from being a fellow Chicagoan. But Reynolds repeatedly emphasized that he was a team player and that he fully expected to support Clinton's agenda, a pledge that he fulfilled. "I am inclined to make the case for Gov. Clinton and his program in all circumstances," he said after the election. "The public won't take it lightly if Congress attempts to block him." That was the kind of music that House leaders liked to hear.

The increased numbers of women and blacks quickly had a legislative impact. One example came when House Democrats discussed the framework of a campaign finance bill with Clinton's aides. The House leaders were under considerable pressure from women members who insisted on carving an exemption in the bill for "EMILY's List," a PAC that had gained wide influence because of its success in electing new Democratic women to Congress, especially in 1992. Despite objections from President Clinton, who said when the bill was unveiled that all PACs should be treated the same way, House leaders supported the viewpoint of the women members. Likewise, the rejuvenated Congressional Black Caucus used its weight to delay passage and to weaken a line-item veto bill that had been advocated by moderate and conservative Democrats to increase the president's authority to withhold spending approved by Congress. Many of these black lawmakers feared that the spending cuts, especially by a future president, could adversely affect their needy constituents. Under the proposal, said Rep. Corinne Brown of Florida, a president "could threaten to rescind funding for a project in a particular member's district if the member did not support the president on another vote of importance to the White House." Other Black Caucus members objected that Clinton and House leaders were taking their support for granted on many other issues. Yet, when the bill finally reached the House floor in April, 14 black Democrats succumbed to pressure from their party's leaders to support the modified line-item veto. If nothing else, they proved that no group within the House is a monolith. Later, Clinton encountered more hostility from the Black Caucus after he withdrew the nomination of law professor Lani Guinier to head the Justice Department's civil rights division. Although he had cited Guinier's controversial writings on voting-rights issues, many of the black members in the House thought that he was too quick in caving in to opposition from many Senate Democrats. The only black senator was freshman Carol Moseley-Braun, the Illinois Democrat.

Not all of the new members moved quickly to center stage. Like other freshmen, many of the new women and blacks gained seats on lower-profile committees like Public Works and Transportation or Banking, Finance and Urban Affairs. Because blacks in the House previously had represented mostly urban districts, it was especially striking to see four black first-termers from the South join the Agriculture Committee. Many of the new black-majority districts were created in the rural South, where black political power had been slower to mature. In addition to focusing on constituent-based issues, they will probably spend their early years in the House learning the institution's customs before taking on more high-profile issues. Rep. Earl Hilliard of Alabama, for example, had an interest in remedying racial abuses by the Federal Bureau of Investigation. But he deferred that concern to focus on economic development for his low-income district. "After two years, I'll know my way around better," Hilliard said.

Many freshman Democrats were well aware of the traditional House axiom that first-termers should spend most of their time assuring that they will win a second term. Especially with the controversy generated by Clinton's economic program, some of them showcased their independence because they feared that 1994 would be a hazardous year for Democrats to be running on their own. A leading example was Marjorie Margolies-Mezvinsky, a freshman who had barely won 50 percent of the vote in her Republican-leaning suburban Philadelphia district and was one of only five House Democrats to vote "no" on each of three key early votes: Clinton's budget, the economic stimulus plan and the initial passage of the deficit-reduction bill. (In contrast to Margolies-Mezvinsky, whose district was one where Clinton finished first the previous November, each of the other four represented a conservative Southern district where Clinton had not fared so well.) She had told voters that she was not a big-spending Democrat.

In the swirl of activity of 1993, the long-term impact of these new members tended to be overlooked. But to observers in the gallery and elsewhere, there was little doubt that the House would never be the same.

The Vote of the Decade

The House's most dramatic showdown during Clinton's early months came in late May, when the Democratic leaders brought to the House floor the budget reconciliation bill that had been prepared by the 13 committees, led by Ways and Means. For new members and old, voting on that proposal posed many challenges. Because the measure included more than $250 billion in tax increases during the next five years, many Democrats were anxious about the political impact in their home districts. It was one thing to support the deficit-reduction goal, at least in principle, as had most Democrats in March; it became more difficult for them to step up to the plate and cast their vote when the result would be real changes in federal spending and tax policies that would affect their constituents. Though Democrats had cheered Clinton when he announced his plan to the House in February, every politician ultimately must make up his or her own mind when faced with a legislative choice. Many factors influence their decision, especially on the tough votes, including the merits of an issue, the swirl of pressures from congressional colleagues, the local impact and politics, and loyalty to the president. Clinton's political arsenal was weak for many of these members because virtually all of them operated on the assumption that they were stronger than the president was in their home district. Evidence of that was there were only four House districts in the nation where Clinton had won a larger share of the local vote in 1992 than did that district's House member; although that weak showing resulted, in part, from the three-way presidential contest, lawmakers traditionally assume that they have a better sense of their district's politics than does a president. That Clinton's popularity had steadily dropped in public-opinion polls during the spring of 1993 made a vote for the budget more difficult and increased the political peril for them with local voters: Now they also had to worry whether Clinton might eventually become a political albatross to them.

Although Foley and other House Democratic leaders had decided weeks earlier to schedule the vote shortly before Memorial Day, they knew a few days before the actual tally that they were not close to the majority required to pass the bill. (With two seats yet to be filled because of vacancies caused by members who had quit to join the Clinton Cabinet, Democrats would need 217 votes on their side; they concluded that they had no hope for any Republican support of the bill.) Although legislative leaders prefer to be confident about the outcome before they schedule the showdown on an important measure, the Democrats were aware that in this case some members would not make their final decision without the intense pressure of the vote staring them in the face. "Our assumption was that we needed to put the lights on the board before we saw who showed up," said House Democratic Caucus vice chairman Vic Fazio of California. He was referring to the tally board on the front wall of the House chamber that lists all members and shows how they have voted when they inserted their plastic card into the electronic system. Under the direction of Majority Whip David Bonior of Michigan, the leaders used a sophisticated "whip" counting system to keep track privately of the intentions of all Democrats and to pressure those who remained uncertain. In the final days before the crucial vote, Bonior and his colleagues met several times each day to compare notes. A few hours before the vote, they were uncertain of the outcome. But they decided to go ahead, in part because they concluded that delay would not work in their favor.

In the final days and hours, a crucial factor was the leadership-sponsored negotiations among a cross section of Democrats over a proposal by party conservatives to control the growth of federal entitlements. Those programs, such as Social Security, Medicare and welfare, do not require annual congressional review, and they have grown so rapidly that they consume more than one-third of government spending. Clinton's earlier failure to make major cuts in these programs had disappointed conservative Democrats such as Charles Stenholm of Texas and Tim Penny of Minnesota. Their displeasure had grown because of their sense that the president and his staff were ignoring their concerns. So, they decided that this was the time to flex their muscle to achieve results. But liberal Democrats resisted any step that would harm senior citizens or the poor. They also objected to the type of automatic across-the-board spending cuts that Republicans had advocated under Reagan and Bush. After several days of intense, back-room negotiations supervised by Majority Leader Gephardt, the two sides finally reached a deal after midnight on the night before the scheduled House vote. Under the agreement, the White House's Office of Management and Budget would annually set targets for all entitlement spending for the coming year. If the ceiling was exceeded by more than 0.5 percent, the president would be required to propose tax increases or spending cuts or, if he favored neither, he would have to explain why he backed the resulting increase in the federal deficit. Conservatives welcomed what they considered the first step toward discipline on entitlements. Liberals were relieved there would be no automatic cuts. Skeptics like Rostenkowski scorned the deal as "bells and whistles." But both sides breathed a sigh of relief that they had made an accommodation, which they recognized was vital to passage of the deficit-reduction bill. It was, Gephardt said, the final act in the cementing of the House Democrats' "family."

Though the agreement on entitlements increased the number of Democrats committed to the overall bill, the Democrats remained short of a firm majority. Gaining the final few votes required a form of hand-to-hand combat by House leaders. The steps to achieve passage included telephone calls and other discussions with recalcitrant members by Clinton, Vice President Gore, Foley, Gephardt and anyone else who could make an effective plea for party unity; informal agreements about future legislative deals, including efforts to back changes to the energy tax when the Senate debated the reconciliation bill; and some deep soul searching by wavering lawmakers. Perhaps the most effective last-minute tactic, which helped to convince at least one uncertain lawmaker to support the bill, was an example of old-fashioned politics: A group of freshman Democrats circulated a petition threatening that their party Caucus would meet and strip a committee or subcommittee chairmanship from any Democrat who voted against the bill. Though the petition was pigeonholed a couple of weeks later, its blunt message had gained some attention. Other members made more personal judgments. Rep. Karen Shepherd, a freshman from a conservative Utah district, was one Democrat who decided to vote for the bill on its merits, regardless of the ominous political consequences, and without much pressure from the White House or congressional leaders. "My reason to run for Congress was to restore the economy and to give our children a better life," Shepherd later said. "There is a pretty good possibility that this could defeat me for re-election. . . . But my highest commitment is to reducing the deficit. I didn't come here to get re-elected." On the other hand, her fellow first-termer Margolies-Mezvinsky said that she voted against the bill, despite her stated support for deficit reduction, because she also had promised the voters in her Pennsylvania district during her election campaign that she would "hold the line on taxes." She failed to explain how she would have preferred to reconcile those two goals. A lonely-looking Margolies-Mezvinsky appeared to be in pain on the House floor as she commiserated with a senior Democrat from her home state in the minutes before the vote. A former television news reporter in Washington, she was not fully prepared for a life in politics.

Speaker Foley announced the result at 9 p.m. on May 27: the proposal passed, 219–213. There were 38 Democrats, including Margolies-Mezvinsky, who joined all 175 Republicans in voting against the bill. The vote was the most dramatic change of policy by the House since 1981, when the House, by an even narrower margin, ratified the Reagan revolution. The drama of the budget vote, which Fazio later called "a defining vote" for the House and its Democrats, was enhanced by the knowledge that the outcome would make and break political careers. Unless they changed their ways, members like Margolies-Mezvinsky who voted against the bill would be outcasts among House Democrats; they could expect to receive fewer benefits from their party for months or years to come. But they gambled that their vote would win them popularity with their constituents at home. Those Democrats such as Shepherd, on the other hand, who cast a difficult vote for the bill would be duly rewarded with party aid in their efforts to win re-election and later, assuming they succeeded. Like all legislators, these two women were playing for two very distinct audiences. By the November 1994 election, they would have a better idea of the wisdom and the impact of their votes. In the meantime, Clinton had scored an essential victory.

Endnotes

1. "The Republicans Strike Back," *The New York Times,* March 11, 1993: A24.
2. Graeme Browning, "The New Reformers," *National Journal,* April 24, 1993: 975.
3. Ibid., 977.
4. Maureen Dowd, "Growing Sorority in Congress Edges Into the Ol' Boys Club," *The New York Times,* March 5, 1993: A1.
5. Browning, "McKinney: Showing 'Em," *National Journal,* Jan. 30, 1993: 250.

6

The Senate Club Crumbles

Sen. Patty Murray of Washington, a self-styled "mom in tennis shoes," was a leading example of the new senators who were determined to change the negative image from the confirmation hearings of Clarence Thomas for the Supreme Court.

One Hundred Independent Contractors

Compared with what lay ahead in the Senate, the House was child's play. With their constant clash of egos and influence, their frequent rambunctiousness and the narrower margin of Democratic control, senators strained the limits of Clinton's political skills and patience. In April, the Senate inflicted the worst setback of his early months. Then, it forced more changes in his economic plan than had the House. Throughout the period, the president was subjected to a barrage of senatorial second-guessing, often from supposed friends from his own party and region: Sam Nunn of Georgia on gays in the military and David Boren of Oklahoma on the budget were the leading examples. Clinton tried several ways to work with senators. First, he stroked some of them with individual attention and other forms of homage. Later, he stated his acceptable guidelines and deferred to them on the details. On other occasions, he used surrogates to negotiate deals. Whatever the outcome, the process was like an obstacle course.

Dealing with the Senate requires endless perseverance, for insiders and outsiders alike. The clash of 100 egos, complex issues and an unstructured setting can produce the equivalent of political mud wrestling, in which extraordinary tenacity is required to achieve results. "I have the best developed patience muscle in America," George Mitchell, a Democrat from Maine, said in 1990, as he reviewed his initial service as Senate majority leader. "It has been remarkably strengthened in the past two years." President Clinton undoubtedly shared similar sentiments, as he met chronic frustration in dealing with senators. In the Senate, time often seems to stand still. Despite all of its fractiousness, the House produces results—for better or worse. But the Senate frequently serves as a courtly television studio in which the disposition of pending legislation is relegated to whatever national or parochial controversy speakers wish to address, often with an air of unbridled drama. Because the Senate's rules guarantee the right to unlimited debate (with a few exceptions), any senator, in effect, can delay the debate or a vote on a bill for virtually any reason. Likewise, senators are free to offer amendments, however irrelevant or spurious, to almost any bill.

All too often, the contemporary Senate has been at war with itself and with its image from a bygone era. Not so many years ago, the Senate was known as a gentlemanly "club" that engendered reverence among both its members and close observers. Although the lore in both historical and semifictional accounts of past eras sometimes added excessive luster, senators often were regarded as "giants" who participated in dramatic debates before hushed galleries. In the 1950s, for example, *The New York Times's* congressional reporter, William S. White, used his close access to many of these figures to write *Citadel: The Story of the U.S. Senate,* an often fawning account that memorialized many of those figures and the institution itself. The Senate is the "one touch of authentic genius in the American system," White wrote. "It is a great and unique human consensus of individual men."[1] In *Advise and Consent,* former reporter Allen Drury recreated Senate personalities of the 1950s to write a riveting best-selling novel about the confirmation of a secretary of state. "As always, when the Senate was about to get into a hot debate, there was an electric tension in the air," Drury wrote.[2]

But the stem-winding oratory and masterful legislative gamesmanship of those days—however valid those accounts may have been—were replaced by a new Senate era of blow-dried, play-it-safe politicians who talk a big game but usually fight on issues at the margins of public interest. Real debate became a forgotten art as senators dashed into the Senate chamber to read prepared statements and then, just as quickly, departed. And starting in the 1960s, with the departure of Majority Leader Lyndon Johnson and the aging of powerful Southern chairmen who had been intent mostly on preserving the status quo, many of the old strictures broke down; younger senators felt greater freedom to challenge the old barons at their game. Although much of the shift was evolutionary as the issues and the times changed, Mike Mansfield also deserved considerable credit for giving junior senators more opportunity to play a role during his 1961–77 tenure as majority leader. The Senate had changed in the prior two decades from an institution where "some held back and kowtowed to others," Mansfield said when he retired. "I can see a Senate with real egalitarianism, the decline of seniority as a major factor, and new senators being seen and heard and not being wallflowers."

In the following years, Mansfield's vision was achieved beyond even his wildest hopes. Whether this served the Senate and the nation well was another question, however. The "100 equals" that Mansfield proudly sought became the curse of what Mitchell has termed "100 independent contractors." With their renowned penchant for independence and the aid of burgeoning staffs, senators typically ignored recommendations of legislative committees and forced further discussions both on and—more often—off the Senate floor. The frequent result was an endurance test for the sponsors of legislation. Although Mitchell himself had been the chief barrier in the eventual failure of one of Bush's top economic priorities—a lower tax rate on capital gains—the Democratic leader skillfully pushed defiant senators toward compromises on many other issues during the Bush presidency. But the election of Clinton produced different and even more difficult dynamics in the Senate. Without the threat of a presidential veto, Senate Republicans typically found themselves as the last barrier to the Democrats' agenda. Because Democrats held only 56 seats after Republican Kay Bailey Hutchison captured the Texas Senate seat from Democrat Bob Krueger in the June 1993 runoff election, they needed to peel off at least four Republicans to gain the 60 votes required for cloture to end debate if the GOP decided to filibuster a bill. The filibuster, which historically had been used sparingly until the 1970s, became a routine part of the legislative process, as Mitchell sometimes resorted on a nearly weekly basis to filing petitions for a vote to end a filibuster. For Mitchell, success also required Democrats to keep their own troops in line. Instead, when some of those Democrats objected to Clinton's economic program, for example, they sought to reshape the legislation to bring it closer to what they pretentiously deemed to be the president's real viewpoints. As a result of these and other practices, it would be a rare occasion that the Senate passed a bill in one day—"the blink of an eye," as Mitchell noted caustically.

It was not only Republicans or junior senators who could make life difficult for Mitchell and Clinton. As they showed dramatically when several of them unceremoniously criticized key parts of the new president's agenda during his first few days in office, the Senate's Democratic committee chairmen also frequently flexed their considerable egos to obstruct Clinton's proposals. Perhaps the most assertive example was Armed Services Committee chairman Nunn, who continued for months to foment opposition to Clinton's announced plan to permit gays in the military, even when the president agreed to a compromise. But Mitchell also had to struggle to keep the muzzle on other chairmen who might cause problems for the White House's legislation. Appropriations Committee chairman Byrd became a one-man wrecking crew for Clinton's favored line-item veto, which the House had passed in modified form. Energy and Natural Resources Committee chairman Bennett Johnston of Louisiana was an early critic of Clinton's proposed energy tax. Sometimes, Clinton found himself attacked from both sides of an issue in the Senate. When Western senators criticized his proposed steep increases in the fees that ranchers and miners pay to use federal lands in the West, Johnston said there was no chance that the Senate would approve such a plan. Then, when Clinton temporarily retreated, senators from environmentally minded Eastern states criticized his decision. Not all the Senate chairmen posed such problems. Budget Committee chairman Jim Sasser of Tennessee and the Finance Committee's Daniel Patrick Moynihan of New York, for example, usually were loyal supporters of Clinton's deficit-reduction plan once it was introduced. Each worked with administration officials to try to keep reluctant colleagues in line.

The problems for Clinton and the Senate Democrats were further complicated by their disappointing results in the November 1992 election. The outcome of no net party change of seats, despite Democrats' hopes of winning the three seats required for them to gain the 60 Democratic votes to break a filibuster, would prove to be a devastating blow to Clinton's hopes for a quick and triumphant legislative start. Most congressional observers, including many Clinton advisers, initially overlooked or minimized the prospective impact of the Senate results. But the result was that Senate Democrats were forced to contend with a new form of divided government, symbolized by the Republicans' filibuster. "After the election, Democrats in the House and Senate threw their hats in the air and stiffed all of us," said Republican Sen. Dave Durenberger of Minnesota. But, he rightly added, their celebration would prove premature. Another election-related element of bad news for Clinton in dealing with the Senate was the realization that the new president's 43 percent victory in November was a signal of his political weakness. "No one is scared of Bill Clinton," said a veteran Senate Democratic aide.

Numbers were not the sole cause of the Senate logjam. It also reflected the more fundamental changes in that chamber resulting from the breakdown of the old seniority-based system that had imposed a form of discipline. In its place was a flowering of power that had run amok. The absence of an orderly structure quickly became apparent to Sen. Patty Murray, the Washington Democrat who won election the previous November as a political novice. With four years of experience in her state legislature and following a campaign in which she pledged to bring a common-sense attitude to Congress, she was not prepared for the gamesmanship and posturing that she soon would encounter. Senators in both parties are too inclined go their own way rather than work as a team, the disappointed Murray concluded after three months in office. "We are 100 individuals," she said. "Too many senators say that they can't vote for something until they get something in return. ... This whole place is built on chits." Rather than work to advance the national interest, she added, senators focus too much on parochial issues related to their home states or pet issues. Also, the Senate's failure to adopt reforms like those in the House that made committee chairmen more accountable meant there was little peer pressure on independent senators. As one of four newly elected Senate Democratic women, Murray hoped that they could encourage their colleagues to soften their usual pomposity and to work together more effectively as a community. As a plain-spoken but shrewd candidate who had succeeded with a message that she would bring to the Senate the views of an average person, she also hoped to remain faithful to that appeal. But it might take considerable time to alter the Senate's deeply ingrained social structure so that all sides would make more effort to seek compromise.

For Senate Republicans, especially, there was little incentive for consensus. After a dozen years in which they had been forced to cooperate with the White House, including an especially painful four years under the muddled Bush, many of them felt liberated by the opportunity to go their own way. Surely, none of them felt any obligation to make Bill Clinton's life easier. Indeed, Clinton's agenda became a welcome opportunity for Republicans to show their unity—in opposition. They quickly realized that it was easier to take a position against a proposal rather than to build a shaky internal agreement for some alternative. On occasion, the Senate Republicans would use their numbers and the filibuster threat as a way to force the Democrats to make significant concessions in legislation on the Senate floor. For example, a half-dozen moderate Republicans, with Minority Leader Robert Dole's encouragement, insisted on and eventually won significant changes in early 1993 on a bill to ease the rules for voter registration in the 50 states. "A determined minority of 41 senators can modify a bill in a significant way," Republican Sen. Mitch McConnell of Kentucky said after that experience. On other occasions, however, the small band of GOP moderates—such as John Chafee of Rhode Island, Dave Durenberger of Minnesota and Arlen Specter of Pennsylvania—would face more heated internal conflicts and tougher choices on whether they should seek changes in Democratic proposals or simply join with other Republicans in voting "no."

As quickly became clear, these complications left Clinton with nothing like the scenario that allowed Reagan and the Republicans to bulldoze their agenda through the Senate in 1981. In that year, the main showdown came in the House, where Republicans and conservative Democrats joined forces to seek control. The minority Senate Democrats largely stood aside or they voted with Reagan on his program of tax and spending cuts; they never seriously worked to stymie its passage. Despite the Democrats' initial hopes in 1993 to emulate the GOP's earlier success, there were few parallels to the earlier situation. Reagan had campaigned and won on a clear-cut national program, in contrast to Clinton's more general appeal for change. The Republicans, who had just captured the Senate majority, were in no mood to challenge their new president in 1981. By contrast, Clinton hardly helped the Senate Democrats in 1992 nor did his spell cast any magic on them in 1993. In addition, Reagan was seeking to cut taxes. Clinton sought to raise them.

Clinton's Spending Plan Meets Three Obstacles

The Senate's idiosyncracies would pose major stumbling blocks to all of Clinton's major legislative proposals, including his economic package. Hardly a day would go by that the president was not held hostage and forced to deal with one self-styled power broker or another in the Senate. Despite the efforts by the White House and congressional Democratic leaders to expedite Senate action by pinning their hopes on the initial House passage, some difficulty inevitably arose. Indeed, the overt pressures often came from several conflicting directions on the same bill, making it virtually impossible to satisfy everyone—or, often, a majority. In the Senate, Clinton often was squeezed from across the ideological spectrum by lawmakers who displayed little restraint in second-guessing him.

But Clinton and Senate Democratic leaders benefitted from one big factor in their favor. Ironically, their efforts to push the economic program through the Senate received a major boost because of intricate procedural changes that Republicans had made in the 1980s when they controlled the Senate and the White House. In particular, during preparation of the several major budget packages of that era, proponents modified the Senate rules to limit the length of time permitted for debate on budget measures. They also restricted the rules so senators could only offer amendments that were germane, or relevant, to those bills. In the interest of budget discipline, they created major exemptions from the Senate tradition of unlimited debate. The impact of those changes was vividly dramatized in late March, when the Senate debated two measures recently passed by the House: the budget plan, which comprised the framework of Clinton's proposed five-year deficit-reduction package, and the separate economic stimulus bill for 1993. Facilitated by its 50-hour debate limitation, the budget plan passed with little suspense, despite votes on more than three dozen amendments that Republicans proposed—each of which was defeated. But the stimulus measure was an appropriations bill for spending, and it had no such procedural protections. So, it languished and ultimately died because the majority Democrats lacked the 60 votes to force a roll call vote on its passage. There were additional complicating factors, of course. But the results reinforced the vital impact of congressional rules, especially in the Senate.

The Senate Democrats' party-line discipline on the budget bill mirrored the action in the House a week earlier on a similar version. The 54–45 final passage on March 25 resulted when only two Democrats jumped ship: Richard Shelby of Alabama, who had flaunted his independence from Clinton and criticized his program, and Bob Krueger of Texas, the appointee to Bentsen's seat, who faced a special election later in the spring and was keeping his distance from the president. Before that vote, Senate Republicans forced separate tallies on many politically volatile issues, in part to set up a record to use against Democrats in later campaigns. (House Republicans had been unable to force comparable choices because the House Rules Committee did not permit such votes when it prepared its resolution on the terms of the budget debate.) Although the Senate Republicans failed to make any changes in the budget numbers, their efforts required the Democrats to walk the legislative plank. Among the GOP amendments were proposals to limit the proposed energy tax and to remove the higher tax on Social Security beneficiaries who also receive sizable income from other sources. Under the management of Budget Committee chairman Sasser, the Democrats held firm. In opposing these amendments, Mitchell—echoing Gephardt's earlier appeal in the House—appealed more to party unity than to the merits of the issues. "If you want change in this country, if you think President Clinton deserves a chance to get his program going," Mitchell said, ". . . you will vote to table this amendment." Although his pleas worked on the budget resolution, members of both parties agreed that tougher votes would follow in coming months, when the Senate would have to implement the specific pieces of Clinton's program. "We start shooting with real bullets from now on," Sen. Dole warned after the vote.

After the budget vote, Clinton told Mitchell in a telephone call, "Finally we've done something to break the gridlock." But the Democrats' victory cheers would prove short-lived. In contrast to the House, where the leadership's firm procedural control barred votes on any amendments, the $19.5 billion economic stimulus bill reached the Senate floor with no limitation on time or votes. The subsequent debate triggered a series of fateful events. From three different directions the president was pounded by senators pursuing their own political agendas, without fully considering the impact on Clinton's program: Some conservative-leaning Democrats said that they sought change to help him, another Democrat overplayed his hand while supposedly working on Clinton's behalf, and Republicans wanted to establish their own record. The resulting unexpected defeat of the bill reshaped the early months of the Clinton administration.

The peril to the spending bill immediately became apparent when Democratic Sens. David Boren of Oklahoma and John Breaux of Louisiana began the debate with hostile speeches that lasted more than four hours. They said that they wanted to defer $10 billion of the new spending until after Congress passed the deficit-reduction parts of Clinton's economic package. The challenge from Breaux was especially intriguing because he was regarded as a faithful Democrat; his colleagues had chosen him at the start of the new Congress for a leadership position as their chief deputy whip. "This is the moment of truth," Breaux told the Senate, as he challenged the economic stimulus bill. "The last several days, as hard as everyone worked, we did not make any real cuts and did not reduce real spending in any specific program, but rather only set out guidelines and targets that Congress will have to meet later. I suggest that we keep faith with the American people, who want us to cut before we spend more." Boren later said that his proposal with Breaux would increase public support for a more balanced presidential program. Although Breaux and Boren threatened to filibuster for days, they proved easy to appease once they discovered the intensity of resistance from senior Democrats. After a weekend respite, Clinton sent them a letter pledging further spending cuts or tax increases if Congress did not meet its deficit-reduction targets. A "substantial amount" of the spending would not occur until after Congress enacted the deficit reduction, Clinton added. With that assurance, Breaux and Boren agreed to drop their threat. As it turned out, however, the political damage was done.

Why had the two senators pushed their initiative? As usual, it is difficult to ascertain fully the motivation for senators' actions. But several factors are worth noting. Breaux had replaced Clinton as chairman of the Democratic Leadership Council, a group that has sought to foster the notion of "new" Democrats who are not wedded to the party's traditional big spending programs. As a Louisiana senator, Breaux was sensitive to the notion that those policies do not play well in the Deep South. And he may have been seeking a middle ground to appease some Republican senators disenchanted with the economic stimulus bill while, at the same time, seeking to not offend Clinton. Some of the same factors influenced Boren. In addition, he often had disdained Democratic dogma during his Senate career. And he had eagerly sought the public notice that comes with taking an independent stance. Consistent with that approach, he had continued to curry favor with former presidential candidate Ross Perot and emulated his anti-spending rhetoric. Like Breaux, Boren also was a member of the Senate Finance Committee that is responsible for tax legislation. In that position, both wanted to assure that they could tell constituents that they had made the necessary federal spending cuts before they voted to raise taxes. Given their oil-state ties, both also were hostile to Clinton's proposed energy tax. And, in the media-conscious Senate, it was commonplace for senators to seek public attention to try to promote their cause. How thoroughly they considered the prospect that their effort would jeopardize continued action on the economic stimulus bill, once they reached agreement with Clinton, was less certain.

Even after Breaux and Boren backed down, the problems had only begun for Clinton and his spending bill. A second major force that altered the debate was the decision by Appropriations Committee chairman Robert Byrd to exercise his procedural wizardry in the Senate on behalf of the proposal. By using an arcane parliamentary device known as an amendment "tree," Byrd effectively eliminated his foes' opportunity to amend the measure. The tactic left his side with the option of a final vote that could override any successful amendments by the bill's opponents. Byrd said that he simply was trying to protect Clinton's bill from the attacks of all sides. "I am the manager of this bill," he told the Senate. "I am doing my job. . . . I want to see him succeed, because if the president succeeds, the country is better off." But one effect, though apparently unenvisioned, was that his scheme created so much anger among Republicans that they grew united and their opposition hardened. Arlen Specter of Pennsylvania, a moderate Republican who had been considered a likely supporter of the additional spending, told the Senate that he objected to the Democrats' steamroller attack. "I do not like the way this body is heading," he told the Senate. "I have not seen the kind of anger that is present in the U.S. Senate that I have seen in the course of the past few weeks, as we move to party-line votes. The way to govern America is not on a party line. The way to govern America is not by having the tree locked up so that nobody can offer an amendment." Although Byrd said that he had informed the White House and Majority Leader Mitchell of his procedural plans and that they had approved, many Democrats, too, were surprised by Byrd's approach. Some worried that Byrd was overplaying his hand as he frustrated other senators. "The White House didn't anticipate how angry senators get when they feel that they are being jerked around on the rules," said a veteran Democratic aide. That became apparent when some Northern Democrats led by Herbert Kohl of Wisconsin sought to offer an amendment requiring that more than half of the economic stimulus package should be paid for with offsetting cuts in other federal spending. Although Kohl's plan received 52 votes, including nine Democrats, that was not enough because Byrd invoked a separate Senate rule that deemed the proposal out of order. Kohl and his Democratic allies, who would have needed 60 votes to prevail, grew even more hostile to the bill.

For Byrd, the setback on the stimulus bill was an unusual rebuff. But he was not prepared to back down. "If they want to make

Robert Byrd the scapegoat, fine," he told the Senate. "I say to the American people, if they want to give this president a chance, they ought to let senators who are obstructing this bill know about it, let them know that the American people want action." From 1977 to 1989, as the Senate Democratic leader, Byrd had labored to accommodate virtually all Democrats, often at the expense of his own views. But his old-school style and partisanship had grated on Republicans; and many Democrats concluded that they needed a party leader who could be more effective in standing up to a Republican president and was more polished in representing their views on television. Eventually, Mitchell proved to be their leader. Rather than being voted out of his leadership position, however, Byrd had the convenient option in 1988 of replacing Appropriations Committee chairman John Stennis of Mississippi, who was in poor health and decided to retire at age 81. Freed of his leadership responsibility and armed with his vast knowledge of Senate rules, Byrd used his powerful new position to advance his own interests, including his firm belief in the benefits of domestic spending and an unquenchable appetite for new federal facilities in his home state of West Virginia. With Bush as president, there had been obvious restraints on Byrd's capacity to dictate results. But once Clinton took office and the veto threat was removed, Byrd's partisan instincts rose to the surface. That combination of factors would prove a deadly contributor to the Clinton setback.

As the conflict over the spending bill extended for several days, with no sign of concessions from either side, Republican partisans began to realize that Byrd's hard-nosed approach was backfiring with swing Senate votes from both parties. So the GOP leaders sought to exploit the resulting anger to rally their own forces against the Democrats' quest for a compromise. Minority Leader Dole and the more outspoken Sen. Phil Gramm of Texas, whose competition for attention and power within their party had created an uneasy tension between them, began to compete to see who could voice the toughest rhetoric in opposing Byrd and Mitchell. After lengthy internal discussions, Dole produced a letter signed by all 43 Republicans pledging to oppose the bill unless it was modified so the proposed $19.5 billion would not add to the deficit. "The American people are asking the Congress to cut spending first and then consider other options to reduce the deficit," the GOP senators wrote to Dole on March 31. Many Democrats had assumed that some Republicans would agree to a lower number once they launched talks about a possible deal. But it soon became apparent that it was too late for making a deal. On four separate attempts to end the filibuster, the Democrats did not gain a single Republican vote. Even when Clinton offered in mid-April to cut his spending plan by more than $4 billion, Republicans did not take the bait. A few weeks earlier, such a deal probably would have been accepted. In the interval, however, the political well had been poisoned.

Several factors triggered the Republicans' revolt. Perhaps the most important was the sentiment by many of their forces that the Democrats, especially Clinton, were ignoring them or taking them for granted on an array of issues. Some Republicans, for example, resented that Clinton had not been consulting with them in the preparation of his health-care bill. It was one thing for Democrats to deem irrelevant the Republicans in the House, where the rules enhanced the power of a disciplined majority. But that advantage was not available in the Senate, a factor that escaped the Democrats' attention when they expected, based on their initial conversations, to pick up at least a few Republican votes on the economic stimulus bill. "We felt erroneously that there would be [an early] compromise with the moderate Republicans," a top White House aide contritely recounted in the middle of the battle. "I wish that I knew then what I know now." Office of Management and Budget director Leon Panetta voiced a similar assessment: "Basically the guidance we got from the Senate side was that it wasn't likely that the Republicans would filibuster" the spending bill.

In fact, a few moderate Republicans like Mark Hatfield of Oregon—Byrd's counterpart at the helm of the Appropriations Committee—worked until the end to seek a bipartisan deal. But they could not secure the approval of the rest of their own party for a conciliatory approach, and they faced intense internal pressure not to compromise. The more conservative Republicans, led by Gramm, saw the opportunity to inflict an early defeat on Clinton and to tag him with the "big spender" label that they had effectively used against earlier Democrats. In closed-door Republican meetings, Gramm and his allies prevailed over the Republican moderates and convinced them not to cut a deal. Though many of these Republicans themselves had frequently voted for the same type of spending that they were now railing against, they correctly perceived that Clinton's failure to effectively sell the stimulus package to the public had paved the way for its defeat. Even Democrats later conceded that they had not done a good job in explaining their case and that the average citizen did not understand why a plan designed to reduce the deficit also included a large chunk of new spending.

Although Senate Democrats had committed their own mistakes—from the Boren-Breaux attack on the plan to Byrd's excessive defense—the responsibility for the setback ultimately rested with Clinton. A leading Democratic senator said, in hindsight, that Clinton's decision to meet with Russian President Boris Yeltsin in Vancouver, Canada, in the midst of the Senate debate was a crucial factor in the setback. Clinton's absence stymied his Senate allies in gaining a White House sign-off in their quest for a compromise, the senator said. That weekend visit was preceded by Clinton's day-long conference in Portland, Oregon, to discuss the problems of the timber industry and government steps to seek a balance between economic and environmental needs in the forests. Although those problems undoubtedly were vital, his failure to consider the timing had adverse consequences for his $19.5 billion spending proposal. Because Clinton was distracted, it was difficult for his Senate allies to make a deal in his absence. "The trip could not have come at a worse time for the bill," the senator said. Once he returned to Washington, where the Senate was preparing for a two-week recess, it was too late for the Democrats to regain the momentum. Clinton turned up the heat by launching several salvos at Republican critics of the stimulus plan. Perhaps his best line was an attack on senators who have their own swimming pool "with taxpayers' money" but would not approve money to give "kids a chance to have recreational opportunities in the summertime." His effort, however, proved to be too little and too late to convince any wavering Republicans. And the resulting failure became a major political turning point for his administration. By making a big investment in a politically tenuous proposal, he opened himself to criticism that he was a conventional Democrat with faulty political judgment.

Stimulus Post-mortems

On April 21, the Senate Democrats gave up the battle for the stimulus bill and accepted a Republican alternative that simply extended federal benefits for unemployed workers. Reluctantly, the House and Clinton went along. The ramifications of this decision to abandon the spending bill became a major focus of Washington's never-ending battle of public relations. With Clinton celebrating the following week his first 100 days in the White House, both parties and the nation's news media engaged in an orgy of assessments of his performance. The White House even joined the exercise by issuing its own glossy pamphlets highlighting his performance on a day-by-day basis. Though he had scored some impressive achievements, including passage of the five-year budget framework, and any such appraisal of the new president was premature, the Senate defeat tended to dominate the outside reviews. In a *USA Today* scorecard, Clinton received an overall grade of C+, including a harsh D+ for his management of the federal budget deficit.[3] *The Washington Post* suggested that, despite deserving credit for attacking the pressing national problems of the budget deficit and health care, Clinton's "stumbles signify not just transitory missteps but evidence of a president who may have continuing difficulty maneuvering in Washington."[4] A national poll commissioned by the *Post* at the same time showed that the public shared those sentiments. The poll showed "little sense of accomplishment and a reversal of the early optimism about ending gridlock in Washington." By 63 percent to 37 percent, respondents said that Clinton had not accomplished much in his first 100 days. They split the blame for the inaction evenly between Clinton and congressional Republicans.

Perhaps most damaging were some candid comments by Clinton's budget director, who had a keen ear for congressional sentiments. During a late April lunch with Washington political reporters and an interview the next morning with the *National Journal,* Leon Panetta warned that Clinton had spread himself too thin and that he risked major legislative defeats unless he focused more directly on his top priorities. Frustrated over the Senate setback, concerned about the dangers that lay ahead and struggling to get the president's attention, the candid Panetta had committed the Washington sin of confessing the truth—that not everything was well with his team. But he accurately pointed out that, despite the problems, all was far from lost. "The principle that came out in the November election is still real," Panetta said. "The president and Congress have to work together to get things done." His comments created something of a firestorm among the political pundits and other cognoscenti in the capital. The reality, however, was less severe. House Ways and Means chairman Rostenkowski, for example, pointed out that the public still wanted Clinton to succeed in addressing the nation's problems. But "he's got to have the courage of his convictions," Rostenkowski added. The far less experienced Sen. Patty Murray voiced a similar comment about Clinton's need to show ideological and political steadfastness on behalf of his goals. "The president has learned that he must be a critical part of the process," she said.

Even Clinton acknowledged that his failure to win support from Senate Republicans showed that he needed to fine tune his political operations. "I thought that at least four of them would vote to break a cloture, and I underestimated that," he told an April 23 press conference. "I did not have an adequate strategy of dealing with that." But he also placed much of the blame on the minority party. Because of the Republicans' success in closing their internal divisions, the plan "acquired a political connotation that got out of proportion to the merits," he added. Although he did not acknowledge his own failure to do a better job of securing passage of the proposal, the president recognized that he needed to improve his salesmanship. Starting in early May, Clinton began frequent travels outside of Washington to sell his economic program and to regain his campaign-style populist appeal. Although his new proposal had nothing to do with the pending budget plan, he advocated the creation of a deficit-reduction trust fund to assure that additional taxes would not be used for federal spending. "Credibility is a difficult thing to come by in Washington today," he told a New York audience. "I don't blame the people for being distrustful of what they hear coming out of Washington." He also stepped up his attack on the capital's special interest groups by unveiling his legislation to reform campaign-finance laws and to require more complete disclosure of lobbying activities.

Caught between these forces was Howard Paster, who gave up a lucrative business as a skillful Washington lobbyist to sign up as Clinton's legislative affairs director. Even in the best of circumstances, serving as the president's chief lobbyist can be a thankless task. When things went wrong in Congress for Clinton's program, Paster found that he became a convenient scapegoat and the target of complaints from unhappy Democrats. "It's a lot easier to be mad at Howard than at the president," said William Cable, a Washington lobbyist who had held a top White House lobbying post under

President Carter. The candid Paster later conceded that he should have done a better job in contacting senators to assess the extent of Senate opposition to the stimulus bill and in seeking acceptable middle ground. Far more often, however, his lengthy experience on Capitol Hill and friendship with many senior Democrats made him a key player in Clinton's legislative successes.

The mid-course corrections by Clinton and his staff showed that they had lost some of the momentum from the unveiling of the president's economic package. In effect, he had bumped belly-to-belly with the Senate on his stimulus bill, and the Senate had forced him to back down and reorganize. Although any presidential defeat in Congress is a sobering experience, it certainly would not have to be a fatal blow to his overall program. For Clinton, the bigger fights were still to come.

The Senate Logjam

The defeat of Clinton's stimulus package was not the only sign of divisions and other woes in the Senate. During his first several months in office, senators offered repeated resistance to the president's program—more than he experienced in the House. Gays in the military, campaign finance legislation and a proposal to give the president line-item veto authority over spending were among the issues that bogged down because of Senate opposition. And senators faced additional internal conflicts of their own. Not even a new president and his front-burner economic program could keep them from addressing other controversial issues, which often had little to do with that agenda. Some of these additional tasks were legitimate and a result of the Senate's unique constitutional roles, including the confirmation of presidential nominees and the greater foreign-policy role that flows from its duty to ratify treaties. But other facets of the Senate's work load resulted from its self-proclaimed role as the "world's greatest deliberative body," a phrase that had acquired a mocking tone. Unlike the House, which deals with legislation in a relatively straightforward fashion and where the rules confine the topics for legislative action, the Senate has a more difficult time completing action and limiting the scope of its endeavors.

Two other Senate events triggered strong public interest—in part, as a consequence of the 1991 Supreme Court confirmation hearings for Clarence Thomas. Although most senators undoubt-edly preferred to forget that painful episode, they also wanted to ensure that they would avoid a repetition of the public disrepute that followed it. So, when former female employees accused Ore-gon Republican Sen. Bob Packwood of sexual harassment that had extended over many years, senators said that they would not lightly dismiss the accusations, as women's groups and other critics said that the Senate had done with Anita Hill's charges against Thomas. With the banner-headline coverage in the nation's news-papers, the Senate could hardly ignore the allegations, which *The Washington Post* revealed days after his narrow re-election. But the Senate's meticulous months-long inquiry, including interviews with dozens of former Packwood aides, showed how carefully it was proceeding in the post-Thomas era.

That caution also became apparent after Supreme Court Jus-tice Byron White in March announced his decision to retire at the end of the 1992–93 term. Senators kept their fingers crossed that they could avoid another national soap opera. With many conserv-atives inside and outside the Senate gearing up for revenge and for giving the liberals a dose of the medicine that had been delivered to Republican nominees, the prospects of a quiet confirmation hear-ing initially appeared remote. But the conservatives' revenge did not come with the Supreme Court nomination; federal Judge Ruth Bader Ginsburg was confirmed, 96–3, after the hearings under-scored her moderate appeal. Instead, conservative lobbyists earlier organized their forces against Lani Guinier, a little-known law pro-fessor at the University of Pennsylvania. She had written provoca-tive scholarly articles about the need for more aggressive legal efforts and remedies to reverse the effects of racial discrimination. But Senate Democrats, including chairman Joseph Biden and some liberals on the Judiciary Committee, concluded that she was out of the legal mainstream. They decided that her nomination was not a fight that they wanted to make—much as some of the same Demo-crats forced the abandonment of Zoe Baird in January. Clinton concluded that he had no choice other than to abandon Guinier, his one-time personal friend. Unlike Anita Hill, this black woman did not even get a public hearing to defend herself. Perhaps surpris-ingly, the Senate's first black woman—Carol Moseley-Braun—did not actively defend Guinier, although her 1992 Illinois campaign was prompted by her unhappiness with how the Senate handled the Thomas-Hill conflict.

The Senate's difficulty in dealing with this array of political problems flowed from what Mitchell had described as tendency of the senators to act like one hundred independent contractors. Increasingly, senators and their offices have drifted from the traditional legislative model of discussion and consensus and have become more like separate baronies with their own cast of crown princes and courtiers. A prime example of this pattern is Biden, a Delaware Democrat who holds the demanding position of chairman of the Senate Judiciary Committee. He has said publicly that he would prefer to chair the Foreign Relations Committee, where he has been the number two Democrat and has actively pursued many causes. Within weeks after Clinton took office, Biden began pressing the administration to exercise a stronger hand in the civil war that began in 1991 when the former Eastern European nation of Yugoslavia divided itself into six republics. To make his case more forcefully, Biden journeyed to the region during the spring and returned to Washington with a 40-page report urging U.S. military intervention to rescue the beleaguered republic of Bosnia. "The United States must lead the West in a decisive response to Serbian aggression, beginning with air attacks on Serb artillery everywhere in Bosnia and on Yugoslav National Army units in Serbia that have participated in this international crime," he concluded. Biden peddled the report not only to Senate colleagues and to reporters but also to the State Department and White House, where his efforts sparked a brief burst of interest by Clinton in late April. As the Bosnian crisis evolved, however, Clinton—lacking support from other Western nations—retreated to a more passive role, and Biden's effort appeared to have had little long-term impact. In a more collegial Senate, perhaps, Biden would have sought Senate hearings and legislative action on his findings in addition to the personal attention generated by his report.

Another senator who gloried in the attention he could generate was Oklahoma Democrat David Boren. On issues ranging from the budget to campaign finance to congressional reform, Boren frequently voiced opinions about the shortcomings of the status quo. Occasionally, he even recommended changes to address those problems. But his "lone warrior" approach was better suited to attracting headlines than to the painstaking work required to craft an agreement. "The senator seems to function on a grandstand," said a House Democrat who had dealt frequently with Boren. "Sometimes, a person who is loud is not always important." By late spring, Boren garnered widespread public attention at the fore-front of several legislative battles, but his efforts proved of limited effectiveness. On campaign-finance reform, he was the chief Dem-ocratic sponsor of a proposal to restrict spending and reduce the influence of special-interest political action committees (PACs). But he showed little skill in attracting Republican support, and he also supported changes that left many Democrats unenthusiastic about their own party's plan. When the Senate—with seven Re-publicans finally voting in favor—passed a campaign reform bill in early June after a three-week debate, the result was a pale version of the original proposal, and it generated little enthusiasm from re-form advocates inside and outside Congress. Democratic leaders had been forced to abandon their goal of public financing of Sen-ate campaigns. And their outlawing of all PAC contributions pro-voked outrage among many House Democrats, who were more dependent on such campaign sources. Meanwhile, Boren's harsh criticism of Clinton's tax plan—especially the energy tax, which would adversely affect oil companies in Boren's home state and elsewhere—angered many Democrats who blamed Boren and other party conservatives for having backed President Reagan's tax cuts in 1981. "For David Boren to lecture Bill Clinton about fiscal responsibility is a national joke," said Rep. David Obey, a Wiscon-sin Democrat and a leader of House liberals. Boren defended him-self by saying that he was trying to prevent Clinton from being dominated by his party's liberal wing. But his unpunished indepen-dence illustrated there were few penalties to keep wayward Demo-crats from abandoning their party's ship. Even more than those of Biden and others, Boren's actions illustrated why everything was so difficult in the Senate.

Salvaging Deficit Reduction

The Senate's handling of the budget reconciliation bill in June showed the institution at both its best and worst. A disgusted ju-nior Democratic senator said privately after the debate that most of his colleagues had shown the backbone of "a towering mountain of jello." Unlike the House during the previous month, where there was extensive peer pressure on wavering Democratic law-makers, the cherished autonomy of senators placed Mitchell and other party leaders at their mercy, with few tools to demand discipline. In the end, however, the Democrats got their act together enough to pass the bill by the narrowest of margins and with little enthusiasm. It was not pretty, but they got the job done.

The first major Senate hurdle for the actual tax increases and spending cuts required to implement Clinton's package was its Finance Committee. That panel had several major differences from its House counterpart, the Ways and Means Committee. One of the most important involved simple numbers. Instead of the 24–14 majority on the House panel, Democrats had to contend with an 11–9 edge on the Senate's tax-writing committee. In effect, because there was no prospect of Republican support, that gave each committee Democrat a veto power over gaining majority support for the bill. And the 11 Democrats included Boren and Breaux, who had led the earlier unsuccessful effort to reduce the size of Clinton's ill-fated economic stimulus bill. For Mitchell, building consensus in the committee was one of the most difficult and consequential aspects of guiding the bill. A few days after the bill's passage, he acknowledged that he had often privately lamented his failure to achieve a three-vote margin in the membership of the Finance Committee. But Minority Leader Dole simply would not agree to such a plan when he and Mitchell bargained at the start of the session over the partisan ratios for membership on Senate committees. And, unlike their House counterparts, Senate Republicans had far more leverage to use the rules to prevent the Democrats from getting their way on organizational matters. "It would have created more problems than it would solve" if he had sought a firmer majority in committee ratios, Mitchell recounted. One effect, however, was that Clinton's allies were forced to abandon key tenets of the president's original package that the House had already accepted.

Another major difference in the Senate was that the Finance Committee chairman—Daniel Patrick Moynihan of New York—was new to that position and not much tested in dealing with the minutiae and high-stakes lobbying that accompanies tax legislation. Clinton's deficit-reduction plan would be the baptism by fire for Moynihan. Although senators respected his intellectual brilliance, his political skills in handling complex and controversial tax legislation remained questionable. One other important distinction between the Finance and the Ways and Means Committees is that the Senate panel had only two new senators at the start of

1993, compared with the 16 fresh faces at the House panel. For both Moynihan and the Clinton administration, that would make it even less likely that they could effectively strong-arm the committee members.

The prime target of internal Democratic opposition was the broad-based "BTU" energy tax, designed to raise $72 billion in the next five years—the second largest amount of deficit reduction in the bill. At the House Ways and Means Committee, the only Democrat who had made major efforts to revise that provision was Bill Brewster of Oklahoma, one of the new committee members. He secured changes in the technical language for the collection of the tax and then bowed to party pressure to go along. On the Senate panel, however, Boren and Breaux were both from major oil-producing states, and they could demand major changes. Neither was shy. Emphasizing the adverse consequences for petroleum-based industries and for businesses engaged in international trade, they made a frontal assault on the proposal before the Finance Committee began its work. After spending the one-week Memorial Day recess pledging to his Louisiana constituents that he would steadfastly oppose the BTU tax, Breaux returned to the Senate with a proposal to tax fuel used for transportation, which he estimated would raise $40 billion over five years. Boren found that acceptable. But senators representing rural states, where residents drive their cars far greater distances than they do elsewhere, objected. Because the Finance Committee included Democrats from Montana, North Dakota and South Dakota, those states had much more clout on the Finance Committee than in the Ways and Means Committee or the House, where sparsely populated states have little influence. (In the Senate, those states have six votes of 100; in the House, they have only three of the 435 seats.) So, when Max Baucus of Montana complained that Breaux's proposed transportation tax was too high and that it would not fairly distribute the burden of a new energy tax, the committee Democrats retreated to an even smaller plan: an increase of 4.3 cents per gallon in the existing gasoline tax. That would raise an estimated $23 billion over five years.

Once the Finance Committee Democrats agreed to the scaled-back energy tax, they faced a new dilemma. The nearly $50 billion reduction in taxes from Clinton's package pleased Democrats like Breaux and Boren who contended that the original plan placed too much emphasis on new taxes instead of spending reductions; but the smaller tax hike meant that they would have to cut more spending to reach Clinton's $500 billion five-year goal. (According to one set of congressional figures, the Senate version would have raised taxes by $243 billion and cut spending by $257 billion over five years; by contrast, the House bill was $273 billion in new taxes and $223 billion in spending cuts.) Their biggest target would be additional spending cuts for the Medicare program, which insures the nation's elderly. The House had agreed to Clinton's nearly $50 billion in cuts, which would have been financed largely by trimming federal reimbursements to doctors and hospitals. The Finance Committee members agreed to increase that amount by an additional $19 billion. Though that amount soon proved higher than many other Democrats could stomach, it was less than the $35 billion that Moynihan had suggested in a televised interview. The chairman's suggestion generated alarms from senior citizens groups and the health industry, which feared not only the direct impact of such large cuts but also the adverse consequences for the shaping of Clinton's subsequent health-care plan. From Moynihan's view, however, those problems were less immediate than the pressing need to pass a $500 billion deficit-reduction package. With the steadying hand of Mitchell, who also serves on the Finance Committee, the Democrats informally agreed to their package after nearly two weeks of private discussion. Then, as was the case at the Ways and Means Committee, they moved to public session, where they remained united under a barrage of attacks from Finance Committee Republicans. On June 18, the committee voted to report the bill on a 11–9 party-line vote.

One striking difference from the handling of the budget package in the House was that Clinton made a deliberate effort in the Senate to limit his personal role in selling the measure. This revised strategy was designed, in part, to allow him to appeal to the nation on behalf of his overall package and its broad goals of deficit reduction, a more progressive tax code and some form of energy tax. During a June 7 meeting with Clinton, Mitchell had informed him there were not enough Senate votes to pass the BTU tax, and he requested that the president authorize him and Moynihan to make the needed revisions. According to Mitchell, Clinton repeated that he favored his own program but "he understood that we had to do what was necessary to pass the bill." Two days later, Clinton told reporters that he expected the Senate to modify his initial energy tax proposal. Given the likelihood that the Senate

would make more changes in his plan than did the House, this lobbying approach also gave the president an opportunity to distance
himself from those changes without directly criticizing Senate
Democrats. Behind the scenes, however, Clinton remained actively
involved in the negotiations and talked frequently with reluctant
Democrats, especially in the final days before the vote. In addition,
his top aides on the issue—Treasury Secretary Bentsen, Office of
Management and Budget Director Panetta, White House Chief of
Staff Thomas (Mack) McLarty and chief legislative aide Howard
Paster—met regularly with Mitchell and his lieutenants at the
Capitol.

In coordinating the bill, especially after it reached the Senate
floor, Mitchell took charge with dozens of private meetings with
Democrats who remained uncertain about their vote. His skills included a well-honed knowledge of the issues, a seemingly limitless
patience, and an ability to tell other senators how much legislative
change they could expect to gain in the bill.[5] He was at the center of
the planning for Democrats, working on several related fronts. "He
was an exceptional negotiator—patient, diplomatic, extremely well
informed," said Sen. Tom Daschle, a South Dakota Democrat who
works closely with Mitchell. "So much of this depended on our communication with the White House, where he has developed an extraordinary credibility. . . . And he had the lead role as spokesman.
This was the most articulate and forceful that I have seen him, on
the [Senate] floor and with the media." Mitchell described his role
as trying to keep open the lines of communication in an institution
where there is too little flexibility and reasoned argument. "You
have to keep your eye on the main objective," he said. "It is a part of
the requirements of leadership . . . to accommodate the concerns of
many members with different viewpoints."

The problems flew at Mitchell from several different directions once the bill left the Finance Committee. About a dozen liberal Democrats objected to the $19 billion in additional Medicare
cuts. Initially, they sought a further increase in taxes to reduce the
cuts. But other Democrats objected. Finally, Mitchell won the liberals' agreement to only $10 billion more in Medicare cuts, with no
compensating reductions in the deficit elsewhere. From another
perspective, several business-oriented Democrats lamented the
cutback of the tax incentives that Clinton had initially proposed as
a way to encourage business investment. Mitchell also agreed to
give this group some of what they wanted: a reduction in the capi-

tal-gains tax rate for small business and more generous deprecia-
tion allowances for new equipment. In exchange, Mitchell won vital votes from both ends of the Democrats' ideological spectrum.
But the outcome remained in doubt until the final hours.

With two senators absent because of illness (Democrat Patty
Murray and Republican Arlen Specter), the Democrats could lose
no more than six of their 55 votes in order to gain a 49–49 tie. In
that case, Vice President Gore would exercise his constitutional
prerogative of breaking the tie. By the afternoon of June 24, the
expected day of the vote, Democratic leaders concluded that they
would gain the 49 votes. But, they later recounted, they were un-
sure exactly who would vote their way until later that evening.
When the votes were finally cast, six Democrats voted against the
bill and Gore did his duty. The six included three senators worried
about their 1994 re-election contest: Richard Bryan of Nevada,
Dennis DeConcini of Arizona and Frank Lautenberg of New Jersey. And three Southern Democrats voted against the plan because, they said, they objected to the excessive taxes. They were
Richard Shelby of Alabama, who had voted against the initial budget plan in March, plus two influential committee chairmen—
Armed Services chairman Nunn of Georgia and Energy and
Natural Resources chairman Johnston of Louisiana. One striking
difference between the House and Senate is that all House committee chairmen voted for the budget bill, in part because of the
fear that they might lose their position if they voted against the
party line. In the Senate, where there are few sanctions for such independence, that would have been an idle threat. Another contrast
was that the seven freshman Democrats in the Senate—including
the four women—all voted for the plan and raised few objections,
in contrast to 11 (of 63) Democratic first-termers in the House who
voted against it. The chief exception was Sen. Feinstein of California, who had won a special election and faced re-election in 1994;
she was more outspoken in raising questions about the bill.

Whatever their political plight, however, the Democrats made
clear that they understood the serious consequences of their
vote—both in economic and political terms. As they were about to
vote at 3 a.m. on June 25, Republican leader Dole closed his
party's side of the debate with a smart-alecky comment that, regardless of the outcome, President Clinton "has already earned his
place on Mount Taxmore." Before the snickers had subsided,
Mitchell quickly responded that the Republican laughter charac-

terized that party's handling of the national debt during the past 12 years. "We have had jokes, not deeds," he said. "It is now time for action." Then, as the roll was called for the vote, Mitchell stood next to the Senate clerks' desk in the front of the chamber and intently watched to make sure there were no mistakes in the tally sheet. Using hand signals and a stage whisper, he also reminded Gore that the result would be 49–49 and that the vice president would cast a "yea" vote to break the tie. That prompted the publicly stiff Gore to scribble a humorous note, which a page delivered to Mitchell, in which he warned, "I'm wavering."

As the sleepy senators left the Capitol in the middle of the night, there was little of the exuberance that marked the House's approval of the same bill a month earlier. With notably less cohesion and camaraderie, senators go their own way, even when they vote similarly. If the personalities had become less riveting than they were a few decades earlier, however, there remained the sense that they had participated in a dramatic and memorable event. The results of that moment might take months and years to unfold. But the senators had cast a rare vote that would have major consequences. After the politically painful defeat two months earlier of the economic stimulus bill, the Senate gave Clinton a victory on a bill that he could ill afford to lose. Yes, he escaped by a razor's edge. But, as Mitchell later said, "the fact of victory is more important than the margin of victory." And in the Senate, Clinton had learned to take whatever he could get.

Endnotes

1. William S. White, *Citadel: The Story of the U.S. Senate* (New York: Harper & Row, 1957), ix–x.
2. Allen Drury, *Advise and Consent* (New York, Doubleday & Co., Inc., 1959), 83.
3. "Clinton: Room for Improvement," *USA Today,* April 28, 1993: A4.
4. Ann Devroy and Ruth Marcus, "Ambitious Agenda and Interruptions Frustrate Efforts to Maintain Focus," *The Washington Post,* April 29, 1993: A1.
5. For further details of Mitchell's leadership style, see Richard E. Cohen, *Washington at Work: Back Rooms and Clean Air* (New York, Macmillan Publishing Co., 1992), 85–90.

7

The Loyal Opposition

☆ ☆ ☆

House Republicans worked hard to gain public attention with press conferences and attacks on Democratic proposals. Featured here is Dick Armey, chairman of the House Republican Conference, with (left to right) House Minority Whip Newt Gingrich , Sen. Don Nickles and Rep. John Kasich.

The Growth of Partisanship

Clinton arrived in Washington without much apparent interest in working with Republicans. After a dozen years as governor of a state where Republicans had little influence, he was comfortable with single-party government. His actions reflected his view that he could succeed without them and that it was not worth the hassle to seek their support. Although this result bruised some of their egos, most Republicans in Congress celebrated the new presidency by basking in their freedom from responsibility. As the unquestioned minority party, they could separate themselves from responsibility for Washington's actions and, when the occasion warranted, they could make proposals or cast votes to position themselves as statesmen. Sometimes, they would get under Clinton's skin and force him to respond. But their alternatives were usually vague and not designed to shape real outcomes. So, Clinton's early dealings with the Republicans were mostly rhetorical, not legislative.

For Republicans, life in 1993 without control of the presidency or Congress had both positive and negative consequences. Among the obvious down sides were the inability to thwart the Democrats whenever that party was united and the loss of the many benefits—from political patronage to attractive photo opportunities—that came with having a friend in the White House. But for many Republicans, especially those serving in Congress, there also was some welcome news. Their failure to control either the White House or Congress meant that they had no accountability for Washington's actions. And no longer burdened with having to defend the departed Bush, they could begin the tricky journey of redefining their own party so it could regain its electoral support of the 1980s. Given the volatile history of 20th century politics, the Republicans could expect to return to the White House before long. Except for the tumultuous period from 1933 to 1953, which included the Great Depression and World War II, no party had retained control of the presidency for more than three consecutive four-year terms.

In the meantime, life as the "loyal opposition" would require adjustments. On their own side, Republicans would have to find and agree on new leaders, new ideas and new tools to sell themselves to the American public. And they would have to take the

measure of the new president and his Democratic allies to determine the other party's political vulnerabilities and the areas where
they could most effectively offer their own alternatives. Clinton
would give them some help with his occasional miscalculations.
And many Republicans were confident that the Democrats' package of big tax increases would provide abundant openings for attack. But Republicans also had to be careful. The constant public
focus on the new president and his shifting fortunes might give the
Republicans a misleading sense of their own long-term prospects.
Although Clinton's historically low public-approval scores in late
spring buoyed the Republicans, they also knew from their bitter
experience with Bush that such ratings defined only a moment in
time and could be ephemeral.

After 12 years of Republican presidents, leaders of both parties found that adjusting to their changed roles was more of a challenge than they had expected. Many Democrats had found that the
responsibilities of governing were a jarring shift from the Reagan
and Bush eras, when they rarely had to worry that their own proposals would become law. Likewise, Republicans acknowledged
that they must grow accustomed to the reality that they often
would be irrelevant to the business of government. They also had
to learn patience. In the first few weeks after Clinton took office,
many congressional Republicans voiced frustration about what
they considered his generous press notices, and they chafed over
their own inability to gain much public attention. At a March
weekend retreat in New Jersey, they asked a panel of Washington
reporters to advise them on how they should cope with their new
condition. As it turned out, the Republican fears were overstated
and Clinton's "Superman" status quickly faded. But Clinton's loss
of mythical standing would not solve all of their problems. The
GOP (the acronym stands for "Grand Old Party") still had to
prove that its members could contribute to the public debate and
sort out the problems that led to the party's rejection in 1992.

The "loyal opposition" has no defined role under the U.S.
Constitution. Mostly, the party outside the White House is defined
nationally by the actions of its congressional leaders. They are in a
stronger position than are state and local officials to address national issues and to sell their ideas to the Washington news media,
which set the tone for national political reporting. The chief exception comes during the year before a presidential election, when the
candidates seeking that office gain the dominant role in defining

their party. In contrast to a parliamentary government like Great Britain, where the majority party in the legislature automatically runs the executive branch and the opposition party has little responsibility other than to prepare for the next election, the American system is less clear-cut. Even if the same party holds the White House and a majority in both chambers of Congress, that does not necessarily mean that the other party operates entirely on the outside. When Lyndon Johnson was president, for example, he had important help from Republicans in the 1965 enactment of the landmark Voting Rights Act and the law establishing the Medicare program. But the nation's politics have changed since then. In both parties, the pressures have mounted against advocates of bipartisanship. With the growth of ideological pressure groups among both liberals and conservatives, politicians have found that the course of least resistance is to hang their hat on one side of the spectrum or the other. The contentious 1990 effort by Bush and congressional Democratic leaders to craft a budget agreement showed that consensus building between the parties has become something of a lost art because participants fear losing their political base of support. The party out of power at the White House, in short, has become more strident and less loyal.

The 12 years of the Reagan–Bush era had prompted more and more hand-wringing—from politicians and scholars, among others—about the impracticalities of divided government. Indeed, the first six years of that period were more productive than the last six years because Republicans controlled the Senate during the earlier time, giving Reagan more leverage with Congress for achieving his goals. After the 1986 election, when Democrats regained control of the Senate and kept their House majority, Republicans were at the Democrats' mercy on legislative action. Occasionally during those dozen years, the Democrats cooperated, especially when Reagan or Bush announced a policy goal that they also supported—such as plans for protecting the solvency of Social Security in 1983, reforming the tax code in 1985 or strengthening the Clean Air Act in 1989. Mostly, however, Democratic leaders used their positions to attack Republican policies and to present occasional alternatives. In 1981–82, when Democrats feared that the Reagan revolution might overrun everything in sight, they also worked to urge their troops to remain loyal to their own party and not to back the Republican program. "So far, the president has effectively focused the argument on overall policy," Rep. Tony Coelho, a California Democrat and key House leader, said in early 1981. "But my guess is the public will become educated and we'll hold our own politically." In the long term, his forecast proved astute.

For the first time in congressional history, the House Speaker—Thomas (Tip) O'Neill Jr. of Massachusetts—would hold widely reported press conferences and would issue statements regularly to highlight Reagan's alleged misdeeds. As the outspoken leader of the opposition party, O'Neill often played the role of the Democratic National Committee chairman. He and other House Democratic leaders also occasionally proposed legislation that was designed, in part, to spotlight the failings of the Reagan administration in dealing with the economy and social issues. When O'Neill retired in 1986, House Democrats had built a wide-ranging communications and political strategy to serve as the opposition voice. In the Senate, meanwhile, Democrats received less press attention because their minority status gave them a diminished role compared with their House counterparts. Until 1989, when Mitchell replaced Byrd as their party leader, the Senate Democrats also were less sophisticated in developing a public strategy to attack Republican policies. During the Bush era, the congressional Democratic team of Mitchell, Foley and Gephardt sought to strike a balance between cooperating with Bush on a few essential legislative issues and defining the differences between the parties on broad problems such as the economy and health care.

When Republicans were relegated to their status as the opposition party in 1993, they did not have to worry about cooperating with the president. They returned to a role similar to the late 1970s, when the Democrats last controlled the presidency and Republicans were locked out of any majority power in Washington. They also looked for other lessons from the Carter era, which many Republicans hoped would be a constructive model for their response to the Clinton presidency. During the earlier period, the GOP's dominant ideology shifted to its conservative wing, which showed little interest in the kind of bipartisan cooperation that had marked the Johnson era. Control of the party—which had been divided between its old-time moderate wing centered in the Northeast and Midwest and its newer, more conservative flank in the South and West—began to move steadily toward the conservatives across the nation. That was best symbolized by the nomination and election of Reagan in 1980. But it was not only the Reagan victory that showed the party's change. That success was based, in part, on a relatively simple idea crafted by congressional Republicans in 1977 and embraced by party leaders: a three-year program of tax cuts that would reduce the rates for individuals by a total of 30 percent. Despite doubts voiced quietly by some Republican moderates, that proposal—crafted by Rep. Jack Kemp of New York and Sen. William Roth of Delaware—became the party's battle cry during the 1980 campaign, and Congress quickly enacted the slightly revised plan after Reagan's election. There were other factors, of course, that led to the GOP's big success in 1980, including an inflation-ridden economy with interest rates reaching 20 percent, the Carter administration's embarrassing failure to free 52 U.S. hostages held captive by Iran for more than a year and the nasty primary challenge to Carter in 1980 by Sen. Edward Kennedy of Massachusetts. But the Kemp-Roth proposal helped the voters to focus on an alternative and gave their party a more populist appeal.

Will Republicans find an equally effective magic button to end the Clinton era? Time will tell. But the early months of 1993 showed both parallels to and differences from the Carter presidency. The chief similarity will be the GOP's emphasis on lower federal spending and opposition to the Democrats' tax increases. Although the huge federal deficit, a legacy from the 1980s, made it more difficult for Republicans to rally around another across-the-board tax cut, they were eager to remind voters of their contrast to the Democrats' "tax and spend" policies. (Democrats like to respond that the GOP practiced "borrow and spend" policies.) Republicans also emphasized their tougher stance on defense and foreign policy, which had marked the Reagan and Bush eras. True, the collapse of communism and the Soviet Union had eliminated much of the public's fear of a dangerous world. But GOP leaders seized on Clinton's support for gays in the military and his own failure to serve in the military during the Vietnam War to appeal to conservative voters, especially in the South.

One significant difference in 1993 was the national party's conscious deemphasizing of the anti-abortion policy that had been a trademark of conservative Republicans since the late 1970s. Recent Supreme Court decisions had moved the nation toward a more centrist position on the issue—i.e., abortion is permissible, but with some state-sponsored restrictions. Following the public's hostile reaction to the anti-abortion tone at their party's 1992 national convention, Republicans decided to tone down their rhetoric on the issue and to emphasize a more inclusive approach. The most successful early example of this approach came in Texas, where Sen. Phil Gramm and many other Republican leaders rallied to the support of state treasurer Kay Bailey Hutchison in the contest to elect a Senate successor to Lloyd Bentsen. Although Hutchison had consistent conservative positions on economic issues, her position for abortion rights helped her to attract many women voters. Despite his own anti-abortion view, Gramm viewed Hutchison as the best prospect to gain the Senate seat. She easily defeated two anti-abortion Republican Congressmen in the first round of voting and then won 67 percent of the vote to defeat Krueger in the June 5 election runoff—the worst defeat in U.S. history for an incumbent senator nominated by a major party. "This election was a clear referendum on president Clinton's tax and spend programs," Gramm said, "and the people of Texas said 'no.'" National Republicans hoped to build on Hutchison's success.

Emphasizing New Leaders, Not Issues

The Republicans' initial effort to overhaul their image and to capture public support focused on placing a new face on their party. In the short term, at least, that was an easier course than developing new policies. And there were plenty of junior GOP lawmakers willing to step forward with something to offer. Although their early steps were not revolutionary political changes, the renewed activism contributed to the Republicans' revitalization.

The first significant change came a few weeks after the November election, when House Republicans reassembled in Washington to select their leaders for the new Congress. The major clash was a challenge by Dick Armey of Texas to Jerry Lewis of California, who held the party's third-ranking leadership post as Republican Conference chairman. Lewis, an ally of Minority Leader Robert Michel of Illinois, was a GOP centrist who had supported Bush and the bipartisan budget deal in 1990. Armey emphasized his conservative appeal and his strong opposition to that agreement. In a slap at other party leaders, he later said, "If I was in the leadership in the summer of 1990, President Bush would have had a clear understanding of what was the problem with the summit." In appealing for his candidacy, which was especially successful with the 47 House GOP freshmen, Armey also emphasized that he had worked to change how Washington did business, especially its big spending. He pointed to his leading role in the bipartisan passage of earlier legislation that led to a closing of nonessential military bases across the nation and to his cooperation with liberal Democrats on cutting subsidies to farmers. Armey's 88–84 victory over Lewis was a signal that Republicans would not allow Clinton and the Democrats to go unchallenged as Washington's new "agents of change." It also sent a message that the House GOP had little interest in working with the new president. Given the Democrats' iron-clad control of House rules and proceedings, the Republicans' judgment appeared realistic, at least for the next two years.

Armey's success was a victory for conservatives as much as it was a change to less senior leaders. An enthusiastic Reagan supporter who believed that Bush's failure resulted from the abandonment of his "no new taxes" pledge, the former economics professor from the Dallas suburbs ardently advocated free-market policies and dismissed the Democratic contention that the 1980s were a decade of greed. Not surprisingly, he voiced confidence that Clinton's program was doomed to failure. "Now, the Democrats can get away with their talk for a while," he said in early 1993. "But eventually they will have to produce more income and job security. And their program won't do it." A few months later, the ever-confident Armey was, if anything, more convinced that Clinton's tax increases, including the higher taxes on the wealthy, would not raise the promised money for the Treasury. "The demagoguery in their class-conflict rhetoric doesn't hold water," he said. "Clinton is driving a train to oblivion." The chief question in Armey's mind was how long the conservative Democrats would wait before abandoning their president. By repeating his economic arguments, he was hoping for at least one of the following results, or maybe both: that the Democrats' legislative success would end soon or that many of them would be defeated in coming elections. In either case, Armey was ready to take the lead in promoting the rejuvenation of Reaganomics. Although he confessed that it had been difficult for Republicans to gain much attention to their own alternatives during Clinton's early months, he had no doubt that the nation would be receptive after seeing the fruits of the Democrats' program.

Another junior House Republican who emerged from relative obscurity during the GOP's December organizing sessions was

John Kasich of Ohio. The brash, 40-year-old lawmaker with a non-Republican blue-collar background defeated North Carolina's silver-haired Alex McMillan, 60, to become the senior Republican at the House Budget Committee. In his new position, Kasich would move aggressively to unite his party around basic budget principles: no new taxes, spending cuts for defense and middle-class programs, and reorganization of the federal bureaucracy. "Republicans lost the [White House] because we had a tendency to manage the government, not to be bold," he said. "I have had a lot of good ideas." With his energetic style, he shared Armey's ability to reach out to a cross section of members in both parties. He had worked closely, for example, with Ronald Dellums, the liberal California Democrat who had replaced Les Aspin as House Armed Services Committee chairman, in their lengthy and successful effort during the Bush presidency to end the production of the new B-2 bomber aircraft. He often emphasized the need to shake up the stodgy Republicans. House members "come and go," he said in early 1993. "So, we should swing for the fences. We shouldn't operate on the margins."

Kasich followed his own advice. Within weeks after Clinton submitted his budget plan to Congress, Kasich won Republican agreement to back his distinctive budget alternative. The plan included cuts in nearly 160 programs that run the gamut of federal spending, from Medicare cuts for wealthy retirees to the cancellation of the annual cost-of-living adjustment for federal employees and the elimination of 162,000 federal jobs. Although the scale of the cuts made even some Republicans nervous about their political impact, 135 House Republicans voted for the plan with 38 opposed. But all 257 Democrats voted against Kasich's proposal. His plan subsequently generated enthusiasm from many Republicans for reasons that were more political than budget-related. Newspaper editorials and political experts, who praised Kasich for offering a credible alternative, generally did not explore the details of the proposal. Instead, they focused on its deficit reduction, which came entirely from lower federal spending, not from higher taxes. So Kasich and his followers were spared, for example, from having to explain precisely how they would have reduced spending for Medicare. "We can work out the details," said Armey, an advocate of the plan. As the Democrats learned and said repeatedly, however, the devil is in the details of the legislative process. The Republicans' ability to avoid a debate on the specifics produced a more receptive audience for Kasich's plan than might have otherwise been the case. As it was, however, the exercise gave a boost to Kasich's profile, both in Washington and in his home state of Ohio.

Another prominent Republican in the spring budget debate was Sen. Phil Gramm of Texas. In contrast to Armey and Kasich, Gramm was far better known by 1993. A former economics professor (like Armey), his penchant for blunt, down-to-earth language has played well in his home state and with the national news media. He first gained public notice in 1981, when as a second-term House Democrat from Texas he led the Southern Democrats who joined forces with House Republicans to pass Reagan's spending cuts. His role, including the leaking of political secrets from Democratic leaders to White House officials, was viewed as apostasy by many Democrats. When they later stripped him of his House Budget Committee seat, Gramm switched parties and was re-elected to the House in 1983 as a Republican. A year later, Gramm easily won the Senate seat from Texas, which had been vacated by the retirement of Republican John Tower. Then, Gramm took on another dramatic challenge. In 1985, he co-sponsored with two other senators the proposal known as Gramm-Rudman-Hollings, billed as a five-year effort to steadily reduce and then eliminate the deficit, with automatic spending cuts required if the annual goals were not met. Although the proposal generated wide publicity and great fears at the time, it proved to have little impact as a fiscal tool: Its goals proved to be unrealistic. Its automatic mechanism covered only a small share of federal spending. And it could be suspended at congressional direction. Eventually, Congress chose to ignore the law, and the deficit continued to grow. But that did not stop the intrepid Gramm.

Freed by Clinton's election of the burden of defending or co-operating with a Republican president, Gramm became the informal leader of the Senate's conservative Republicans on budget issues. Although he did not copy Kasich in proposing a comprehensive alternative budget, he issued several statements criticizing the additional spending and taxes in Clinton's budget. His proposal to drop all of those changes, Gramm told reporters, presented a "very clear choice" that everyone can understand. Later, Gramm and Armey introduced a plan to increase tax incentives for businesses and individuals that was designed to increase savings and encourage corporate investment. The Senate did not accept any of Gramm's proposals. But that was not his point. Instead, the peripatetic senator—who had stated his interest in a 1996 presidential candidacy—took his case to the Senate floor, to New Hampshire, and to almost any other place where he could find an audience. His goal, he said, was to urge Clinton to review his proposals, "find a common ground and come back and work with us." Gramm, surely, was not surprised that the president failed to respond. But the senator was hoping to start a political debate that would extend beyond the legislative debate on the budget.

For Gramm and the other Republicans, however, their hopes to gain attention to themselves and their ideas were constantly over-shadowed by the party's dominant figure in Washington, Senate Minority Leader Robert Dole of Kansas. A major presence on the national political stage for a quarter century, Dole had earlier served as Republican National Committee chairman, had been President Gerald Ford's running mate in the unsuccessful 1976 campaign, and had sought his party's nomination for president in 1988 in what became a bitter challenge to Bush. He also had been one of the leading power brokers in Congress for much of that period. After eight years in the House, he had been first elected to the Senate in 1968. His work in the early years focused on the Agriculture Committee, whose work has obvious interest to his home state, and the Finance Committee, with its broad jurisdiction over taxes, Social Security, trade and other issues. From 1981 to 1985, as Finance Committee chairman, he shepherded much of Reagan's major legislation. Then, when Howard Baker of Tennessee retired in 1984, Dole defeated four other Republicans to become Senate majority leader. Unhappily for Dole, the Republicans lost their Senate majority in 1986 and he was relegated to minority leader. But, under both Reagan and Bush, he developed a good working relationship with Senate Democrats to move essential presidential proposals. Once Bush was defeated, it was Dole's turn to move to the limelight. And he was not reluctant to claim the authority. "It's unfortunate, but that's politics," he said, with little remorse, about Bush's defeat a few days after the election. "Having said that, I can't change any of that. I am sort of looking forward to a little different opportunity, I guess."[1]

The election of a Democratic president posed new challenges for Dole. For the previous dozen years, he usually faced the need to unite the party around a proposal or viewpoint defined by the White House. That had left Dole little flexibility to put his own stamp on the party's effort and also required him to work to keep all Republican factions backing the president. Now, Dole would be calling the shots on what position to take. Likewise, because party unity would no longer be so vital, he had to spend less time accommodating each Republican senator. That the rules of the Senate give the minority party far more influence and ability to disrupt the proceedings than in the House was another reason why Dole would become the center of attention—within both the party and the Senate. His House counterpart, Minority Leader Robert Michel of Illinois, kept a low profile and had few opportunities to significantly influence House business. By contrast, when Dole wanted to place his imprint on legislation, Mitchell and the Democrats usually were not able to refuse. His own skills and experience provided several other reasons for his move to the top. Despite his frequently acerbic personality, Dole was a skillful and eager guest on television news programs, where he often served as party spokesman. His years of legislative experience and his quick mind gave him the expertise to comment knowledgeably about a broad array of issues. And he had shown the ability to understand the views of and reach out to Republicans across his party's ideological spectrum. Over the years, for example, he had worked with GOP moderates and with Democrats on food stamps for the poor and civil rights. With conservatives, he usually took an aggressive posture on crime issues and on foreign policy. On the economy, he was more pragmatic and took positions that were attuned to the politics of the time and to all sides of his party. Finally, Dole's broad hints that he might run again for president in 1996 were another reason few Republicans were willing to defy him. With this background and his obvious desire to play on center stage, Dole would be hard to ignore. He even hoped that, on occasion, Clinton would be willing to work with him.

Armey, Kasich, Gramm and Dole shared something in common as Republican leaders: They were legislative activists who also knew how to play politically to a national audience. For a time, at least while they had few legislative options, the latter role would prove more productive.

Seeking Legislative Opportunities

For the loyal opposition, it is one thing to have the opportunity to attack the president in a legislative forum. But it is not always so easy to succeed, even rhetorically. As the Republicans would discover in the weeks immediately after Clinton's election and inauguration, the new president was skillful in defining the economic agenda and in sustaining favorable news coverage, at least until he had to put forward and gain action on specific proposals. Without actual Clinton plans to shoot at, the Republicans were frustrated in their early efforts to define and attack him. They also realized that they had to move carefully soon after the election, lest they offend the public with too quick of a return to partisan "politics as usual," which voters had decisively rejected in the election. By early spring, however, the constraints were off, and Republicans moved aggressively to undermine Clinton and to show the president's shortcomings.

The ineffective Republican efforts at the Senate hearings in January on the nominations of members of Clinton's Cabinet illustrated the difficulty of finding the proper political balance in criticizing a new president. The Republicans believed that the personal backgrounds of some of the nominees might provide an opening for attack. The GOP leaders also were still fuming about the bitter 1989 battle that led to the Democrats' defeat of former Sen. John Tower, who had been President Bush's first choice for Defense Secretary. When Dole in December appointed feisty conservative Sen. Trent Lott of Mississippi to coordinate their strategy for the forthcoming confirmation hearings, some Republicans said that they would apply the "Tower test" to Clinton nominees suspected of ethical misdeeds in their public life.[2] Sen. John McCain, an Arizona Republican, warned at the time that Democrats would be reminded of their earlier statements that Tower's personal ethics were as relevant to a review of his qualifications for the post as his professional record was.

After Clinton announced his Cabinet selections, Lott and his allies focused their attention chiefly on Ronald Brown, the president's choice for Commerce Secretary. As chairman of the Democratic National Committee for the previous four years, Brown had remained a partner in Washington's high-powered law firm of Patton, Boggs and Blow, where he advised several overseas clients. But when the hearings began, the Republican assault was surprisingly tame. In response to questions from Lott and others on the Senate Commerce, Science and Transportation Committee, Brown agreed to stricter standards for keeping his distance from previous clients. But many Senate Republicans were wary of pressing too aggressively; they feared committing the same excesses for which they had criticized the Democrats four years earlier. Oddly, Brown's most embarrassing concession came when Clinton's publicly stated objections forced the cancellation of an expensive Inaugural week gala in Brown's honor, which would have been paid for by many corporate donors. And the only nominee who ran into serious problems during the initial confirmation process—Zoe Baird, Clinton's choice for Attorney General—was forced to withdraw chiefly because of opposition from Democrats when she told the Senate Judiciary Committee about her failure to meet federal requirements for reporting the services of her child's "nanny." McCain conceded, in his post-mortem on the confirmation hearings, that Republicans deserved "blame" for not pressing harder on ethics questions, especially on Brown. "There is clearly some confusion" in their ranks about how to respond to a Democratic president, he said.

Republicans also were divided in early 1993 about how aggressively they should move to recast their own identity rather than simply to attack Clinton and the Democrats. House Minority Whip Newt Gingrich of Georgia, a conservative leader, said that members of his party would have failed if they spent more time talking about Clinton than about their own ideas. Rep. Marge Roukema of New Jersey, a moderate Republican, echoed that viewpoint with her contention that Republicans can succeed only if they present credible policies of their own. "There is no magic bullet here," she said. "That would be the worst thing. . . . We have to go back to old-fashioned fiscal management." But many Republicans disagreed. Armey, the newly elected chairman of the House Republican Conference, said that the GOP was in less need of new ideas than of reinforcing their successful themes of the 1980s. "We had our champion with Ronald Reagan, who made good things happen," he said. Faced with these differences and the difficult challenge of crafting a new party message, the Republicans generally agreed to sit back and criticize. When they chose their new chairman of the Republican National Committee in late January, the winner was Haley Barbour, a Washington lobbyist known for his skills as a television spokesman but lacking any significant policy background. Several other party leaders distanced themselves from their earlier emphasis on ideology when they said that the sometimes shrill, anti-abortion tone at their 1992 national convention had been a mistake. Rich Bond, Barbour's predecessor, told

Republicans that they must "not cling to zealotry masquerading as principle."

Clinton's decision to ignore the Republicans after he took office reinforced their own inclination to stand on the sidelines. Despite his many meetings with congressional Democrats before he announced his economic program on Feb. 17, the president did not meet with GOP leaders until the day of his speech. "They have no obligation to bring us down [here] at all," Gingrich told reporters at the White House after the meeting. "They can try to ram things through on a partisan basis. But I think, hopefully, as they get through this experience, one of the things they're learning is that it would actually be better to consult with us earlier." After Clinton unveiled his economic plan in the speech to Congress that night, Dole took the gloves off by describing it as "a tax-heavy package that fails to make the tough choices on spending controls." When Clinton traveled to the Capitol in early March in a good-will gesture to meet separately with House and Senate Republicans, the discussions were friendly but there were few substantive exchanges. At the House, he helped Republicans to cut a large cake to celebrate the 70th birthday of Robert Michel of Illinois, their party leader, and he gave an old Chicago Cubs baseball cap to Michel. In the Senate, the big news the same day was that Clinton joined the Republicans in eating one of his favorite meals—a Big Mac and french fries. "The president of the United States is a charming fellow," Kasich told reporters. But the meetings had little impact on the legislative debates that would soon follow.

There were other reasons Republicans chose to sit on the sidelines during the Democrats' early budget debates. One was that it was a politically safer route, at least for the time being, to keep the focus of attention on the Democrats' plan and their internal struggles. Some Republicans, Dole said, believed that the nation's problems were no longer their responsibility and that the GOP should stand aside as the Democrats advanced their own proposal and "let them have it." The Democrats understood that, too, but they were not inclined to allow the Republicans simply to lob political grenades. That was why Clinton and other Democrats quickly challenged Republicans to enter the fray. When budget director Panetta testified before the Senate Budget Committee in late February, Republican Lott pulled from his pocket a list of proposed spending cuts that he claimed added up to $216 billion. But Lott declined to share it with Panetta or with the nation because he conceded there are political risks in offering what may have been controversial alternatives. Also, as the Republicans had painfully learned during the Bush years, deficit reduction was no easy task and was not a subject on which their party could easily agree. For example, some deficit "hawks" like Sen. Pete Domenici of New Mexico, the senior Republican on the Budget Committee, were willing to join Democrats in proposing limits on annual increases for Social Security beneficiaries. But other Republicans were reluctant to take what they considered a political risk, especially after Clinton's election moved the weight of responsibility to the Democrats. Instead, they coalesced in the Senate behind a proposal for "entitlement controls" that promised large savings in programs like Medicare and welfare but deferred the details to future legislation. Likewise, some Republicans were more willing to consider defense cuts than were such leading GOP experts on the Pentagon as Strom Thurmond of South Carolina and John Warner of Virginia, both of whom—not coincidentally—had many major defense facilities in their home states. Even Sen. Gramm of Texas, the arch-proponent of federal spending cuts, drew the line when it came to cutbacks on two costly projects, the supercollider science project and NASA's space station, both of which were based in his home state. Indeed, the largely unspoken divisions on the Republican side illustrated why it was remarkable that Clinton was able to keep his usually fractious party mostly unified on budget issues.

Besides their splits over policy, Republicans also suffered from personality differences that made it difficult for them to seek a consensus for legislative action. For years, there had been little coordination between senior House and Senate Republicans. Gingrich and Armey, for example, mistrusted Dole's willingness to deal with the Democrats. For his part, Dole had spoken contemptuously of how the House conservatives were unwilling to face the realities of governing. Their respective presidential ambitions also were a source of conflict between Dole and Gramm, the two most active Senate Republican spokesmen. The conflicts were not only among the party leaders. In California, for example, the internal warfare was so intense that most of the state's House Republicans opposed their fellow Californian Jerry Lewis in the contest he lost to Armey. Following the defeat, Lewis issued a bitter statement, claiming that a "divided California delegation" had given Armey the victory. The result, he added, confirmed "one important fact: In times of important decisions relating to the economic and political future of our states, Texans stick together and Californians do not."

Even the Republicans' success in defeating Clinton's economic stimulus bill highlighted many of these internal problems. Much as they welcomed the result, GOP senators had done little planning to encourage their success. The Democrats' tactical errors, as discussed in chapter six, placed the victory in the Republicans' lap. True, Dole and his team finally succeeded in keeping their troops united despite the belated efforts by Clinton and the Senate Democrats to forge a compromise. But Republicans like Specter and Hatfield, who eventually voted for the filibuster that killed the bill, had also discussed possible Senate compromises with the Democrats. They and a handful of other GOP moderates had a history of abandoning their party on spending bills—in part, to secure added federal funds for programs in their home states. But, partly through their own political shrewdness, these swing votes in the Senate had been able to develop a sense of where the political winds were blowing. When they saw the Democrats' weak and belated defense of Clinton's economic stimulus bill and the heavy-handed tactics that the Democrats used to try to pass it, they realized the modest political support for the proposal. As loyal Republicans, they were not deaf to the voices in their party who saw that bill as an opportunity to impose an unexpected and stinging defeat on Clinton, which could have significant consequences. But the GOP efforts on the stimulus bill, like most of their other activities during Clinton's early months, did not seek to offer a meaningful alternative. They voiced, instead, what is often the loyal opposition's most potent response: "No."

Political Opportunities

To regain power, the "loyal opposition" ultimately must turn its attention from Washington and try to make its case with the voters. A party's prospects in electoral politics depend, in part, on the success of its legislative efforts. But the rhetorical fog that typically accompanies debate in the Capitol usually requires political leaders—both national and local—to take their message directly to the grass roots. From the national perspective in 1993, Republicans hoped to create a favorable climate for the hundreds of potential

GOP candidates who might consider running in subsequent campaigns. The results of local elections, including for Congress, usually are determined by a series of parochial factors, not the least of which are the candidates' skills. But several national conditions—including the state of the economy, the president's popularity and the national mood—often play an important role in encouraging candidates to make the race and, then, helping them to find the right combination of factors for success.

Despite the convincing defeat of Bush in the 1992 election, Republicans found grounds for confidence that the Clinton presidency would bring good tidings to their own party. First, Clinton's 43 percent of the popular vote hardly represented a ringing vote of confidence in a party that had been experiencing problems at the national level. That share was within a few percentage points of the Democratic presidential vote in each of the three previous elections. Second, the Democrats' election loss of 10 House seats in 1992 and the break-even Senate results provided little cause for their satisfaction. Beyond those results, the difficult economic and political challenges facing the president's party in managing the U.S. government gave the Republicans additional cause for hope as they looked ahead to the 1994 and 1996 elections. As had happened during the Carter presidency—which was marked by a series of economic and foreign-policy woes, not all of which were controllable from Washington—some Republicans believed that the 1993–96 period would be a good time for their party to be out of power, recharging its batteries and waiting for the Democrats to fail. The day-to-day burdens of governing—on issues ranging from civil rights to foreign policy—posed strains for Democrats not only in gaining new supporters but also in accommodating the sometimes conflicting views of their own constituencies. And the 19 percent of the national voters who supported Ross Perot represented a political wild card that was up for grabs between the two parties. But Perot's activities and rhetoric, both before and after the 1992 election, represented an anti-Washington message that did not augur good news for Democrats, once Clinton was elected.

The continuing appeal of Perot also carried ominous warnings for Republicans. When national polls in the spring of 1993 showed that he was virtually even in a hypothetical 1996 match-up with Clinton and that Dole was running third, the implication was that Perot was outperforming Republican leaders in making the case as the logical alternative. Republican leaders told reporters that

Perot's celebrity status was based more on imagery than on real ideas and that, without a conventional political organization, he was likely to fade under the public spotlight in the many months until the 1996 election. They noted, for example, that he attacked Clinton's proposed tax increases though Perot during his 1992 campaign had proposed new taxes that would have been even more painful for the middle class, including an additional 50 cents for a gallon of gasoline. For national Republican leaders, one of their greatest fears was that Perot would move into their party and try to use his unlimited financial resources to secure the 1996 presidential nomination. That did not prevent junior congressional Republicans from lining up to identify with Perot, however, during his occasional visits to Washington in which he took on issues ranging from the proposed trade agreement with Mexico and Canada to congressional procedures.

Some Republicans, meanwhile, focused on more immediate election contests. In Congress, the resignations of three House Democrats—Les Aspin, Mike Espy and Leon Panetta—who joined Clinton's Cabinet created vacancies and competitive contests during the next few months in distinct regions of the nation. In each case, Republicans ran an aggressive campaign and the outcome was close, but Democrats again proved their skill in winning House contests. Their success was based, in part, on the Democrats' proven formula of maintaining a stronger "farm team" than the Republicans. Each of the Democratic winners had served as a state or county elected official, while the three Republican losers—though each had some experience in appointed positions—had never been elected to office. For House Republicans, the only good news that they could draw from the contests was that none of the winning Democrats gained more than 55 percent of the vote, a result GOP insiders attributed to Clinton's steadily declining popularity throughout the spring. Rep. Vic Fazio of California, the House Democrats' chief campaign strategist, took solace in the voters' continuing message that they "want the government—President Clinton and the Congress—to take responsible action and put the country on track and people back to work."

But Republicans fared far better in another spring election, giving them high hopes for the future. When Gov. Ann Richards of Texas, after failing to convince several stronger candidates to run, appointed Robert Krueger to the Senate seat vacated by Treasury Secretary Bentsen, the Democrats found themselves in an all too familiar dilemma. In November 1991, they had basked in the outcome of the Pennsylvania Senate campaign, heralding Harris Wofford's victory over Richard Thornburgh as ominous news for Bush and the Republicans. Now, the Texas campaign posed similar dangers to their own party. Although Democrats held most statewide elected offices and 21 seats in the 30-member House delegation, their strength in Texas had been slipping in national contests. Clinton had lost the state the previous November with only 37 percent of the vote, his worst showing in any of the nation's 10 largest states and a sharp contrast to Jimmy Carter's victory in Texas in 1976. In addition, Republican Phil Gramm had gained two convincing Senate campaign victories with his calls to reduce federal spending.

Krueger had been in public life for nearly two decades, including two previous unsuccessful campaigns for the Senate. His shortcomings were readily apparent. A Shakespearean scholar, he had acknowledged his modest skills as a candidate in the often rough-and-tumble world of Texas politics. His stiff political style and his experience in Washington had some of the features that had backfired on Thornburgh in 1991. Democrats, relieved that no other Democratic official had entered the contest, initially predicted that Krueger might win 50 percent of the vote in the non-partisan primary contest, which would avoid the need for a runoff against the runner-up. Republicans, for their part, had three well-known elected officials in the contest: two House members and the state's Treasurer, Kay Bailey Hutchison. During the initial contest, they vigorously attacked each other, raising GOP fears that the front-runner among the Republicans would be damaged in a runoff against Krueger. But Hutchison won with her support for abortion rights, which appealed to women, and with her backing from mainstream Republican leaders in Texas; it was well known, for example, that Gramm had encouraged her candidacy. What was most significant about the May 1 primary was not only that she had a big lead over her two GOP foes but that she also led Krueger. The Democrats' initial hopes that he would gain 50 percent in the first contest faded to the reality of a dismal 29 percent. During the following five weeks to the runoff contest, Krueger tried some desperate tactics to appeal to voters, including a television commercial in which he mockingly portrayed himself as "The Terminator" and confessed that he was "a terrible politician." His hope to convince Texans that he was, instead, "a good senator" who cared about issues fell flat. During the runoff campaign, Hutchison focused on her opposition to the new taxes in Clinton's economic package and emphasized that she would cut spending when the voters sent her to Washington. As had Democratic women who sought Senate seats in 1992, she benefitted from her gender and the unspoken message that she was not simply "another politician."

When Hutchison trounced Krueger, 67 percent to 33 percent, her victory had several potentially profound consequences. For Texas politics, that she had won by the biggest margin for a Republican in a statewide race during the 20th century was a further sign of the deterioration of the Democrats' coalition there. Nationally, the devastating outcome was a powerful warning to Democrats about the perils that they faced in high-profile Senate elections in 1994. Though Krueger had sought to distance himself from Clinton's unpopular views on issues such as taxes and gays in the military, many voters did not make the distinction. The conclusion that they were stuck with Clinton, in effect, confirmed the warning that their party leaders had made since the 1992 election: Democrats would sink or swim as a party. That prescription delighted Gramm. "This election is a rejection of everything that Bill Clinton is trying to do in Washington," he said. For his part, Sen. Boren of Oklahoma warned that liberals in his party would have to pay more attention to the views of the conservative voters who supported him and other Southern Democrats in Congress. "If we want to lose the Senate in 1994, let's have more headlines about punishing the moderates," he said in a caustic reference to the effort by some House Democrats to strip the chairmanships from Democrats who had voted against Clinton's economic package. In depriving Democrats of a badly needed Senate seat, the outcome also raised questions anew about the wisdom of Clinton's decision to move Bentsen to Treasury Secretary from his former position as Senate Finance Committee chairman. As for Hutchison, she became one of her party's celebrities, knocking Clinton's economic policies at partisan events across the nation.

For Republicans, the welcome result confirmed the wisdom of their efforts to focus on the Democrats "tax and spend" policies. The prospect of scoring additional gains in the 1994 election also buttressed their decision to resist compromise with Clinton even as they urged him to moderate his views. At the same time that the legislative battles were becoming more intense, the political lines were drawing sharper. Even when Clinton signaled that he wanted to move to the political center, the immediate and heated resistance from the liberal wing of the party reminded him and other Democrats of the risks in that course. Those signs were troubling, especially to the many vulnerable Democratic senators and House members planning to seek re-election in 1994.

Endnotes

1. Helen Dewar, "Bush's Loss Moves 'Unshackled' Dole to Center Stage Among Republicans," *The Washington Post,* Nov. 8, 1992: A30.
2. Sara Fritz, "GOP Plans 'Tower Test' for Grilling Clinton Nominees," *Los Angeles Times,* Dec. 16, 1992: A4.

8

The Inside and
Outside Views

☆ ☆ ☆

No matter the political season, members of Congress and Washington lobbyists conduct business on the Capitol steps.

Inside the Beltway

For President Clinton, battling with the House and Senate or even the Republicans provided continuing challenges. These adversaries were surely part of the business of government. Sometimes he would win; sometimes he would lose. But the rules of engagement usually were straightforward. Dealing with the leaders of the permanent Washington, on the other hand, would prove more frustrating. These were the private and often self-appointed citizens who have worked inside the capital Beltway, an interstate highway that encircles Washington. Many of these individuals have moved comfortably from dealing with one administration to another—requesting favors, dispensing advice and making life difficult for the powers that be. The lines between friendship and hostility were not always precise when these vested powers took on the new leaders. But they were difficult to ignore. And their self-importance often came at the expense of consistency and sincerity. Within two weeks of the election, for example, novelist and socialite Sally Quinn—who is the wife of Benjamin Bradlee, the retired executive editor of *The Washington Post*—greeted Clinton with a cheeky article in that newspaper explaining why it was important for him to acknowledge the informal local customs. "Welcome to Washington, but play by our rules," Quinn admonished. "Like any other culture, Washington has its own totems and taboos. It would serve the newcomers well to learn them and abide by them."[1]

Clinton brought some of his problems with these groups on himself. Though he had lived enjoyably in the city for four years as an undergraduate at Georgetown University, worked during that time for Sen. William Fulbright of Arkansas, and later made frequent visits as governor of Arkansas pleading for federal aid or changes in policy, his campaign distanced himself from the Washington community. By attacking the congressional pay raise as a symbol of what ailed the capital during the Reagan-Bush era, he raised congressional anxieties. But Clinton could hardly criticize the nation's capital of the Reagan-Bush era without also pointing a finger at his own party. Republican control of the White House for the past dozen years had relegated Democrats to outsiders in the city's political culture. But given their significant influence in Congress during that period, Democrats had hardly disappeared from the official scene. Informally, they were thriving as lawyers, lobbyists, consultants and the tens of thousands of others who help Washington to function—or muck it up—from day to day. No better evidence of the Democrats' continuing influence in Washington came after Clinton was elected president, when he selected Vernon Jordan, a prominent local attorney, as the chairman of his transition committee. Later, he mingled with area "big shots" during his pre-Inaugural visits to the capital.

But, even before the blossoming of billionaire populist Ross Perot, attacks on Washington had become a favorite national sport, often with reason. Government leaders were viewed as royal figures, who could command an audience with business leaders and entertainment celebrities from across the nation and whose everyday actions drew the attention of "pop culture" magazines. With an increasing presence in citizens' daily life—from its dollars to its regulations that affected virtually every citizen—Washington's demands could hardly be ignored. And its bloated lifestyle and arrogance made the area an apt target for attack and mockery. Yes, other cities such as New York and Los Angeles had pockets of affluence that put the nation's capital to shame. But Washington was different, if only because it was supposed to represent the nation and not to stand above it like a royal palace. Fueled by the growth of federal programs, the metropolitan area had become one of the nation's wealthiest regions. Government was not the only factor in the growth. During the prior two decades, the region had become a national center for high-tech and other computer-era industries. The wealthy lifestyle also invited many expensive retail stores, restaurants and hotels to accommodate local demands. The Kennedy Center for the Performing Arts was one of the nation's entertainment meccas. No longer was Washington the sleepy Southern town of the 1950s, which President Kennedy once joked to be "a city of Southern efficiency and Northern charm."

Despite these changes, Washington continued to pull on the nation's emotions, as millions of tourists annually discover. The public likes to see where its laws are made and how its money is spent. Magnificent living monuments, especially the White House and the Capitol, take the breath away even from the area's lifelong and often jaded residents. The power and majesty of its democratic institutions attest to the nation's strength, even when they operate in awkward fashion. Members of Congress, who are all too fallible to those who regularly watch or deal with them in the larger arena of the capital, gain more authenticity when they speak on their own to groups in Washington or in their home states. And a new president enters Washington with a special mystique that derives, in part, from receiving the stamp of approval from voters across the nation.

From the sometimes jaundiced perspective of Washington's political community, however, a change in the presidency is not quite so magical as it seems to the new lead performers. The nation's problems remain largely intact, as do the rules—formal and informal—for dealing with them. The capital's permanent insiders disdainfully eye the novice players with an attitude of, "This too shall pass." After the excitement of the initial weeks, a president and his team must face their real rites of passage: They encounter a rigorous initiation as they test their plans and ideals against both the established ways of doing business and the forces who have spent years learning and playing by those rules. Those old-timers have sharpened their skills not only in Congress but also in the permanent Washington that includes lobbyists, image-makers and the news media. The same newly arrived president and his advisers who were eager and hard working soon become, to some of these natives, sophomoric and unable to make a decision. Ideas that were bold and imaginative become, instead, overreaching and unrealistic. And citizens across the nation who had heard so many positive comments about the new president must prepare themselves for more critical reviews.

So it happened to Bill Clinton. No doubt, he made some errors during his initial months in office, as would any person—including past presidents—in any job, new or old. Some of those mistakes had consequences for his administration's policies and for real Americans, including the cloudy circumstances that led to his abandonment of the $19 billion economic stimulus program. Others were fluff or cosmetic, such as his widely publicized decision to get a $200 haircut from a Hollywood stylist while inside Air Force One on a Los Angeles International Airport tarmac. To Washington's graybeards, however, each Clinton action or inaction provided yet another excuse to criticize him, pull him down the ladder a peg or speculate about the latest political ditch into which he was driving his administration. The most publicized source of this second-guessing came from the news media, especially television, where the Clinton who could do no wrong in the fall of 1992 suddenly became politically inept. His failures were magnified and catalogued on an almost daily basis; his successes were virtually overlooked. Analysis of underlying trends was sacrificed to the affairs of the moment, as self-critical press analyses later acknowledged. Evolving changes in the press corps also contributed to this phenomenon, which has turned coverage of the White House into a national soap opera. The daily developments are viewed through the prism of a story line, which may change every few weeks or as events warrant. Washington's lobbyists—or influence peddlers, as they are not so fondly described by their many critics—also contribute to the eroding power of a president by offering alternatives that chip away at his own proposals. "Death by a thousand cuts" is their approach in dealing with a president who shows the slightest hesitation or willingness to compromise his presumed ideals.

Although the permanent Washington is almost certain to outlast any president, the two sides usually find that it is in their respective interests to strike at least the appearance of an accommodation. Despite the mutual expressions of contempt, they all need each other to do their business. They also must convince their respective constituencies across the nation—voters, readers, viewers, contributors, private members and so on—that they are working diligently to address the public's business. At times in 1993, the attempts at cooperation seemed phony and unconvincing, as when the beleaguered president decided that he must invite several hundred reporters and their friends for an amiable Sunday barbecue under a tent on the White House lawn. They responded that, of course, the opportunity to rub shoulders with the powerful did not influence them. But, maybe, they will mention it to their family, neighbors or, especially, their boss. And the president responded the next day with a biting attack on the press's hostile tone. Yes, the relationships can have an incestuous fragrance. But, they are all part of doing business, even for a president who is a self-styled patron of change.

The Lobbyists on the Defensive

Lobbyists have been part of the Washington scene for as long as the Capitol building has existed. In principle, they have a legitimate task of representing the many diverse factions of America, each of whom is fully entitled to hire private agents to influence government decisions that may affect them. Indeed, many of the millions of Americans who view lobbyists with contempt have also been helping to finance them through membership in the thousands of organizations with an active Washington presence—from the Chamber of Commerce to the AFL-CIO, from the National Rifle Association to Common Cause, from billion-dollar foreign and domestic companies seeking to cut their tax and regulatory burdens to individuals seeking help on an immigration visa. Clinton's election placed all of them on the defensive. But they showed their usual resourcefulness in responding.

Although their critics decry the influence and venality of contemporary lobbyists in terms that suggest they are a threat to democracy, the modern breed actually has become rather tame. When then-Rep. Lyndon Johnson, for example, became a leading Democratic fundraiser during Franklin Roosevelt's presidency, he raised hundreds of thousands of dollars in illegal contributions from political allies who ran a big Texas construction company that had received huge federal contracts.[2] Some laws that seek to restrict and disclose both lobbying operations and the donation of political funds remain filled with loopholes. But stricter enforcement and the potential glare of publicity make it much less likely that the Roosevelt-era abuses prevail among today's lobbyists. Indeed, savvy lobbyists know that they must use more sophisticated techniques these days to garner support from members of Congress. For example, some Washington lobbying firms now charge a client more than $1 million to generate local "grass roots" contacts with members of Congress. "These firms use phone banks to drum up constituent support in key congressional districts or find a small group of community leaders who can put the arm on a Member," according to a recent study of these new-style firms.[3]

The most successful lobbying sometimes is performed for free. Hillary Rodham Clinton sanctioned a notable example of this genre when she invited John Sculley, the chief executive of Apple Computer Inc., to sit next to her in the House gallery as her husband unveiled his economic package to Congress in February. Imagine the indignation along Washington's lobbying corridors the next morning when the bosses from other major companies compared notes about the publicity bonanza gained by their competitor. Sculley, of course, did not have to pay for the high-powered access and publicity that he received that evening. But surely it was no coincidence that he had supported Clinton during the campaign and outlined his view of the industrial future at the post-election economic summit in Little Rock. And he already had endorsed the president's plan and had "ladled praise on Clinton as a big-picture thinker with a grasp of the future."[4] Many other lobbyists also believed it was no coincidence that a few days later the president agreed to pleas from Sculley, among others, to water down his proposal to tax the overseas operations of multinational companies like Apple. But the self-effacing Sculley sought to cast his efforts in loftier terms. "I'm not in the lobbying business," Sculley protested to *National Journal.* "When I'm involved with anyone in the Administration, it's almost always focused on broad issues."

The task of lobbyists, whether they are the corporate bosses or hired guns, is to persuade public officials about the merits of their cause, whether broad or narrow. The most effective lobbyist, like a Sculley, operates subtly so the decision-maker does not focus on whether government policy has sacrificed something to the private interest. Indeed, many lobbyists claim that they are advocating the broad public interest, not some greedy parochial concern. And they may be right, at least sometimes. Influential lobbyists often operate on the margins of a debate, where they do not necessarily contest the broader proposal. Instead, they seek to add, drop or change a minor detail to make a switch that may save that company or some other interest group millions—or billions—of dollars. To succeed in that sort of appeal, a lobbyist typically cannot rely on bluster and must have a well-marshaled argument with the facts in order. At the same time, it surely does not hurt for lobbyists to have some well-placed lawmakers on their side in key congressional power centers.

The aluminum industry provided an example of how lobbyists work most effectively. During the House debate on Clinton's proposed energy tax, its leaders gained an obscure change that exempted energy used in an "electrolytic process." Because aluminum is produced by this complex manufacturing process, which consumes large quantities of energy, its lobbyists claimed that the tax would place their industry at a competitive disadvantage in dealing with aluminum produced by companies in other nations. So, they urged an exemption from that fee for the electricity that is used to generate heat required for the smelting process. Treasury Secretary Bentsen initially rejected their request. He was concerned that granting an exemption to one industry would lead to a "slippery slope" that would exempt other industries and eventually gut the proposal. But the Aluminum Association and its large membership would not take "no" for an answer. After having secured the initial agreement of House members with aluminum plants in their districts to send a letter to Bentsen urging the change, they followed up with a closed-door campaign in which those House members lobbied their colleagues on the Ways and Means Committee. Rostenkowski had opposed exemptions in the bill. In this case, however, he showed a greater receptivity. He was, no doubt, influenced by the fact that a leading supporter of the aluminum exemption was Speaker Thomas Foley; his district, based in Spokane, Washington, included two large facilities of the Kaiser Aluminum Company, with a combined payroll of about 3,000 employees. In addition to the contacts by Foley, another key player was Ways and Means member Mike Kopetski, an Oregon Democrat whose district also included many aluminum workers. He negotiated with Rostenkowski and with Howard Paster, the chief White House legislative aide, the details of a deal that cut roughly in half the energy tax for aluminum manufacturing. As is usual when thousands of their constituents' jobs are at stake, these and other lawmakers claimed that they were working to protect the local economy and the livelihood of their workers, not the narrow interests of a large company. In a large and complex national economy, that line certainly can be hard to decipher, as can the boundaries between the private lobbyists and their congressional advocates.

The aluminum industry's exemption was far from resolved, however. By the time that the House had approved the energy tax as part of its deficit-reduction package, it was riddled with several other exemptions and qualifications to the tax—which was to be based on the heat content of energy, known as a British thermal unit (BTU). Diesel fuel used for farming was exempt from the tax, for example, but diesel fuel used for passenger automobiles would be fully taxed. Pleasure boats would pay more for fuel than would commercial boats. The result was a legislative hodgepodge that *The New York Times* described as "one of the most exemption-loaded, head-scratchingly complicated, brow-furrowing revenue raisers in history."[5] And, surely, it was no coincidence that those farmers and shipping companies had far more active and better-paid legislative advocates in Washington than did ordinary citizens. When the bill reached the Senate, opponents of the tax cleverly turned the tables by citing the proposal's convoluted legislative history to make their successful case to replace the so-called BTU tax with an increase in the gasoline tax that fell most heavily on consumers. They got their way—both in the Senate and in the final version of the bill. Ironically, therefore, the lobbyists who had succeeded in gaining the special provisions inserted into the measure produced so many complications that the original package had to be entirely scuttled and replaced in the Senate with a tax that raised one-third of the earlier amount. The outcome hardly dismayed them.

Even with the energy tax, however, the lobbyists were limited in how much they could achieve. Because President Clinton and most congressional Democrats had committed themselves to the enactment of a package reducing the deficit by a total of about $500 billion in five years, they obviously had to find the savings somewhere. If the $70 billion that Clinton envisioned from an energy tax was eliminated, the lawmakers would have to find substitute sources—from either other new taxes or additional spending cuts. That was no easy task, of course, as senators painfully learned. Skillful lobbyists, therefore, often find that they are competing with each other in a zero-sum game, especially in tax and spending issues. These contests can consume congressional attention and provide spicy news stories, and they certainly can be financially costly for the groups soliciting the changes—and lucrative for the lobbyists. But the results often do not produce the kinds of sweeping policy impact that all of the often self-serving brouhaha suggests. Still, politicians usually prefer to avoid these conflicts, which make them choose between competing forces. So, the Clinton team and congressional Democrats often had to cater to the lobbyists—speaking to their clients, reviewing their proposals, making vague promises of accommodation—even if their ideas had little merit or future.

White House aides occasionally said nice things about the interest groups and their hired guns, especially when they were seeking endorsement of their proposals or financial support for the Democratic Party. Indeed, a planeload of Washington lobbyists flew to Little Rock on Election Day to celebrate the victory with their supposed pal. And, the next month, Clinton reciprocated by telling a crowd of 2,200 Washington insiders—each of whom paid $1,500 for the privilege of dining with him—that, "I know that most Americans are pretty down on Washington . . . [but] I think that most Americans who serve here are better, perhaps, than the country thinks." But Clinton was not shy about crossing the street to cast them as the enemy, when the occasion was appropriate. As part of the preparation of his health-care package, for example, he visited a suburban Virginia health clinic in February and castigated the nation's drug companies for pursuing "profits at the expense of our children." In addition, he sought to draw the connection between their corporate shortcomings and their influence peddling in Washington: "The pharmaceutical industry is spending $1 billion more each year on advertising and lobbying than it does on developing new and better drugs." Clinton's early efforts to make a symbolic clean sweep of the old ways also featured the imposition of strict ethics rules on his top officials, making it more difficult for them to represent interest groups after they left government service.

Clinton's most publicized blow at Washington's culture came with his support of legislation to overhaul the campaign-finance law. Arguing that political reform was vital to achieving economic reform, he said "the influence industry" was challenging his policy goals. As he unveiled his campaign-finance proposal on May 7, he told students on the White House lawn, "The more we seek to change things, the more we draw lobbyists to Washington to see if they can stop the change." Although he acknowledged that their viewpoints deserved to be heard, he added, "there are times when these powerful interests turn debate into delay, and exert more influence over decisions in Washington than the people we were elected to serve do." His original proposal would have barred lobbyists from making contributions to lawmakers whom they lobby, would have ended the tax deductibility of lobbying expenses and would have reduced the money that political action committees, many of which are operated by lobbyists as part of their legislative strategy, could contribute to candidates. Savvy insiders quickly pointed out that the effort to restrict the lobbyists' donations was filled with loopholes and could be easily evaded. Likewise, a Clinton-backed congressional initiative to force more complete disclosure of lobbying activities drew criticism from reform advocates, who complained, for example, about its failure to prohibit gifts from lobbyists to lawmakers. The reformers also criticized the continuing efforts by Clinton's political operatives to raise large sums of money at Democratic fundraising events. Nor, as we saw in Chapter Five, did many members of Congress greet these restrictions on their own operating styles with unbounded enthusiasm.

Even some lobbyists had trouble figuring out which side of the fence they were on. Days before Clinton unveiled his political-reform agenda, his aides joined lobbyists at a breakfast meeting to sell $1,500 tickets for a Democratic National Committee dinner, which eventually raised more than $4 million. One of the lobbyists later told an Associated Press reporter, "Somebody spoke up and said, 'You guys are kickin' the [expletive] out of Washington lobbyists. How do you expect us to try and sell tickets for you?'"[6] For public consumption, however, Clinton was on the side of the reformers when it came to reducing their influence and their large contributions. "This proposal can change the status quo," he said of his campaign-reform plan. "And the special interests surely will mobilize against it. . . . But when we do overcome the forces of inertia, we can once again make our political system work—work more quickly, work more efficiently, work less expensively, and most importantly, work for the people who work hard and play by the rules." Many lobbyists and other Washington insiders, who had often heard this type of rhetoric, could only shrug their shoulders at the conflicts, both real and staged, that come with their territory. With some necessary modifications, they continued business as usual.

The Press Shapes the Story

Reporters and editors do not view themselves as just another Washington interest group. After all, the Constitution gave them special status in the First Amendment's protection for freedom of the press. With the growth in the size of the Washington press corps, its role has changed in the Capitol culture, much as the lobbyists have been forced to adopt new techniques to get their viewpoints across. No more than three decades ago, for example, the public received much of its news from a few wire services—such as the Associated Press and United Press International—and large metropolitan newspapers, many of which had their own Washington staffs. But the financially troubled UPI, for example, has substantially pared its operations, and big-city papers in Philadelphia, Washington, Dallas and Los Angeles, among others, have closed down. In their place have grown more specialized news services that serve smaller suburban communities and typically do not have much national news coverage, and chain newspapers whose journalistic formula—less hard news and more features—was copied across the nation.

Those changes in the national news-business had vital consequences for the Washington press corps. One of the most important has been that, as the number of large newspapers diminished, those that survived gained more journalistic influence—chiefly, *The Washington Post, The New York Times, The Wall Street Journal* and the *Los Angeles Times.* These organizations, whose reports also are distributed in news services that hundreds of smaller newspapers subscribe to, have sought staffers and a style that moved from old-fashioned reporting to more feature writing and instant analysis. In part, newspapers were forced to adjust to their readers already having heard the basic facts of major stories from television, including the decade-old Cable News Network, which updated the news at least every half-hour. In addition, television producers gave increased time to analysts and commentators, who offered their own view of events and their news significance. Sometimes, those roles have become confusing to television viewers. The same reporters who wrote or edited the news in the morning newspaper or report on television at the dinner hour sometimes broadcast their sharp-edged opinion of its meaning later that night or on weekend "talk" shows, which have become a growing part of the news scene. All too often, these exaggerated exchanges have sacrificed journalistic integrity to the demands of contrived entertainment.

Using some of his successful campaign techniques, Clinton and his aides initially hoped to avoid some of these personalities who filter the way that public officials want to communicate their story. They envisioned, for example, the frequent use of local town meetings and sophisticated satellite hookups for the White House to speak to the public without going through the national news media. But that campaign-style salesmanship had limited impact once Clinton was in office. Not only did such efforts take time to organize, they also did not reckon with the continuing influence of some of the news media in shaping public opinion. Network-television reporters, for example, in late spring ran repeated stories about Clinton's mishaps and his difficulties with Congress; at the same time, national news magazines ran cover stories criticizing his conduct. (*Time* seized upon White House snafus such as the $200 haircut and the firing of White House travel aides—whose chief job was to help reporters with their travel connections—to run a curious cover story headlined, "The Incredible Shrinking President."[7]) White House reporters delighted in taking Clinton down a notch or two. "The White House press room has never been as relentlessly petty and mean as it is today," *Newsweek* reported during the same week in early June. "Clinton's press staff made the mistake of not only ignoring White House reporters but actively disdaining them. . . . No surprise, then, that when Clinton began to stumble this spring, the White House press corps was positively gleeful."[8] Another measure—admittedly unscientific—of Clinton's problems was that he became a butt of ridicule on late-night television entertainment programs. According to a survey by the nonpartisan, Washington-based Center for Media and Public Affairs, Clinton was the subject of more than 250 such jokes between January 1 and May 15, 1993. During a comparable period in 1989, there were about 50 jokes about President Bush. Press coverage improved somewhat in June, perhaps coincidentally when Clinton hired David Gergen to take charge of shaping the White House message; he had been a White House press aide under three Republican presidents before becoming a magazine editor and television commentator. And, White House officials hoped that their mid-June picnic for reporters would have a subtle impact in improving relations. But they were reminded later the same week that they were at the mercy of other forces, when ABC and CBS refused to broadcast Clinton's first prime-time news conference. NBC, the third national television network, cut off the president midway through his appearance and switched to its regular programming.

The contentiousness between Clinton and the White House press corps produced some soul searching within the news media. In *The New York Times,* its reporter covering the news media said that the coverage "raised, somewhat earlier than usual, the question that arises in every administration: whether the nation's news organizations are being fair to the President."[9] Academic experts interviewed by the *Times* concluded that the press criticism had taken a hostile tone at an unusually quick pace. A media critic for *The Washington Post* noted that "the zeal with which every presidential gaffe of recent weeks has been exploited lends credibility to the charge [of reporters' excesses] and to our habit of going into feeding frenzies whenever there is a scent of blood in the water."[10] Even Sally Quinn, who had earlier greeted Clinton with a dollop of contempt, showed a new form of patronizing sympathy for his plight and joined in second-guessing the press's earlier hard edge. "The press corps, interacting with Bill Clinton when he was on the ropes, became sorry for him" in recent weeks, she wrote in July. "Worrying that the patient was in extremis, the press, as observer-participant, took on his feelings of sadness and hurt. And it helped bring him back from the dead."[11] But these pseudo-psychological self-examinations may have missed a larger problem with the coverage by White House reporters: By examining the day-to-day ups and downs, they often missed the bigger picture. The *Time* and *Newsweek* reports, which focused on alleged gaffes and stylistic problems, inexplicably paid short shrift to the previous week's narrow, but vital, House passage of the president's economic package. Surely, that legislative action was far more important to the outcome of the Clinton presidency than was an airport haircut. Even the more respected newspapers succumbed to the constant search for conflict. When the House or Senate passed Clinton's economic package, albeit narrowly, the next day's stories often focused on how difficult the following step would be rather than on the significance of the immediate accomplishment. And, for that matter, there were few news stories that sought to examine the hostile public reaction to the early months of the Clinton presidency. The Republican landslide in the Texas Senate election, for example, generated little news review of its significant political implications for both parties.

The analysis of the press coverage also produced some introspection from leading congressional Democrats. Those with experience in dealing with Washington reporters revealed an understanding that good news gets less coverage than do the usual problems; they have learned that the press loves controversy. Reviewing the coverage of the Clinton White House, House Speaker Foley said, with an air of resignation: "I think that we have gone from very enthusiastic and maybe even hyperbolic praise for the president, to somewhat steady criticism. But that is part of being in public life." Senate Majority Leader Mitchell lamented that one of the most surprising things that he must face is "the degree of misinformation [from the press] about what occurs here." Seeking to explain this problem, House Majority Leader Gephardt said that some administration officials and leading Democrats in Congress shared responsibility for the unfavorable news coverage of its economic package because some of them had been inconsistent with their message. "I will never say that we are communicating perfectly," Gephardt told reporters in his office while the Senate was enmeshed in debate on the bill. He stressed the importance of internal discipline by Democrats in conveying a coherent message. But he also offered advice for reporters, as they reported on the actions of Congress. "Somewhere down the line, I hope that we can give the American people a sense that this is working well, . . . that men and women are coming together to make courageous decisions," Gephardt said. "I'm asking that reporters who write interpretive pieces [make the point] that it's working."

The increased presence of media celebrities and the more adversarial coverage were only part of the change in the Washington press corps. A substantial increase in its size came from the staffs of smaller newspapers interested mostly in how the federal government affected parochial local interests. Likewise, the growth in magazines and newsletters that reported on specific industries or issues emphasized the tendency of both the press and the public to examine isolated events rather than the big picture. In Congress, especially, many lawmakers have found that reporters have become like another interest group that focuses on narrow concerns rather than on the broad scope of congressional duties. Only a handful of reporters take an institutional view of how Congress performs.

Even with the many shortcomings in the press corps and with the public's declining attention span, citizens rely heavily on news organizations for information on how public officials are conducting themselves. As the conflict between the national press and politicians has become an ever-greater subject of frustration and tension between the two sides, one consequence has been that public approval of both camps has dropped to low levels, according to national polls. Resolving that dilemma and improving their relationship poses difficult and important long-term problems for the nation and its political discourse. But it also has more immediate consequences for the president and his party.

The Sour Public Opinion of Washington

Clinton generated the worst public-approval ratings for a newly elected president in the modern history of public-opinion polls. By late May, less than 40 percent of respondents in several polls said that they approved of his job performance, while about 60 percent disapproved. By contrast, Clinton had started his term—as have most presidents—with support scores that exceeded

60 percent. But other modern presidents generally have kept their positive scores at least twice as high as their negatives during their first several months in office. Several factors contributed to Clinton's slide. The criticisms and second-guessing from lobbyists and the press corps, no doubt, had a cumulative impact. Clinton's often slow and unsteady course in taking charge of the executive branch—with new policies and second-level appointees—created doubts whether he was ready for prime time. The lingering public cynicism toward all politicians, fueled by hectoring of the new president by Republicans and Ross Perot, also took its toll. And the inevitable public unhappiness over tax increases and spending cuts would have made it difficult for any president to sell such a program, no matter how skillfully handled.

But Clinton and his allies made their plight more difficult by failing to respond effectively to their opponents' criticism of the economic plan. When he unveiled the package in February, a national poll by the *Los Angeles Times* found that 50 percent considered the president's approach "bold and innovative," while only 35 percent criticized it as "tax and spend." By June, however, those scores had flipped: Only 28 percent said that the plan was "bold and innovative," while the critics had jumped to 53 percent. "Ominously for Clinton, discontent over the nation's direction has increased dramatically even though the public's views about the economy have not substantially deteriorated since February," the *Times* concluded.[12]

Senior Democrats candidly conceded that they had compounded many of their own problems. During the early months of his tenure, the once peripatetic president had surprisingly abandoned his campaign style of reaching out and identifying with the voters. Following his February announcement of his economic package, he did not formally address the nation on the issue again until the eve of the final razor-thin House and Senate votes in August. His public pleas for the plan, both in Washington and across the nation, were few and perfunctory—especially given the scope of the package and the intensity of political opposition. Despite his earlier admiration of Reagan's communications skills, Clinton acted more like Bush—working as a Washington insider rather than rallying the public at large. "We have not responded as aggressively or as effectively as we might have to attacks," Democratic National Committee chairman David Wilhelm conceded in June during a meeting of state party chairmen.

Whatever the cause, Clinton's low scores not only mirrored the public sourness, they also caused additional deterioration of the political climate for Democrats. These sentiments were monitored closely at the White House. Politicians—including presidents and members of Congress—typically use many measurements to keep a finger close to the political pulse. And Clinton has probably been as sensitive to the public mood as any recent president. He met weekly with his campaign pollster, Stanley Greenberg, and his aides spoke with Greenberg nearly every day; the Democratic National Committee paid for those services. Clinton, for example, followed his pollster's advice in late spring to reframe how he described his economic package so that he emphasized that chiefly the wealthy would pay for the tax increases.[13] But the president's options were limited. He would not have been credible if he had followed Sen. Dole's conclusion to "start over" following the release of the *Los Angeles Times* poll in June. Although it is easy for an opposing politician to offer that advice, there would have been no reason to believe that Republicans would have joined hands with the weakened president if he had decided to sit down with GOP leaders. After all, they had said for months that the 1992 election results left the Democrats accountable for government actions. Moreover, a radical change in policy likely would have angered and befuddled Clinton's Democratic allies, who had been struggling to pass his program. In any case, his official powers were undiminished by the polls. And he probably would have worsened his plight if he allowed the hostile public to intimidate him and prevent him from acting as he deemed appropriate.

So, the Democrats decided to play the hand that they had dealt themselves early in the year: the legislative agenda for economic change and health-care reform, calibrated moves to refine the nation's social policy to make it more inclusive of groups that had felt abandoned under the Republican presidents, and a downplaying of foreign policy. But one step that Clinton could take, without making overt changes in policy, would be to refine how he sold his program to the nation. That course gained momentum in late May with the hiring of Gergen as presidential counselor. Given his background as both a press commentator and a former White House aide, a major part of his task was to coordinate the delicate task of reshaping the presidential image. George Stephanopoulos, who was President Clinton's first communications director, had lacked needed skills in dealing with White

House reporters and in managing his large office. He shifted to providing more behind-the-scenes advice for Clinton and, in a version of musical chairs, Clinton's deputy chief of staff Mark Gearan became communications director. Because Gergen had worked for three Republican presidents, his hiring itself sent an unmistakable message that Clinton wanted to move to the center. Clinton and his aides had to be careful not to make the shift too jarring. But the changes in tone and personnel were quickly felt at the White House, both internally and in the president's message. "After the air of chaos that suffused the White House for most of the spring," a White House reporter wrote, "the reshuffling has lent 'a better focus to what's going on with the presidency and with the President himself,' [a senior White House aide] said."[14]

How that would affect the public remained to be seen, however. Even if he could secure less hostile press coverage, that would not assure that Clinton would win back the hearts of concerned citizens. The Democrats knew that, ultimately, the test of their program's success would be whether it improved the tepid economic growth rate of recent years. Although they had little choice but to offer such hope, they were willing to bet that they would succeed. "I'll wager that this time next year, you are likely to see the individuals who had the courage to vote for this economic plan taking credit for the economic recovery and the progress that it makes possible," Vice President Gore told reporters at the Capitol in the early morning of June 25 after he had cast the deciding vote for Senate passage of Clinton's economic plan.

Congressional Democrats wanted to believe Gore. But Clinton's failure to sell his case more effectively frustrated many of them. They repeatedly pleaded with him during the spring to try to resurrect his populist appeal of the campaign. These lawmakers wanted him to become more visible, not only to bolster his appeal but also to strengthen themselves with their own constituents who remained dubious of the economic plan's merits and ignorant of its key details. As some of them had said even before Clinton took office, they recognized that their political fates were inextricably linked to his. Consequently, many of them grew especially fearful during the following months as his popularity decreased. A June poll by Public Opinion Strategies, a Washington-area Republican polling firm, reinforced their fear that events were running out of their control. The poll found that 78 percent of the public agreed "Congress isn't doing the job we elected it to do." That striking result, which came in the midst of the debate on Clinton's economic plan, was an increase from 70 percent two years earlier, when Congress and the president were in legislative gridlock. Democrats worried about not only their separate political futures but also the possibility that Democrats could lose their working control of the House or Senate, or both, after the 1994 election. In that case, the opportunity for achieving further significant policy changes would diminish and Clinton himself would have a less compelling record to cite, assuming he sought re-election in 1996. But the confident and self-styled "Comeback Kid" might prefer to move at his own pace and to assume the public eventually would fall in line. If so, that was a peculiar risk, after the consequences of President Bush's earlier failure to rally public support behind his own leadership.

Despite their gains in the polls, uncertainty also plagued the Republicans. Although they saw, by the summer of 1993, good prospects for major gains in upcoming congressional and presidential elections, some of their strategists worried that they were too dependent on Clinton's ups and downs and that they were not doing enough to advance their own fortunes. Newspaper editorials continued to criticize the GOP's failure to advance alternatives to the Democrats' proposals. Meanwhile, party factions failed to address their own significant internal differences on issues such as how much to cooperate with the Democrats and whether to propose detailed alternatives. And some Republicans quietly worried that they did not see on the horizon the type of presidential candidate who could coalesce their party and rally the nation. For both parties, in short, the sour public mood created a political volatility that befuddled them but that they could ignore only at their peril.

Connecting the Insiders and Outsiders

Any president faces a major challenge in seeking to satisfy the needs and the views of the varied groups whose livelihood or fate depends, in part, on what he does. As they separately observe and react to his actions, he can expect that they will emphasize the problems—real or imagined—that may ensue and that their public comments will largely overlook or take for granted the positive aspects of his decisions. Further complicating a president's task is that efforts to satisfy one group often will offend another. Thus, for example, Clinton's agreements to modify minor provisions of his economic package to reduce opposition from an interest group with influential congressional allies, such as the aluminum industry, frequently generated hostile press coverage. Like other presidents in such a situation, he was accused, in effect, of selling out. But if he had failed to make such concessions, he ran the risk of jeopardizing the passage of his plan, which might have made him appear even weaker with the public at large. Those types of irreconcilable forces help to explain why all but one of the six presidents since the assassination of John Kennedy left office under adverse political circumstances—an unpopular Johnson decided not to seek another term; Nixon resigned because of the Watergate scandal; and Ford, Carter and Bush lost bids for a second term. Only Reagan, the president who worked most skillfully to distance himself from the details of deal-cutting, managed to survive and prosper politically, despite the considerable scorn of many of the so-called elites.

Clinton hoped to do better than his recent predecessors. In seeking to balance the interests of the competing forces outside the government—including lobbyists, reporters and citizens—he sought during his initial months to bring a new approach to the burdensome job of president. That did not assure, of course, that he would benefit or succeed. But he made some incremental changes in the rules of the political game. As a politician with considerable intellectual skills, who had given deeper thought than had his recent predecessors to the complex tasks facing him, Clinton tried to present himself as an activist president on his own terms. Thus, he became more personally involved than had any president since Johnson in preparing the details of new policies and negotiating compromises with Congress and key interest groups. Unlike Johnson, however, Clinton tried to maintain his status as a political outsider untainted by years of Washington experience and deal-cutting. Likewise, he made less use of the traditional White House forums of Oval Office speeches and East Room press conferences as he sought to communicate with the public. Instead, he wanted to establish a more informal connection—from televised meetings with young children at the White House to active use of electronic mail and other high-tech services. These changes would take time to carry out and, as Clinton and his aides learned, could not fully replace the more conventional tools.

Regardless of his fate, Clinton's efforts sought a more modern context for the exercise of presidential power. Facing a society where technology was significantly changing how individuals acquired information and communicated with each other, he wanted to develop new tools that would occasionally allow him to circumvent the old strictures. Although the old-line powers offered the expected resistance to what they viewed as threats to their vested interests, Clinton was not trying to put them out of business. Instead, his goal seemed to be a more direct form of democracy in which he could communicate with the public without being subject to constant interpretation by outside forces. Some of his techniques were similar to those used by Ross Perot, who was able to use his personal fortune to buy direct access. Clinton, of course, was limited financially by the constraints of government procedures and political party financing. Like Perot, however, he was operating on the premise that voters were tired of the traditional forms of political discourse and that they wanted straight talk from public officials and other leaders. In this context, Clinton's political difficulties after he took office largely resulted from other political factors and had little do with his new modes of communication. Whether Clinton—or Perot, for that matter—could develop tools for more successful and sustained attempts to talk with the voters about the nation's problems remained to be seen.

As for the public at large, there was continuing evidence that its cynicism toward virtually all politicians raised the barriers between the nation and Washington. Sen. Harris Wofford of Pennsylvania, who had campaigned as an outsider to win the important special election in late 1991, commented on how the political environment had changed since the early 1960s, when he was an aide to President Kennedy. In those days, he said, the nation's leaders could command public attention. Now, citizens have become so skeptical of calls for action and a litany of promises that a president must address an issue several times before he can hope to gain a response. "It is much harder today to get consent than during the last time I was in Washington," Wofford said. "Then, the president could call to the nation one time and it worked. Now, it's much more complicated because of the cynicism and our failure in government to get things done." Citizens' hostility resulted in part from an overload of information from both public and private sources and a frustration about not knowing whom to believe. Repeated government failures and lies to the public—on conflicts ranging from the Vietnam War to the federal budget deficit—undoubtedly compounded that attitude. The immediacy of information was a dual-edged sword. On the one hand, the public had an opportunity to be far better educated about their nation's problems and their possible solutions. But the flip side included a growing impatience by average Americans that those conflicts be addressed and a fear of the possible impact on their own daily lives.

Within Washington, the business of government continued. But the start of the Clinton administration raised anew the question of whether the nation's problems and policy-making, as well as the federal apparatus itself, had become so cumbersome that it was virtually impossible to get anything done. Passage of the economic package both reinforced that impression and showed that, in the end, the federal government was not entirely gridlocked. But looming ahead was health care. If anything, this issue was even more intractable. With their huge stake in the national economy, the myriad sectors of the medical industry were lining up to demand their piece of the action and to frustrate solutions that were adverse to their parochial interests. The health-care dilemma, like the economic debate, would show the limits that face even a new president who had an unlimited patience and ability to try to make sense of the nation's problems and to find some new answers. On these issues and others, the lobbyists, reporters and other persistent agents of permanent Washington often made it more difficult to forge consensus. Sometimes, they contributed to such an overload of information that they were stretching the ability of a democratic system to respond.

Endnotes

1. Sally Quinn, "Making Capital Gains," *The Washington Post,* Nov. 15, 1992: C1.
2. Robert A. Caro, *The Years of Lyndon Johnson: The Path to Power* (New York: Alfred A. Knopf, 1983): 743–53.
3. Peter H. Stone, "Green, Green Grass," *National Journal,* March 27, 1993: 754.
4. Paul Starobin, "Some Apple-Polisher," *National Journal,* April 17, 1993: 921.
5. Michael Wines, "Congress's Twists and Turns Reshape Bill on Energy Tax," *The New York Times,* June 2, 1993: A1.

6. Jim Drinkard, "Are Lobbyists Good or Bad Guys in the Clinton Administration?" *Associated Press,* May 6, 1993.
7. "The Incredible Shrinking President," *Time,* June 7, 1993: 22.
8. Eleanor Clift, "Don't Mess with the 'Media,'" *Newsweek,* June 7, 1993: 23.
9. William Glaberson, "The Capitol Press vs. the President: Fair Coverage or Unreined Adversity," *The New York Times,* June 17, 1993: A22.
10. Richard Harwood, "The Press's Revenge," *The Washington Post,* June 16, 1993: A21.
11. Sally Quinn, "To the Couch, Mr. Clinton!" *The Washington Post,* July 18, 1993: C1.
12. Ronald Brownstein, "Public Loses Faith in Clinton Economic Plan," *Los Angeles Times,* June 16, 1993: A1.
13. James A. Barnes, "Polls Apart," *National Journal,* July 10, 1993: 1750.
14. Burt Solomon, "Musical Chairs in the West Wing May Bring Order from Cacophony," *National Journal,* June 26, 1993: 1660.

9

Struggling to the Finish Line

☆ ☆ ☆

Democratic leaders announce House-Senate agreement on the deficit-reduction plan at a Capitol Hill press conference. Included are Senate Budget Committee chairman Jim Sasser, Senate Majority Leader George Mitchell, House Speaker Tom Foley and Senate Finance chairman Dan Moynihan.

Accommodating Many Viewpoints

Before his administration could move ahead at full speed to other issues, especially health-care reform, President Clinton had to secure final congressional approval of his economic program. Because that plan's defeat would have been politically devastating, top Democrats did not want to contemplate the consequences of such a setback. Ultimately, they would achieve their goal, by the absolute barest of margins, in both the House and Senate. But the tortuous final road to enactment of the bill underlined Clinton's shaky grasp of the power levers. The debate also starkly revealed the Democrats' internal differences, which they had worked for months to paper over. Those varied difficulties were an apt metaphor for the growing problems that the Clinton administration faced in Congress as the two branches settled down to the daily routine of trying to steer the federal government. As the initial bloom of election victory and the early weeks in office faded, Clinton and his party began to pay the price for several shortcomings of the previous months: their often ambiguous campaign agenda, the 43 percent election victory, the administration's awkward start and the continued infighting among Democratic factions in Congress. Because governing is such a difficult process, even under the best of circumstances, these various political and legislative constraints became heavy burdens to carry. Still, a win is a win. And Clinton and his partners had every right to glory in the passage of their economic plan—and to breathe deep sighs of relief.

As its months in office passed, the Clinton administration also began to learn what each new team must face: Congress will grant a fresh start to a president, but most lawmakers—even supposed allies—will not wait long before they assert their own prerogatives. The House and Senate decisions in March to defer to the basic outlines of Clinton's budget plan would soon become a quaint and forgotten token of respect. When Congress reached the point of writing the final details of the new budget, hand-to-hand legislative combat was required to resolve many issues. Clinton's once-robust new energy tax was whittled to a far more modest increase in the gasoline tax, and even that plan endured harsh attacks. A similar congressional response also asserted itself on other issues, as vague campaign pledges met the realities of stark policy choices.

Abortion-rights supporters, for example, were startled by a House vote that imposed continued restrictions on federal funding of abortions for low-income women. "I was shocked to learn that this is not a pro-choice Congress," said first-term Rep. Lynn Schenk, a California Democrat. "With all the hype of 'the year of the woman,' I was lulled into a false sense of change." And Clinton's promise of campaign-finance reform bogged down in the House, a victim of internal disagreements among Democrats and of the party's focus on the budget. On a few issues, however, the president was more successful. In addition to the easy Senate confirmation of Ruth Bader Ginsburg to the Supreme Court, he won final congressional approval in September of the first genuine "Clinton" proposal—a national service program to encourage volunteers to participate in community activities.

Several significant patterns began to emerge in how Clinton and Congress handled these and other issues. Prominent among them was his reliance on the Democrats' congressional leaders and key committee chairmen. Mostly, these lawmakers strongly supported his plans, and their efforts were essential to his legislative accomplishments. Although most White House officials believe that such backing ought to be unequivocal, the vital cooperation provided by Speaker Foley and Majority Leader Mitchell and their lieutenants exceeded the liaisons with several recent presidents and rescued Clinton on several occasions. By summer, however, some warning signals appeared on this horizon. When House Majority Whip David Bonior of Michigan and, later, Majority Leader Gephardt voiced strong opposition to Clinton's bid to win approval of the proposed North American Free Trade Agreement, they showed that the party leaders would not always act as a monolith. The mounting legal problems faced by House Ways and Means Committee chairman Dan Rostenkowski also were a reminder that the vital help of a few key players could prove ephemeral and that their successors might prove less effective. And the opposition to the final deficit-reduction bill by senior Southern Democrats in both the House and Senate warned of legislative and political problems that lay down the road. Even stalwart partners like Foley and Mitchell made pointed remarks about the White House's mishandling of congressional business.

The growing willingness of many rank-and-file congressional Democrats to criticize and vote against Clinton's program was in stark contrast to the early weeks of his administration. At that time, such opposition came chiefly from a few senior Senate Democrats, especially the independent-minded committee chairmen. With Clinton's continued decline in public-opinion polls and the need for many senators and all House members to focus on their own re-election in November 1994, however, their respect for presidential loyalty diminished. On issues ranging from the gasoline tax and the North American trade deal to gays in the military, many congressional Democrats began to define their distance from Clinton. In doing so, they hoped to show that their chief allegiance was to local constituents. One example was Democratic Rep. Collin Peterson of Minnesota. In strongly opposing the proposed trade agreement because he feared that it would cost thousands of local farming jobs, he warned that if the president tried to twist arms to secure its passage, "he won't get a lot of support from me on anything." Peterson was true to his word: After having voted for the initial House passage of the deficit-reduction plan, he was one of the 11 Democrats who switched to oppose the final House-Senate agreement.

That Clinton and the House and Senate leaders were forced to focus virtually all their attention on the deficit-reduction plan until Congress began its month-long August recess also showed the difficulties facing a president who had campaigned on the need for extensive changes in Washington. When Congress returned after Labor Day, the political cycle had moved inexorably to the point where it was almost halfway to the next set of House and Senate elections. Those campaign results and the prospect of significant Republican gains, of course, could have a major bearing on the remainder of Clinton's term. The calendar was growing short for action not only for Clinton's plan for health-care reform but also on a variety of other campaign pledges, such as "reinventing" government to make it work more efficiently and strengthening the nation's industrial sector at the same time that the military was being significantly downsized.

Given the strife that Clinton was encountering as Washington sought to complete work on his economic plan in the summer of 1993, these political limitations became a subject for deeper political concern. At a time when his legislative influence should have been at a peak, the grueling and exhausting challenge of reshaping federal policies and priorities had sapped much of the initial good will from Congress and the nation. And they forced the young president to struggle for each victory.

Wrapping Up the Economic Package

When the House and Senate have passed contrasting versions of the same bill, the task of resolving those differences often falls to a House-Senate conference committee. Such a committee usually is a straightforward affair and often can complete its work in a few meetings among the senior members of the House and Senate committees that initially drafted the bill. But the budget reconciliation bill was a more complicated matter for several reasons, and it would severely test the legislative skills of congressional leaders and White House officials. During a three-week period in July, they would be forced to resolve thousands of details on hundreds of issues in a way that would gain the votes of a majority of both the House and Senate for the final bill. There would be little margin to spare.

The sheer size of the conference committee required daunting logistics. Because 16 committees from the House and 12 more from the Senate drafted at least a small part of the conference report on the massive bill, party leaders and the White House had to closely monitor and spur completion of the conference committee deliberations, which actually took place in dozens of subconferences. (The final version of the legislative language and the accompanying explanatory statement filled 255 pages of the *Congressional Record,* in small type.[1]) The House and Senate Budget Committees had the formal responsibility of coordinating the conference. But most of the key decisions rested with the House Ways and Means Committee and the Senate Finance Committee, which had jurisdiction over more than $335 billion of deficit reduction plus another $56 billion in tax cuts and new spending. Much of the rest of Clinton's deficit-reduction program, which congressional number-crunchers initially calculated at $496 billion over the next five years, came outside the reconciliation bill. That included $102 billion in discretionary spending cuts, which would be handled in separate appropriations bills, plus $65 billion in reduced interest and other costs to finance the federal debt.

Conference committees, in theory, are supposed to meet in public and exchange compromise proposals between their House and Senate members. But the reality often has been that most of the key discussions are held in private among the House and Senate committee and subcommittee chairmen. They, in turn, keep in close contact with other conferees from their committees, a majority of whom must ratify the deal before it is officially sealed. Sens. Mitchell and Moynihan carefully appointed Finance Committee conferees whom they believed that they could rely on as loyalists. As a result, they pointedly excluded Sen. Boren of Oklahoma, whose outspoken opposition to the proposed energy tax had created so many difficulties for them during the initial bill-drafting; though he was third in seniority on the Finance Committee, he was not among the seven Democratic conferees. That decision eased the leaders' task in managing the conference committee. But the one-vote margin by which the Senate initially passed the bill plus its highly controversial circumstances meant that this would be no ordinary conference committee. In effect, Boren and every other Democratic senator who had voted for the measure would hold a veto power over the bill if they objected so strongly to a particular provision that they would vote against the final deal. Similar dynamics prevailed in the larger House, although there was less public focus on specific individuals than in the Senate. In short, the Democratic managers of the bill in both chambers would be forced to constantly monitor the views of their party comrades on potential compromises.

The conference committee's work also was complicated by the unexpected announcement on July 19—as the final deliberations began—that Robert Rota, the former House postmaster, had pleaded guilty to three criminal charges as part of a broader federal grand jury investigation into embezzlements at the House post office. The political significance was that the prosecutors had made clear in the evidence they released that Ways and Means Committee chairman Dan Rostenkowski had been a prime target of their inquiry and he was implicated in the charges against Rota. Their incriminating documents, although they removed the Congressman's name, were identical to materials that had been earlier produced from Rostenkowski's files. Some Democrats feared that an indictment of Rostenkowski might be imminent, in which case the House Democratic Caucus rules would require him to step down immediately as Ways and Means Committee chairman. Such a development, in turn, would have disrupted the conference committee's ability to successfully complete its work before the August recess. As it turned out, that fear proved unwarranted and, participants later said, Rostenkowski acted well focused during the deliberations. But even the threat of an indictment cast a shadow over the conference committee's deliberations.

On the other side of the conference-committee table from Rostenkowski sat Daniel Patrick Moynihan, the new chairman of the Senate Finance Committee. As the negotiations convened, several news stories focused on this political odd couple—the rough-hewn ethnic politician from Chicago and the erudite former Harvard University professor from New York—and their ability to work together. "Mr. Moynihan, it is said on Capitol Hill, has written more books (16 at last count) than Mr. Rostenkowski has read," *The New York Times* noted. "Mr. Rostenkowski, it is said, is so savvy that he can pick the eccentric Senator's pockets."[2] But the two principals downplayed these stereotypes as well as their stylistic differences. They aptly pointed out that they shared the goal of reaching agreement on a compromise as close as possible to Clinton's original plan. They also recognized that they had little room for ego clashes. If Rostenkowski played his cards so he trumped Moynihan, the result might be that the Senate would defeat the entire deal. For Moynihan, the challenge was especially severe. He was new to his position and many of the complex tax issues. He had to contend with a corps of senatorial prima donnas, many of whom were intent on showing their own importance. And, unlike Rostenkowski, he had not worked closely with Clinton. Like Rostenkowski, however, he told reporters that he could not make demands that might force the House or Senate to defeat the bill.

From the start, both realized that the most difficult issue would be resolving the differences on a so-called energy tax: The House had passed the broad-based tax designed to raise $72 billion over five years, while the Senate had approved a far more limited increase of 4.3 cents per gallon of gasoline, which would raise about $23 billion during the same period. Because Clinton and congressional leaders continued to insist on a total deficit reduction of about $500 billion, the fate of several other tax provisions and proposed spending cuts would be influenced by the handling of that nearly $50 billion disparity. The higher the energy tax, the less pressure there would be on other provisions. "We have only one difficult problem: what form of energy tax we can agree to," Moynihan said. "And that problem is not determining what is a good energy tax, but what can pass the House and the Senate."[3]

To determine what would work politically, Rostenkowski and Moynihan kept in regular contact with Foley, Mitchell and the other party leaders to review possible changes. Their private discussions typically focused more on whether an alternative could gain the needed support than on whether it made good policy sense. Much of the work was driven by symbolism. For example, when Sen. John Breaux, the Louisiana Democrat, publicly questioned the need to attain the roughly $500 billion in deficit reduction that Clinton had originally sought, he elicited a quick response from Treasury Secretary Bentsen, Speaker Foley and others about the sanctity of that goal. Likewise, a key demand on which many conservative Democrats insisted was that the final package—unlike the House-passed version—embrace a higher total in spending cuts than in new taxes. Most of all, the Democratic legislative chiefs kept in mind the overriding need to give Clinton the victory that would be crucial to establishing momentum for his presidency, which had encountered a shaky start. The impact of defeat "would have had more serious consequences" politically than would the details of the bill, said Sen. Tom Daschle, the South Dakota Democrat.

The Bottom-Up Conference

As the conference committee on the deficit-reduction bill moved into high gear, the various factions began to flex their muscles to seek their share of the legislative pie. Their demands for fine tuning the product highlighted the conflicting pressures that Democratic leaders were forced to resolve. Although such pressure tactics are a ritualistic part of the legislative bargaining process, the many advocates posed a greater threat than usual because of the slim margins by which the House and Senate had initially passed the measure. And it often was difficult for the decision-makers to predict how much change they would have to make to win the votes of the Democrats who remained undecided. Most of the wayward lawmakers who caused the greatest consternation among the chief conferees did not even serve on the conference committee reconciling the tax provisions.

The chief source of Democratic nervousness came from members in conservative Deep South states. Not coincidentally, that was the area where Clinton's popularity had dipped to particularly weak levels, as the Democrats' devastating loss in the special election for the Texas Senate seat in early June had revealed. Although many of these conservative Democrats privately worried about the impact to the oil industry of the House-passed energy tax, they publicly focused their unhappiness on what they said was the unsatisfactory response to their demands for more spending cuts. Sen. David Boren of Oklahoma made the first significant move when he said on July 27 that he intended to oppose the final agreement. "This decision is far too important to be defined by shortsighted partisan political considerations," Boren told the Senate. "It is a basic decision about the future of our country. . . . I voted to send [the Senate bill] to conference in the hope that it would be changed in a major way through presidential leadership and bipartisan cooperation." But Boren, despite his earlier success in helping to scuttle the broad-based energy tax and insisting on more spending cuts, concluded that success on his overall goal was unlikely. Indeed, his call for a new round of budget negotiations with the Republicans fell flat. Moreover, the pressures in the conference committee were to increase spending above the Senate-passed levels. To pass the bill, as a result, Democrats apparently would need to switch a senator who had voted against it.

In the House, Rep. Charles Stenholm of Texas, who had originally voted for the much larger energy tax, said a few days later that he would oppose the bill because of its gasoline-tax increase. In a statement, he called it "unwise for substantive as well as political reasons for us to raise taxes on middle-class working men and women in order to pay for increased spending as this conference report does." Other Democrats reported that Stenholm's switch was based, in part, on the growing political opposition to the measure in his conservative district. His decision was important, at least symbolically, because he had influenced Gephardt's earlier House efforts to craft a spending-limits agreement between party conservatives and liberals. His defection was a warning to Clinton that conservative Democrats were restless.

Meanwhile, members of the Congressional Black Caucus pressed their case for fewer spending cuts, especially in programs that benefitted low-income groups. "If we're going to find a way to cushion the effect on the middle class and the working poor, if we are honest about clear deficit reduction, then we have got to be very honest about raising the revenues to do that," Rep. Kweisi Mfume of Maryland, the Caucus chairman, told reporters at the White House after a July 21 meeting with Clinton. The Black Caucus members also fought for Clinton's proposed expansion of the earned income tax credit. Designed to raise working families out of poverty, this tax-code tool was consuming a rapidly growing share of the federal budget; it also had gained support in recent years from many Republicans, who viewed it as a work incentive. The conference committee's agreement to add several billion dollars a year to its annual benefits, in effect, amounted to a significant welfare expansion and showed that a "deficit-reduction" bill can also include new federal costs and policy initiatives. The credit "has won praise from liberals and conservatives alike as an effective tool for combating poverty and rewarding work," according to an analysis of its new terms. "The $20.8 billion to be spent expanding the program over the next five years is a sizable down payment on Clinton's vow to reform conventional welfare policy."[4] The expanded credit and other smaller spending increases for the poor also proved to be an important political inducement. In the end, all 37 House Democrats in the Black Caucus voted for the plan. (The only black Republican—Gary Franks of Connecticut—voted "no," while he and several black Democrats feuded publicly about whether he should continue his membership in the Caucus.)

In these and other cases, the conflict among Democrats often appeared to be a collision of the irresistible force and the immovable object. In seeking to reconcile these forces, Rostenkowski and his House Ways and Means Committee colleagues hoped to salvage as much as possible of the increased revenues from Clinton's original energy tax. But other lawmakers—especially those from large states where more people drove long distances to work—wanted to limit the Senate-passed gasoline-tax increase. Once again, a striking feature was the control that junior lawmakers exercised over the outcome. Consensus on the deficit-reduction bill required a "bottom-up" agreement, said a Rostenkowski aide. He meant that, in contrast to the typical deal that was imposed from atop the legislative hierarchy, the rank-and-file members, in effect, dictated the results on this bill because the narrow margin forced the leaders to solicit their views.

Resolving the details of the energy tax provided a striking reversal of the customary legislative pattern. Rostenkowski recognized a few days after the start of the negotiations that the broad-based "BTU" tax was a dead letter in the Senate. So, he then pressed for a nine-cent increase in the tax on a gallon of gasoline, perhaps in combination with a nationwide tax on consumers' home-utility bills. His hope was to raise from energy taxes an amount at least halfway between the House- and Senate-passed bills. After several Senate Democrats said that such a total was too high to approve and that they were increasingly skittish about any consumer-based tax, however, the House and Senate leaders tentatively reached a consensus for a gasoline-tax increase of 6.5 cents. Finally, they thought that they had a deal, which *The Washington Post* and other newspapers predicted on July 29 was close to approval. At that point, Rostenkowski said that the leaders were checking to see "if we can get the votes at 6 [cents per gallon], but I'd like to get 7."[5]

Unfortunately for Rostenkowski and the senior Democrats, they did not account for the stubbornness of several Democratic senators, chiefly Herbert Kohl of Wisconsin. When Kohl, a multi-millionaire businessman whose impact during his first five years in the Senate had been negligible, stated that he would vote against anything higher than the increase of 4.3 cents in the Senate-passed bill, he killed efforts to raise added revenues. "I don't think we should tax the middle class," Kohl told reporters. He did not offer specific alternatives. That the increase was modest had become less important than the symbolism of the issue. For the average American driver, the annual cost of the 6.5 cent increase would have been about $42 annually, or 80 cents a week. That was about 25 cents per week more than the Senate version. Yes, it was a tax increase. But was it worth one senator's stout resistance? Kohl's objection to the small sum fit the portrayal by the disgruntled freshman Sen. Patty Murray, the Democrat from Washington. "Individual senators assert their power to show their influence back home," she said. "Too many senators don't understand what compromise is about."

The result was a political victory for Kohl, who faced re-election in 1994 and began to trumpet his achievement a few days later with a campaign-style advertisement in Wisconsin. But it was a setback for Democratic leaders in trying to craft a balanced bill, which Clinton had said would demand "shared sacrifice" by most Americans. After all, this small gasoline-tax increase was the only defined new burden on most of the middle class. Rostenkowski summarized his unhappiness with the result: "The closer the vote, the more members become prima donnas," he said. Legislatively, the outcome also further eroded the admittedly outdated image of a legislative system in which powerful chairmen cracked the whip to get their way. "It is not unusual for a floor majority to drive" how Congress handles a tax bill, said Steven Smith, a political science professor at the University of Minnesota. "The main thing that has been different with this year's bill has been that all of this has been in the open and that the flexing of muscle has seemed more conspicuous than in the past."

The Rest of the Agenda

Meanwhile, as the Democrats struggled to resolve their differences on the crucial deficit-reduction bill, the House and Senate moved during the late spring and summer on several other fronts. In some cases, they were engaged in the routine business of passing bills to keep the federal government functioning. In others, they were responding to Clinton's initiatives to put his own stamp on government. Whatever the case, the many conflicts demonstrated both the array of issues that the new players had to address and the difficulty of changing how Washington works. Although these debates received less public attention than did Clinton's economic program, the various issues might ultimately play a greater role in defining his presidency.

On other domestic debates, members of Congress could not shake free of problems resulting from the large federal debt. By a larger than expected vote of 280–150, the House voted to kill further funds for the superconducting supercollider, based in Texas. And it sustained, by only a one-vote margin, a downsized space station for the National Aeronautics and Space Administration. Although supporters counted on stronger support for those projects in the Senate, a senior Senate Republican aide responsible for budget issues voiced amazement over what he said was "some fiscal austerity that I would never have expected." Even the devastating floods in the Midwest that resulted when the Mississippi and Missouri Rivers reached record levels produced penny-pinching symbolism. Some lawmakers, including a few from affected regions in the Midwest, delayed the nearly $6 billion relief legislation for a few days in a largely unsuccessful effort to force a debate on whether Congress should find the money elsewhere to pay for the additional costs.

Congress also began work on what some termed "Phase Two" of Clinton's domestic agenda—his initiatives that moved beyond the budget debate and sought to reshape and bolster various federal initiatives. The first proposals that made it through the legislative mills both were designed to appeal to college students. The national service plan, passed with a few Republican votes, encouraged students and other individuals to participate in community service programs, with a modest stipend. Before passing this program, Congress considerably scaled back Clinton's promises to cover as many as 150,000 participants annually. Clinton scored greater success with his proposal to revamp the federal student-loan program with a federal financing mechanism to replace the role of commercial banks and to provide cheaper rates. One interesting feature of these two bills, and others that were starting to move down the pipeline, was that Sen. Edward Kennedy of Massachusetts was a prime advocate of several Clinton initiatives in his position as chairman of the Senate Labor and Human Resources Committee. "I enjoy working closely with the president. We have serious men and women [in the White House] who are open to ideas . . . and are interested in practical solutions." Kennedy's enthusiasm reflected that Clinton's election allowed the senator to gain action on legislative ideas he had long supported but that had been frustrated during the 12 years of a Republican White House. Despite Clinton's self-depiction as a "new Democrat" who opposed the liberal dogma that Kennedy had long advanced, their cooperation appeared to be genuine. Speaking to a Kennedy fundraiser in Boston during June, Clinton said, "Every effort to bring the American people together across that which divides us has the imprint of Ted Kennedy." The senator also hoped to play an important role on health-care reform, which loomed as the most significant feature of Clinton's "Phase Two."

For Clinton, what could be called the gender-related issues generally went smoothly. In addition to the uncontroversial confirmation of Ruth Bader Ginsburg to the Supreme Court, Clinton succeeded in winning Senate confirmation of Joycelyn Elders as Surgeon General, despite her controversial views on issues such as teen-age pregnancy and condom use. But efforts to relax certain restrictions on abortion, especially those dealing with federal funds for low-income women, proved less successful. The advocates suffered from a continuing national ambivalence on how far the government should go to encourage a pro-choice policy and from some dissension among the advocates of that viewpoint, both on and off Capitol Hill. In addition, the unexpectedly firm opposition to their cause by Rep. William Natcher of Kentucky, the 83-year-old House Appropriations Committee chairman, posed severe procedural obstacles during debate on legislation in June. That setback led many women lawmakers of the House to intensify their demands that Clinton's health-care plan include abortion and other reproductive services. On racial issues, the tension between Clinton and the Congressional Black Caucus following his decision to drop the nomination of Lani Guinier faded as the attention of both sides shifted to the economic debate, where they shared broader agreement.

Several foreign-policy problems remained largely immune from the political debate during Clinton's first year. After the brief flare-up during the spring, the continuing disintegration of the Bosnian nation and the threats posed by neighboring Serbia in the European Balkans prompted occasional threats by Clinton and a few members of Congress. But Congress reflected the national mood of wariness over getting involved in the potential quagmire. The replacement of Bush by Clinton produced no change in the lingering tension with Iraq over that nation's failure to comply with United Nations resolutions following the 1991 Persian Gulf War. When Clinton ordered in June a sea-launched missile attack on a major intelligence facility in Baghdad, the public focus briefly returned to that region. But the tension subsided within a few days. Perhaps the most significant foreign-policy action by Congress during Clinton's initial months in office was the decision to support his request for $1.6 billion in U.S. aid to Russia and other nations of the former Soviet Union. At a time when Congress was scrimping on funds for domestic programs, many lawmakers did not want to highlight the foreign aid, though it received broad bipartisan support. The consequences flowing from the end of the Cold War also received little attention at home. Even the decision by President Clinton to endorse a federal commission's recommendations to close or substantially pare 62 major military bases and other facilities in the United States generated surprisingly little controversy in Congress. On another military matter, Clinton's decision to make less sweeping changes in restrictions on gay servicemen and women disappointed many of his campaign supporters but was generally well received in Congress. Indeed, that step generated less opposition from gay-rights supporters on Capitol Hill than from groups who claimed that the relaxations would undermine military morale.

One important feature on many of these other issues was that the unified Republican opposition that had been waged against

Clinton's economic plans cracked—albeit sometimes modestly. Although occasional efforts from each side to encourage more bipartisanship remained largely talk, the end of the deficit-reduction debate encouraged some hope and efforts to develop cooperation. Given the prospect that Clinton could not assume the same high level of support from congressional Democrats on other issues, such as the North American trade pact, some White House officials began to take more concerted initiatives to reach across the political aisle. That became especially apparent when he unveiled his health-care plan in September.

Making the Final Sales

But a serious revision of White House legislative tactics, including an extended hand to the Republicans, would have to wait. When it came time during the first week of August to find the few votes required to gain a bare majority for the deficit-reduction bill in both the House and Senate, Clinton and his congressional allies pursued a two-front strategy. Publicly, they intensified their sales campaign in an effort to increase citizen understanding and support of the deal. And, on Capitol Hill, they engaged in a form of hand-to-hand combat with the "swing" lawmakers. In neither case was their effort a work of classic beauty. But they got the job done. In contrast to the efforts to find a compromise during the previous weeks, these final efforts focused less on modifying additional provisions of the economic package. Instead, the late sales effort was more of a political effort to make wavering Democrats comfortable with the package and attuned to the imperative of a presidential victory. "There is a moment of truth when some members have to decide why they are here," Speaker Foley commented following the final sales pitch. "Support of your president is important." But some congressional Democrats had other priorities.

Clinton attempted to set the framework for the final push with his first nationally televised speech urging support of his economic plan since he delivered his Feb. 17 speech to Congress. In the 20-minute evening address on Tuesday, Aug. 3, broadcast live by the major television networks, he copied the tactic of Ross Perot in using several charts to show the scope of the deficit problems and the fairness for the middle class of the Democrats' effort to reduce the deficit. "As this chart shows, we ask the well off to pay their fair share, requiring that at least 80 percent of the new tax burden fall on those making more than $200,000 a year and very little on any other Americans," he said. "This plan is fair. It's balanced. And it will work." Clinton also sought to invoke his campaign appeal as a political outsider working to break the nation's political gridlock. "At this exceptional moment of promise, why are so many in Washington so reluctant to take action? Why is it so hard for so many in this city to break the bad habits of the past and take the steps we all know we have to take," he asked. "I need your help. I need for you to tell the peoples' representatives to get on with the people's business."

But Clinton's message may have been diluted a few minutes later by the televised response by Senate Minority Leader Dole, who delivered a no-holds-barred attack on the Democrats' proposal. "As you wade through all of the numbers and promises, keep in mind that passage of this bill will affect your job, your business, your family and your retirement," Dole said. "The president's economic plan calls for more taxes, more spending and higher deficits. That is why we oppose the bill—and why you should oppose it. And you should immediately contact your senators and representatives by calling 202–224–3121," the number of the Capitol switchboard. During the next 24 hours, the local telephone company reported, more than 3 million calls overloaded the Capitol—several times the typical load. And, most offices reported, a sizable majority of those callers getting through to the jammed phone lines were opposed to the Democrats' plan. Nor were the subsequent public-opinion polls reassuring to the Democrats. According to a Gallup Poll for *USA Today* and the Cable News Network, taken immediately following the two speeches, 33 percent said that Congress should pass the budget plan and 44 percent said that it should not. To make things worse for the Democrats, Clinton's failure to sell his message was revealed by the poll's finding that 68 percent of the public believed that the middle class would pay most of the plan's taxes. A CBS News poll after the speech found that 25 percent of the respondents said that the Clinton plan would help the economy and that 32 percent said that the economy would be hurt. Foley later suggested that the low polling numbers resulted, in part, because Clinton—in his early desire to spread the "shared sacrifice" theme—rhetorically "may have overstated what the middle class will have to do." (See Table 10.1)

Table 9.1 Highlights of budget-reconciliation bill as passed by Congress—and projected five-year impact on the deficit. (Figures are in billion of dollars)

Net spending cuts	**$255**
Freeze in all federal discretionary spending	$102
Interest on the federal deficit and related management savings	65
Medicare reductions, chiefly in lower payments to doctors and hospitals	56
Delay annual increases for federal retirees	12
Auction the use of the federal telecommunications spectrum	10
Medicaid reductions, chiefly for hospital care for the poor	7
Student-loan program reform	6
Net tax increases	**$241**
Raise income-tax rates for the wealthy	$115
Subject all earnings for the wealthy to medicare payroll tax	29
Increase taxes on social security benefits for certain retirees	25
Increase federal tax on gasoline	24
Increase federal corporate-tax rate	24

Clinton also took his appeal directly to members of Congress. On the morning following his televised speech, he spoke to a closed-door meeting in the Capitol of the House Democratic Caucus, where he emphasized the closeness of the expected vote and appealed for support. He also promised to make further spending cuts. Back at the White House that afternoon, accompanied by more than a dozen members of Congress, he signed executive orders pledging adherence to the deficit targets and controls on entitlement spending. Meanwhile, working with lists provided to White House aides by top House and Senate aides, Clinton was making many telephone calls to the undecided lawmakers whose votes would determine the bill's fate. Although Clinton aides later said that those calls produced the needed results, his soft-spoken message surprised some Democratic lawmakers. "To the dismay of many supporters, the president is approaching his task with surprising diffidence," the *Los Angeles Times* reported a week before the vote. "In defiance of the most basic tenets of personal salesmanship, he seems unable to 'close the deal' or 'ask for the sale.'"[6] A then-uncertain California Sen. Dianne Feinstein told the *Times* that, during a 45-minute meeting with Clinton and his aides, they did not specifically ask for her vote. Feinstein eventually cast her vote with Clinton, but the sales effort was further evidence that Clinton was something less than a Lyndon Johnson in his sales effort. Perhaps the president thought that a more heavy-handed effort would be unproductive with the modern breed of lawmakers.

Following Boren's announcement that he would oppose the final agreement, Democratic leaders recognized that they needed to reverse at least one of the six Democrats who had voted "no" when the Senate originally passed the bill in late June. (For that 49–49 vote, on which Vice President Gore had broken the tie, one senator from each party had been absent because of health problems; both had returned and they were certain to divide along party lines.) The list of potential switchers was not promising. Furthermore, the prospect of finding even a single Republican to support the bill remained virtually nil, given the GOP's intense internal pressure to keep a unified front. As for the Democrats, they had written off Shelby of Alabama at the start of the economic debate. Lautenberg of New Jersey was running for re-election during 1994 in a state where tax increases had become politically lethal in recent years. And Johnston of Louisiana and Nunn of Georgia, two proud committee chairmen, gave no sign that they would yield ground. That left Bryan of Nevada and DeConcini of Arizona. Both were centrist swing votes for Democrats, and they were facing re-election jeopardy in 1994.

Of those two, the more experienced DeConcini showed greater interest in negotiating a possible deal for his support. Meeting with reporters in the Senate press gallery on July 30, for example, he said that it was "most unlikely" that he would vote for the plan, but he added, "I never say never." He briefly outlined three conditions that would have to be met before he switched his vote: assurances that President Clinton would keep an earlier pledge to create a trust fund so all of the new taxes would be used for deficit reduction, an increase smaller than 4.3 cents per gallon in the gasoline tax and a smaller increase in the taxes on wealthy Social Security recipients. In fact, the Arizona senator already had begun private discussions with the president and leading Senate Democrats about signing on with the economic package. Five days later, DeConcini announced following a meeting with Clinton at the Oval Office that he was on board. "I was not sent here to be a

part of gridlock," DeConcini told reporters. "I was sent here to reduce the deficit in my last election, and I'll continue to work for
that." That the trust fund was essentially a gimmick that would
have no real impact on the federal deficit and that his other two
demands would reduce the total of deficit reduction were of less
concern to DeConcini and Clinton than was the senator's decision
to switch his vote. Some Democrats said that he was looking for
Clinton's support in discouraging a likely Democratic primary
challenger to his re-election bid. Others said that he was consider-
ing Senate retirement and was hoping to put himself in line for an
ambassadorship. DeConcini's only response to such questions was
a Cheshire cat smile. In September, however, he announced that
he would not seek re-election.

While DeConcini, Kohl and other senators were kicking up
dirt to force changes in the bill, an unheralded House Democrat
who had often battled with his party's leaders made a lower-key
contribution to reaching the final compromise. When a worried
Speaker Foley concluded 24 hours before the expected showdown
vote in the House that there were probably not enough votes to pass
the bill, he summoned the still-uncommitted Rep. Timothy Penny
of Minnesota in a telephone call to meet with him and other top
party leaders at a high-level meeting in the Capitol. Their purpose
was to discuss Penny's desire for more spending cuts. "I felt that
they either would wrestle me to the ground or ask for my help,"
Penny recounted. "They needed extra votes, so they asked for my
advice." After several intensive meetings during that evening and
early the next day, Foley joined Penny, Office of Management and
Budget director Panetta and others at the House press gallery to
announce their agreement—a few hours before the crucial vote—
on a plan to work with Clinton to seek additional cuts in federal
programs during the following months. On the day after the vote,
Foley said that he had called Penny because "he is very straight" in
his advocacy of spending cuts and that the House speaker had
found that he could deal forthrightly with him. Foley did not need
to state the obvious: He had gone to Penny because of a desperate
need to guarantee not only his essential vote but also those of several of his allies among conservative Democrats. Penny's decision
to support the bill was accompanied by surprising news on the
morning after the vote, which revealed the ambivalence among
some of the plan's supporters. The 41-year-old Democrat, who had
been elected to his sixth term, announced that he would not seek

re-election the next year. Calling that budget "far short of the plan I envisioned and well short of what is needed to balance the budget and restore economic growth," Penny said that he had voted for it because of his fear that the alternative would be even less deficit reduction, not more. He added that he did not want to become like too many politicians who "end up staying far too long."

The Cliffhanger Votes

With the summer recess set to begin on Friday, Aug. 6, the final hours before the House and Senate votes were among the most spine-tingling in recent congressional memory. The fate of the Clinton presidency was on the line. Likewise, Clinton and his aides warned, defeat of the plan could produce a sharp turnaround in the record-high levels of the New York Stock Exchange averages and would jeopardize interest rates, which were at the lowest levels for borrowers in two decades. And, as Speaker Foley later said, a defeat would have triggered angry "recriminations about who brought about the failure" among congressional Democrats. The votes were scheduled for Thursday evening in the House and the next evening in the Senate. Everyone knew that they would be close. Few expected the drama that was about to unfold, especially in the House.

In a narrow sense, some of the hype surrounding the vote was overstated. Between the Clinton and Dole speeches, *The New York Times* reported, "more claims and counterclaims were made Tuesday night than were staked out in the Oklahoma land rush, and some of them just as suspect."[7] Clinton's contention that the bill was the largest deficit-reduction plan in history, for example, was subject to dispute. Its estimated $496 billion down payment on the deficit during the next five years was actually smaller—on an inflation-adjusted basis—than the controversial $482 billion package that President Bush signed, with bipartisan support, in 1990. (A month later, the Congressional Budget Office reported that the projected five-year deficit reduction would be $477 billion.) Dole's claim that the $241 billion in new taxes was the world's largest-ever tax increase also was suspect. It actually was less than the $215 billion—which would have been $286 billion in 1993 dollars—in a 1982 bill that Dole played a major role in writing as Senate Finance Committee chairman and that President Reagan signed. And when

Dole said that Clinton's estimate of the new jobs generated by the plan was smaller than the Congressional Budget Office had forecast in January, the president apparently was using dated numbers. As in many legislative debates, however, the facts sometimes proved less important than the perceptions.

As the House neared its vote on the conference committee report, Democratic leaders grew increasingly apprehensive as they closely monitored their vote count and checked with undecided lawmakers. Foley said that he had been occasionally "discouraged" by unexpected Democratic defections and worried that the House might not pass the measure. Among the lawmakers who had voted for the bill on May 27 and decided to switch in the final hours on Aug. 5 were Rep. Bill Brewster of Oklahoma, the Ways and Means member who had won some concessions in the earlier energy tax, and his Oklahoma colleague Dave McCurdy. Both privately told colleagues that Sen. Boren's opposition in their home state had made it more difficult for them to maintain their support for the bill. Perhaps the biggest surprise, and one that angered Clinton, was the decision by fifth-term Rep. Ray Thornton of Arkansas to turn against the bill. Not only did he represent Little Rock, where Clinton had lived for nearly two decades, but Thornton also had a safe Democratic seat, having won re-election with 74 percent of the vote. "There was no good explanation for his vote," said a top Democrat who spoke with Thornton on the crucial day.

During the final hours, Clinton worked the telephone furiously from the White House. At his side, senior aides Howard Paster and George Stephanopoulos—keeping close contact with key House Democrats and their aides—organized and monitored the calls to and from the Oval Office. Among other things, they kept an open phone line to the Democratic cloakroom just off the House chamber, where members typically relax and hold private conversations. In contrast to his earlier conversations, these last-minute calls featured Clinton's strong appeals for support. In several cases, he promised hesitant Democrats that he would propose more spending cuts when Congress reconvened after Labor Day. Still, when the switchers were combined with several undecided members who decided to vote "no," the proponents were short of a majority as the 15-minute vote was about to start. By contrast, House Democratic leaders learned moments before the vote in May that they had a firm, if narrow, majority.

During the final speeches before the votes were cast, there was the unusual sight of most members seated quietly in the chamber, listening to the final remarks. Such speeches rarely influence how members vote. But the hushed assembly showed that the lawmakers were well aware of the significance of what was about to happen. Minority Leader Robert Michel of Illinois, apparently believing that his side would lose, said that "the die is cast here in the House tonight, but it will be close." He told the Democrats that his side "will be back another day to remind you of your folly." Finally, Foley ended all the talk. First, he graciously noted the announcement the previous day by two junior House Republicans from New York—Susan Molinari and Bill Paxon—that they would soon marry. Then, he voiced a direct appeal to Democrats. "After many years of indulgence and avoidance and delay and excuse," he urged, "take a hard road back to fiscal responsibility and a sound economic future for all of our people. . . . Tonight is the night to vote. Let us not break faith with our people. Let us pass this plan. Let us move forward to a better day for our country."

As members inserted their plastic cards into the electronic boxes attached to the seat backs throughout the House chamber, the recorded tally initially favored the bill's proponents. "149–134" after the first minute of the 15-minute vote. "192–165" after 8 minutes. "202–184" after 12 minutes. Then, the vote started to narrow. "209–196" with a minute left. As the buzz in the chamber grew louder, more Democrats voted "no" and the margin closed to "210–209." Finally, after the clock had expired, the count appeared to freeze at 216–214. But four Democrats had not yet voted. (There was one vacancy following the death earlier in the week of Paul Henry, a Michigan Republican, who had endured a long battle with cancer.) All of a sudden, many eyes on the House floor and in the press gallery focused on Marjorie Margolies-Mezvinsky, the freshman from Pennsylvania, who had had an agonizing and highly visible chat on the House vote with Rep. John Murtha in reaching her decision to vote "no" moments before the May vote. This time, she had set herself up for an even more pointed—and, in many ways, embarrassing—act. Hours earlier, she had told Philadelphia-area reporters that she planned to vote against the bill. Later, however, she pledged in a telephone call with Clinton shortly before the vote that she would support the bill if her vote was needed. The razor-thin margin meant that she would have to deliver. Surrounded by several reassuring colleagues, who accompanied her to the front of the House to cast her vote, she appeared shell-shocked. First, she consulted briefly with Democratic Rep. Sander Levin. Then, as if on cue, she joined veteran Rep. Pat Williams of Montana, as each signed and submitted to the House clerk a green card, which meant an "aye" vote. At nearly the same time, Thornton of Arkansas and freshman David Minge of Minnesota signed red cards to vote "no." The final vote: 218–216. As a few Republicans briefly chanted, "Goodbye, Marjorie," the presiding officer—Rep. Gerry Studds of Massachusetts—announced the result. Veteran House officials said that they had never viewed such a chaotic scene on the House floor. In a somewhat calmer format the next day in an interview on National Public Radio, Margolies-Mezvinsky explained her vote, including the commitment she extracted from Clinton to hold a conference in her suburban district to focus on further cuts in entitlement spending. "I just think that I did what I had to do, and I think that I learned a very important lesson last night," she said. "If, in this period of time as a freshman woman, I can redefine the conversation—and we are talking about something as important as entitlements—then it's worth going to the mat for."

Compared with this spectacle, the next day's finale in the Senate was more button-downed. But there was still an element of drama. Once DeConcini announced his support, Democrats had 50 votes—plus Vice President Gore to break the tie—assuming that no other senator switched. But Sen. Robert Kerrey, a first-termer from Nebraska who had been a harsh opponent of Clinton during his own 1992 presidential candidacy, made it known that he was reconsidering his support. Like Penny and other conservative House Democrats, Kerrey said that the package needed more spending cuts and he futilely tried to find a way for Congress to hold a special session to consider such a plan. Although many of his colleagues and other experts around the Senate assumed that he would support Clinton, Kerrey made the Democrats sweat. He had several lengthy phone calls with the president and his aides in the two days before the vote and also held a vital meeting with his friend, Finance Committee chairman Daniel Patrick Moynihan. Finally, an hour before the scheduled Senate vote, Kerrey took to the Senate floor and announced his decision. "I will vote 'yes' for a bill which challenges America too little, because I do not trust what my colleagues on the other side of the aisle will do if I say no," he said. "President Clinton, if you are watching now, as I suspect you are, I tell you this: I could not and should not cast a vote that brings down your presidency. You have made mistakes and know it far better than I. But you do not deserve, and America cannot afford, to have you spend the next 60 days quibbling over whether or not we should have this cut or this tax increase." He criticized Clinton for allowing the Senate to jettison the broad-based energy tax—a decision that Kerrey had not sought to reverse. He also called on the president and his own colleagues to return to the political high road. It was a riveting speech. But its greatest significance, of course, was simply that it ended the suspense over the bill's passage. Shortly after 10 p.m., senators finished casting their voice votes, with Gore again providing the margin of survival. The deed was done. There were no more surprises.

In an interview earlier that afternoon, Speaker Foley gave a fitting summary to the week's dramatic events. The outcome in the House—and, later, in the Senate—was "a test of whether the Democratic Party could govern," he said. "Having passed that bill, there is a sense of satisfaction. There would have been disillusionment and disappointment . . . if we had failed." Clinton and the Democratic Party, while narrowly avoiding the abyss of failure, scored one of the most remarkable legislative victories by a single party in congressional history. The result could not have been closer. But, as Sen. Mitchell had said earlier, "the fact of victory is more important than the margin of victory." The Democrats left town for a month's recess—exhausted, relieved and more than a bit worried about the electoral consequences of their legislative action.

Endnotes

1. *Congressional Record,* Aug. 4, 1993: H-5792—6047.
2. David E. Rosenbaum, "On Budget's Razor Edge, Opposites March in Step," *The New York Times,* July 6, 1993: A1.
3. Eric Pianin, "Hill Budget Negotiations to Test Democrats' Ability to Govern," *The Washington Post,* July 11, 1993: A6.
4. Viveca Novak and Paul Starobin, "Spreading the Money," *National Journal,* Aug. 14, 1993: 2016.
5. Eric Pianin and Ann Devroy, "Conferees Near Deal to Raise Gasoline Tax 6–7 Cents," *The Washington Post,* July 29, 1993: A1.
6. Paul Richter and Karen Tumulty, "Clinton's Soft Sell on Budget Upsets Allies," *Los Angeles Times,* July 30, 1993: A1.
7. David E. Rosenbaum, "Beyond the Superlatives," *The New York Times,* Aug. 5, 1993: A1.

10

Unified Government at Work

At a ceremony on the White House's south lawn, President Clinton writes his signature on his budget package.

A Victory over Gridlock

A nation's political cycle is rarely allowed to rest. When a long-sought goal is achieved and the task completed, the antagonists briefly pause before they carry their conflict to new levels and new issues. Thus, on a bright sunny August day, when Clinton and most of the Democratic congressional leaders assembled on the spacious South Lawn of the White House to celebrate the signing of the deficit-reduction bill, they exuded satisfaction and a sense of accomplishment. In contrast to the events of recent days and weeks, Clinton was in full control and his congressional guests sat respectfully. The heavy lifting was over. Now, all sides would await the potentially broad ramifications. And Clinton sought to emphasize the scale of the accomplishment. "We come here to begin a new direction for our nation," he said. "We are taking steps necessary and long overdue to revive our economy, to renew our American dream, to restore confidence in our ability to take charge of our own affairs." The president's rhetorical bravado sounded strikingly like that of a political campaign event, with his promise of change and his attack on the forces of the status quo. He did not want to dwell on the fine-print details and the various claims and counterclaims that had dogged Congress for months. Too much of the debate, he said, came from "those who oversimplified and downright misrepresented the questions of tax increases and spending cuts because they had narrow economic or political or personal reasons to do so."

After he painstakingly signed his name to the bill with about a dozen different pens, he stepped away from the desk and plunged into the audience to hand the cherished instruments as mementos to several of his key partners. Speaker Foley was first. Then, chairmen Rostenkowski and Moynihan. As Clinton casually walked down the line shaking hands, he greeted about two dozen lawmakers—all Democrats, of course—and scores of other guests gathered for the noontime event. They included White House and legislative aides who had labored on the bill for thousands of hours, sympathetic lobbyists and various friends of the president. Serenaded by the U.S. Marine Band, they warmly embraced as they relived their recent experiences and joined in the ceremony.

The Aug. 10 bill signing celebrated the completion of a goal that the president formally launched during his Feb. 17 speech to

At the White House bill signing, the President's chief legislative aide Howard Paster (right) greets Sen. Paul Sarbanes, an important ally on economic issues.

Congress. In reality, however, that process had begun several months earlier, during the 1992 campaign, when Clinton and the Democrats pledged new economic directions and a reordering of the nation's priorities if they won the presidential election. Given the vagueness of those promises, the American people had not been fully informed about the specific consequences. But their votes had shown their desire for change. Because of the winning candidate's message and because political campaigns have consequences, they should not have been surprised with the post-election results. Many citizens, however, were unhappy with the consequences—the tax increases and the cuts in favored programs. That response shows why governing is more difficult than campaigning. As a nation, we are constantly reminded of that reality, especially during an era when politicians have proved more adept at criticizing their opponents than at providing their own action plans. Partly because of the staggering federal deficits, public officials have few easy choices if they are committed to changing national policy. And voters are quick to pounce on these politicians for their alleged shortcomings and fabrications. The resulting tension between voters and their elected representatives is a natural and longstanding part of the political process. Following the enactment of Clinton's economic plan, the partisan resolution of the conflict would remain unclear until, at least, the November 1994 election.

Meanwhile, before those returns could be counted, the legislative results had produced important lessons about how Washington works and, more specifically, about the relationship between the new president and Congress. Such an assessment must begin with several basic premises:

*Under Clinton's leadership, in his early months, the Democrats showed that Congress could respond to pressing national problems after the president took the initiative.

*But legislating has remained an inherently demanding process even under the best of circumstances. It became all the more difficult when there was much pain and few rewards for the public at large and when the president had done little before the election to prepare the voters for his plan to reduce the deficit. "The problem for Bill Clinton is that he answered a call that was never made during the campaign," said a veteran Senate Democratic aide.

*Likewise, the internal politics of the House and Senate and the growing entrepreneurship among lawmakers have made it more and more difficult for party leaders and committee chairmen—despite some new and effective tools—to press for action on controversial issues.

*And the partisan conflict, which had flourished during much of the past decade, became even more contentious under the pressures of the Democrats' initiatives and single-party control of the White House and Congress.

So, yes, Washington's gridlock was broken and Washington changed course, at least in a narrow sense. But the grueling, often exhausting, efforts that were required to achieve those results demonstrated anew the challenge of leading a politically diverse and complex nation. "You are not going to have public enthusiasm for any of this," Speaker Foley said, in hindsight. Especially with the "campaigns of misinformation and opposition," he added, it was surprising that so many lawmakers supported the final deal.

Some Democrats dismissed the caveats and complained that such quibbling diminished the significance of what they had accomplished. "I have a hard time analyzing what went wrong," said a weary Howard Paster, Clinton's legislative director, as he reviewed the previous six months, while preparing for the vacation-time exodus of most White House aides. "The key is that we won on a tough vote for many members." With all sides agreeing that defeat of Clinton's program would have dealt a serious blow to his presidency, the reverse should also be true: Victory gave an important political lift. Paster took special note of the historically high level of support that Clinton received within his own party. The sole similar recent event was the virtually unanimous Republican backing that Reagan received on the major budget and tax-cut bills in 1981. In that case, however, Democratic control of the House meant that the president also needed significant help from the other party. Indeed, congressional historians could not recall a prior instance in which, as in 1993, major legislation had been enacted without any help from one of the two major parties. Adding to that significance, of course, was the narrow margin on final passage, in which the shift of one vote would have reversed the outcome in either the House or Senate.

However tenuous and hard-fought the victory, the initial months of Clinton's presidency demonstrated anew that the nation's legislative engines can run. After the dismal deadlocks during the second half of the Bush administration and the critics' overstated claims that Congress was tied in knots and needed radical overhaul, passage of the deficit-reduction bill constituted a vote of self-confidence in that institution's ability to perform. Members of Congress have difficulty passing legislation on their own initiative. But they have fewer problems accommodating a newly elected president, especially from their own party, who is intent on changing the nation's direction and has taken his case to the people. Sufficient respect remains for the office and the power of the presidency that enough lawmakers accepted the wisdom of House Ways and Means chairman Rostenkowski when he asked, "Who am I to say that I won't support the president?" In that sense, the Democrats showed that single-party control is a more efficient form for running the federal government, especially given the growing difficulties of attaining bipartisanship. The willingness of Rostenkowski and party leaders such as Foley, Gephardt and Mitchell to sublimate their own political egos and considerable influence to the president's interests in placing his imprint on economic policy marked a vital return step toward strong presidential leadership without sacrificing a disciplined legislative role. After 12 years with a confrontational Republican White House, congressional Democrats were more prepared to accept the president's vital role in commanding the legislative process, while they reserved for themselves the power to write many of the details. That was a stark contrast to 1977, when an earlier team of Democratic leaders kept their distance from the new Carter presidency and ultimately shared responsibility for its failure. The contemporary team of congressional leaders had a greater understanding of the need for cooperation between the two branches. Even the Republican-driven Senate defeat of Clinton's economic stimulus bill, which had marked a jarring political setback to the young administration, did not fundamentally stifle its economic program.

Still, there were second-guessers, both inside and outside Congress. Rep. Karen Shepherd, the freshman Democrat from Utah who pleased party leaders with her early support of the deficit-reduction bill, later lamented the difficulty in building consensus within the House. "We have very bad communications within this body, at almost every level," she said. "It's very hard to build consensus and to find what different groups have in common. . . . Instead, we yell at each other and reach the lowest common denominator." Rep. Eric Fingerhut, an Ohio first-termer who had worked with Shepherd on a Democratic reform task force, complained that junior members like themselves had not been fully consulted on legislative details until far too late in the process, "after the rubber hits the road." In the news media, commentators focused on the lack of public enthusiasm. Clinton's narrow victories in Congress mirrored the public's indifference toward him, including "the very large number of voters who don't seem interested in Clinton at all," according to a political columnist.[1] Another experienced news analyst concluded that the president faced a "pervasive lack of confidence" throughout the nation. "Much of the country doesn't like this budget, thinks it will hurt the middle class, whatever Mr. Clinton says, thinks the President is doing a lackluster job and mistrusts most things the government does."[2] Public-opinion polls reinforced this sense that the top Democrats' satisfaction over a job well done was not widely shared by the public. A mid-August Gallup Poll for the Cable News Network and *USA Today* found that 64 percent of the respondents considered the new budget "business as usual"; a separate question found that only 17 percent believed that Clinton had reduced Washington's gridlock.

Given the delay and endless haggling, much of it under the glare of the public spotlight, that was required to pass Clinton's first big bill, continued national cynicism toward Congress was understandable. Still, compared with the embarrassments a year or two earlier—the Clarence Thomas hearings and the House bank scandal—Congress, at last, comported itself as a serious legislative body. It was probably too much to expect that the lawmakers also would handle their work in an efficient and peaceful fashion. But that most of the American public did not take a more positive view of the results was a sign of the depths to which public scorn of Congress had dipped.

The Political Battle Continues

That public displeasure with Washington failed to abate following the legislative successes revealed more of the political volatility that had been so prominent during the 1992 campaign. Although Republicans were more likely to benefit in subsequent elections because they were the opposition party, both parties were uncertain about their own direction and future. They could only guess at how the voters would respond. The low public approval scores for the two major parties, combined with the continuing appeal of Ross Perot, also were a warning that unhappiness with business as usual posed the prospect of more fundamental changes in the political system. For example, in response to a question in the mid-August Gallup Poll of who has the best ideas for improving the economy, 35 percent responded Clinton, 30 percent said Perot and only 24 percent favored the Republicans. The support for Perot reflected what political analyst Kevin Phillips termed "an anger/frustration alternative" for many middle-class voters who had soured on Clinton.[3] Stanley Greenberg, Clinton's veteran pollster, said that the public had become "extremely rootless," which helped to explain the president's difficulty in building stable support for his agenda in Congress.[4] Some second-guessing Democrats, looking back at the success of Clinton's campaign message, voiced regret that the president and his advisers had apparently forgotten the lesson that political victories required constant voter education. In his first few months in the White House, Clinton relinquished much of that battleground to the rejuvenated Republicans. For their part, however, the GOP leaders were more effective in tearing down Clinton than in offering their own compelling alternatives.

The public's growing unhappiness with the two parties came at a time when, ironically, both of them were acting with an unusually high level of solidarity. The Senate Republicans' success in using the filibuster to stymie or force major changes in many bills gave them greater legislative influence than they had expected in the jarring weeks after Bush's defeat. And the Democratic leaders were able to keep about 85 percent of their House members and nearly 90 percent of their senators lined up behind their program. That was better than their record under the two previous Democratic presidents, both Southerners, when conservative Democratic lawmakers often cooperated with Republicans in the "conservative coalition." Several major political changes—including the increased influence of Southern moderates in the Democratic Party, redistricting changes that have produced many new black lawmakers from the South and increased pressure for party discipline, especially in the House—have produced a gradual reshaping of the political lines in Congress. One result has been that bipartisanship has become more difficult to achieve, especially on the hot-button issues of taxes and spending.

Some Southern Democrats took advantage of the redrawn landscape and their party's narrower House and Senate majorities to wield major influence on the details of the deficit-reduction plan, though they finally voted against it. Sen. David Boren of Oklahoma and Rep. Charles Stenholm of Texas, for example, were instrumental in forcing their party leaders to abandon the broad-based energy tax and to approve additional cuts in Medicare and other spending programs. But each then voted against the final House-Senate conference report, though both had supported initial Senate and House passage. Not surprisingly, these reversals by Boren, Stenholm and other conservative Democrats triggered some unhappiness among their party colleagues. "They worked with the lobbyists to make the energy tax hollow," complained a Democratic strategist. "Then, when they hit it with a bat, there was nothing to hold it up. . . . They got away with playing both sides of the fence. That has made their colleagues very resentful and suspicious of them."

For other members of Congress, especially those who were newcomers or from vulnerable seats, the public mood was ominous. Among those placed in the greatest jeopardy were other Southern Democrats who had been at the center of the political spectrum and decided to stick with Clinton. Take, for example, first-term Rep. Don Johnson, a Georgia Democrat. Immediately after his vote for final approval of Clinton's economic plan in August, he became the target of harsh criticism in his district, which includes suburban and rural pockets between Atlanta and Augusta. With organizational help from conservative Christian religious groups, protesters unhappy with his budget vote picketed Johnson's local appearances and demanded his recall from office. "I've never seen anything like this before," he said after a raucous town-hall meeting with 350 people in the small community of Grovetown, during which he was repeatedly booed and shouted down with catcalls. "People have a strong cynicism about what's happening in Washington." Johnson's position may have become especially precarious because he had decided to vote for the bill literally at the last minute, following a telephone conversation with Clinton that ended as the House was voting on the package. Earlier that day, Johnson had announced that he would vote against the legislation. But Clinton, who was desperate for support, finally convinced Johnson that he would deliver on promises for additional spending cuts. *The Augusta Chronicle,* the largest newspaper in Johnson's district, was not impressed, claiming that Johnson and other reluctant Democrats had "horse-traded away their vow to fight the deficit for empty promises."[5] The newspaper, which had endorsed Johnson during the 1992 election, declared that it "regrets" that decision. Even Johnson's Democratic predecessor in the seat—Doug Barnard Jr., who had retired in 1992—joined the second-guessing, claiming that Johnson's last-minute switch had "compounded his problem" politically back home.

How serious were such warnings? For a politician, trying to comprehend what motivates citizen protesters and how widely and strongly their opinions are shared can be an important but difficult exercise. For Johnson and other congressional Democrats who had reluctantly supported Clinton's plan, the vocal opposition might have represented the efforts of fringe groups among their constituencies. But these officials could not be sure. Besides, the national public-opinion polls suggested that the public objections probably ran deeper than that. In this environment, lawmakers who had taken a political risk to support Clinton's initiative probably would be less likely to take his side on the next issue that forced them to choose between party loyalty and constituent pressure.

As for congressional Republicans, their strong party unity meant that they faced few difficult decisions during Clinton's early months. With the comfortable expectation that votes against new taxes and spending likely would benefit them personally, at least so long as Clinton's popularity was down and the Democrats were struggling, they stayed on the political sidelines. But many Republicans also understood the warnings in the public-opinion polls that they faced danger if they offered only a negative message about the nation's direction. As was shown by the sorry performance of President Bush's re-election campaign, the ever-shifting political dynamics eventually would force them to show what they stood for—or else, face the public demand for change.

The Legislative Beat Moves to Health Care

With the completion of the deficit-reduction bill, Clinton and most members of Congress heaved a sigh of relief that they could move on to other issues that voters might find more rewarding. Each of the next round of legislative initiatives—including the North American free trade agreement (NAFTA), crime and welfare reform—raised new sets of political problems. But at least, the politicians hoped, these proposals offered potential benefits to some constituents. And each of these proposals would produce new political coalitions in which Clinton could count on support from some Republicans. Indeed, the prospect of shifting alliances left some politicians with a case of political seasickness. "Just when Republicans worried that their image was too negative, along comes an issue [NAFTA] that lets them help President Clinton while hurting his party at the same time," according to a news story, which reported that a Democratic pollster viewed the proposal as "a dream come true for Republican tacticians."[6] Some congressional Democrats worried that intensive opposition in their own party to the proposed deal with Mexico would produce a political nightmare.

For most Democrats, the more exciting prospect for policy and political change came in September with Clinton's unveiling of his health-care plan. But that proposal loomed as a titanic legislative struggle that would affect the pocketbooks and lifestyles of virtually all citizens. Those stakes could have profound political consequences. Many Democrats believed that it was no overstatement to claim that the fates of their party and of Clinton's presidency were on the line. Resolving the many conflicts and reaching agreement would produce "the biggest and most complicated legislation in more than 50 years," said House Majority Leader Gephardt. Even more than the struggles over Clinton's plans for the economy and deficit reduction, the health-care debate would dominate the attention of both the nation and the Washington community. The health-care industry consumed nearly a trillion dollars in annual spending and affects virtually every American. It had mushroomed to 14 percent of the gross domestic product, several percentage points higher than in other industrialized nations. The growing political focus on the issue was accompanied and nurtured by increased public anxiety over specific problems: Employers and employees worried about the cost and scope of their insurance coverage, and family members struggled to find adequate and affordable care for themselves and aging relatives.

The difficulty in resolving these problems was obvious, if only because presidents and Congress would have agreed to solutions years earlier if they could have. Although health-care costs were soaring, polls showed that most people were happy with their existing insurance coverage and many balked at any change that would affect their current care and relationship with their doctors. Although there was agreement by many health-care providers—hospitals, doctors and the like—that change was needed, there was wide disagreement among the so-called experts over what could or should be done. Compounding these problems was the continuing public skepticism about government's ability to solve national problems and the political reluctance to spend more tax dollars. In addition, the debate over the problems and the solutions was complicated by technical jargon and terms such as "managed competition" and "purchasing cooperatives" that the professional insiders could barely agree on, let alone the average citizen. And, despite their professed desire to reform the system, many congressional Democrats were nervous about confronting the details, especially their financial implications. When pressed to take a position, they differed widely over what should be done and how much political risk they were willing to take while imposing major reforms.

Clinton highlighted the scope of the problem and his own commitment to action when he announced five days after he took office his decision to place his wife, Hillary Rodham Clinton, in charge of the newly created White House Task Force on National Health Care Reform. At the time, he said, the task force would study the options and prepare recommendations within 100 days of when he took office, following which Clinton planned to submit his proposal to Congress. "It's time to make sense of America's health care system," he told reporters at the White House. "It's time to bring costs under control and to make our families and businesses secure." The appointment of the "first lady" was extraordinary and dramatized the high political stakes. The task force itself became one of the most intensive efforts ever in Washington to review a problem and propose solutions. Its work was divided into many groups, whose mostly closed-door meetings often lasted well into the nights and continued on weekends. By including many private-sector experts and congressional aides in the task force's work, the White House also sought to develop a proposal that would generate wide support. But the task force became a topic of controversy because of its complexity and secrecy and its delays in preparing its recommendations. And when Clinton finally announced his plan to Congress on Sept. 22, more than four months late, he acknowledged that step only began what would likely be the arduous task of crafting legislation that would satisfy House and Senate majorities. But he laid down a familiar challenge in his nationally telecast prime-time speech: "When you hear all of these [opposing] arguments, ask yourself whether the cost of staying on the same course isn't greater than the cost of change."

On Capitol Hill, meanwhile, most congressional Democrats acted like good soldiers during the months they awaited Clinton's plan. Not only did they practice an uncommon public silence on its details and timing, the key players also took organizational steps to prepare for speedy action once Clinton submitted his proposal. They kept mostly private their discussions on the substance of the proposal, the handling of the plan once it reached Congress, and the best communications tools to educate the public and advance the proposal. Once Clinton unveiled his proposal, they wanted to move quickly and with as much cohesion as possible.

Their abundant differences on policy were downplayed on Capitol Hill during the months leading to Clinton's unveiling of his plan, as advocates privately argued their case before White House aides. Much of this debate centered around the mechanism for the new health policy rather than policy goals. On those, Democrats could generally agree with three broad principles: decent access to medical treatment for all Americans, affordable service and quality care. And many of them acknowledged that, as had been the case with Social Security and Medicare decades earlier, they would not pass a complete program from the start.

In contrast to their unified opposition to Clinton's economic package, many Republicans said that they wanted to cooperate on the health-care plan. White House advisers, who were eager to avoid another highly partisan conflict, welcomed the initial overtures, and they also sought support from some of the influential interest groups that work on health issues. They had come to realize the tight margin for error they faced in passing legislation when they had to depend entirely on support from Democratic lawmakers, including the many party factions that might seek to veto various plans. "I never want to go through another six months where we have to get all of our votes within one party," Clinton told the nation's governors on Aug. 16. Administration policy-makers also recognized that, on such a complex and sweeping issue, it would be to their advantage to have the political cover of bipartisan support. "Health care is an issue that goes beyond politics," Mrs. Clinton said in April, following a meeting with a large group of senators from both parties. "The American people want us to work together."

But achieving that cooperation would require more than wishful thinking. In partisan terms, Republican successes during the first half of 1993 had emboldened them, and they had no reason to make quick concessions to the Democrats. And many of the key GOP players had significant policy differences from leading Democrats. There also were internal pressures on Republicans to craft and stick to a party-line position. Even before the 1992 election, they had sought, with limited success, to craft a partisan response on health care—much as had been the case with the Democrats. Following Bush's defeat, they gained more flexibility to move on their own course. But the Republicans faced many obstacles with the many technical and political issues that also had divided the Democrats. A group of moderate Senate Republicans, for example, sought to promote cooperation with the White House by meeting with the Clintons and promoting their own alternative, which included some of the free-market reform features that Clinton had encouraged. "Republican senators want to be helpful in the solution of this problem," said Sen. John Chafee of Rhode Island, the chairman of the Senate GOP health-care task force. Despite that cooperative spirit, however, many conservative Republicans had little interest in joining hands with the Democrats, and they spent their time attacking the big-tax, big-spending features of Clinton's views on health care. They preferred to make incremental changes in the current system, without a major change in the federal role. For example, Rep. John Kasich of Ohio, the Republican leader on the House Budget Committee, issued a report that claimed that U.S. health care "suffers not from a lack of resources, but from inefficient use of the resources available." And Sen. Gramm, with his presidential-candidacy aspirations, backed an alternative that would allow individuals to have a tax-subsidized medical savings account. Some moderate Democrats encouraged the middle-ground position by Chafee and his allies. That potential bipartisan agreement not only strengthened the centrist forces, it also sent a message to Democratic advocates of a more activist view that compromise would be essential within their party.

Can We Govern?

The prospect of bipartisanship added a new set of political complications for Clinton and Congress. The 1992 campaign and the 1993 budget debate had left considerable ill will and suspicions between the two parties plus fears from each side that the other would seek to gain political advantage in their dealings. In addition, Clinton's inexperience as Arkansas governor in working with a sizable corps of Republican legislators created some doubts about his ability to work both sides of the fence in the Capitol. But many Democrats felt that it was time to scrap the partisan fireworks. "The last thing the country needs is party politics-as-usual but that is exactly what we are getting from Republicans," Rostenkowski told a Chicago business meeting. "Parties are a means to doing public business, not ends in themselves. Whenever party considerations take precedence over all else, it's a sure signal that the public's well-being is ignored, if not damaged."

Regardless of the political alliances, the conclusion of the budget debate left a haunting sense in Washington. The problem of the federal deficit had not been defanged and the needed revenues would continue to remain unavailable, even for meritorious new spending programs. In short, all of the squabbling over budget plans yielded some reduction of projected deficits, but even under optimistic projections the annual deficits likely would remain around $200 billion by the start of the next administration in 1997—compared with the roughly $300 billion that Bush bequeathed to Clinton. "After months of handwringing and fiery debate over the benefits and drawbacks of the Clinton economic plan, Congress has passed a package that analysts contend will have only a limited influence on the economy," according to an economic appraisal. "The consensus among some of the nation's leading forecasters is that the plan will slightly crimp economic performance in the short run, while providing a modest boost over the long run."[7] Some economists also worried that the higher tax rates on the wealthy would reduce the already weak economic growth at a potentially vulnerable point. But economists more sympathetic to the Clinton administration countered that the legacy of the Reagan-Bush years left no alternative but a lengthy and sustained attack on the record federal deficits of the 1980s.

Perhaps the greatest irony in the assessments of the Democrats' budget deal was the conclusion of many political and economic analysts that the deal bore marked similarities to their appraisals of the one Bush and the Democratic-controlled Congress signed in 1990: Both deals reduced the deficit by about $500 billion over five years. Both raised taxes primarily on the wealthy. Both raised the federal gasoline tax by about a nickel per gallon. Both also took sizable whacks at defense and Medicare spending, while failing to eliminate any major domestic programs. The main difference, of course, is that the 1990 plan was a model of bipartisanship, with opposition from both ends of the political spectrum, while the 1993 deal was passed with no Republican support. Whether Clinton will suffer as much political damage for his support of tax increases as Bush did for breaking his "no new taxes" pledge remains to be seen, of course. For these two very different presidents working with very different legislative scenarios, however, the similarities of their policies was a striking commentary on the limited options available to the federal government in the 1990s.

The many legislative, political and economic obstacles that frustrated the Democrats' ability to change the government's direction after Clinton's election were a reminder of the difficulty of reshaping national policy. In retrospect, many scholars agree, that should not have been a surprise. "What has made the President's first months so rocky has been less his own performance, which includes real achievements as well as failures, than the character of the contemporary political environment," wrote Alan Brinkley, an American historian at Columbia University. He cited the absence of consensus among Democrats on most major domestic issues, the weakness of Clinton's 43 percent election victory, and the lack of a popular mandate. But Brinkley listed larger factors, as well: "the legacy of nearly three decades of social, economic and ideological disappointment, a legacy of political frustration and popular cynicism symbolized for the moment by the irritatingly persistent popularity of Ross Perot." The changes in the news media, spawned by the official miscalculations of the Vietnam War and the Watergate scandal, exacerbated that public skepticism, he added.[8]

Students of the Lyndon Johnson presidency must have been struck when news reporters in the summer of 1993 described Clinton's "credibility gap," a term that once referred to Johnson's failure to tell the truth about the scale and effectiveness of the U.S. military commitment in Vietnam. "Plainly put, lots of people don't believe what Mr. Clinton told them about the deficit-reduction plan," wrote a reporter for *The Wall Street Journal.* "This amounts to a kind of deficit in public trust, which is an enormous problem for a president, and one that transcends any single issue."[9] When a large majority of the public does not accept what a president says—for example, Clinton's accurate statement that the new taxes would heavily target the most wealthy taxpayers—that makes it difficult for political leaders to rally the support that is needed for national "shared sacrifice." From his different perspective, House Speaker Foley raised a similar concern, after the passage of the deficit-reduction plan, when he talked about the decline in the "credibility of political institutions." The average citizen, barraged by an array of political hyperbole and broadcast commentary, is "easy prey" for critics, Foley said. "Once [political leaders] get behind the envelope, it's hard to catch up."

Facing these challenges, political leaders have limited choices. They can follow the model of President Bush during his final two years in office, when he pursued an essentially status quo approach to governing and hoped that the nation's problems would take care of themselves. They can try to educate the public about the challenges that the nation faces, as Clinton did to some degree during the 1992 campaign. Or they can work legislatively to craft change, as the Democrats did in 1993, and hope that their efforts succeed and that the public finds the results acceptable. In any case, there is no guarantee of political success. And the nature of a democratic system is that the voters have every right to remove the incumbents in favor of a new team and to demand new directions.

Senate Majority Leader Mitchell, displaying what may have been a weariness with the political burdens of his task, said that public officials ultimately must follow their conscience and that they should be willing to pay the consequences. "Most of us [senators] are here for a relatively short time," he said. "You simply must do what you think is right. . . . If I'm unable to do what I know is right for our country, then what has all the energy and work been for?" Politicians, of course, have not always followed such advice. But the increased strains of governing in the late 20th century may have left them with little alternative. And the end of divided government in 1992 forced a return to political accountability that, at least for a time, left more definite lines of responsibility for the results.

In his more positive moments, Mitchell heralded the Democrats' achievements, not only on the economy but on several other issues where they had resolved deadlocks from the Bush presidency. The enactment of long-deadlocked proposals for unpaid leave to many employees with a family or medical emergency and for easier voter-registration procedures demonstrated the legislative results of the president and Congress working from the same script. "This year's record demonstrates that gridlock is largely over," Mitchell concluded.

The legislative process, in many cases, was not pretty. And the public cynicism was unabated. As they continued to work on changing course, however, Washington's officialdom—at least, the Democrats—derived some satisfaction from their ability to move the government off dead center. Although the economic and political consequences could only be guessed, they had delivered the promised change.

Endnotes

1. Michael Barone, "His Problem: Indifference, Not Hate," *U.S. News & World Report,* Aug. 16, 1993: 37.
2. R. W. Apple Jr., "Clinton Is Pulled from the Brink. He'll Be Back," *The New York Times,* Aug. 8. 1993: Sect. 4, p. 1.
3. *American Political Report,* Aug. 13, 1993: 7.
4. David Lauter and Ronald Brownstein, "America's Vanishing Majority," *The Los Angeles Times,* June 30, 1993: A1.
5. "Johnson Sells Out," *The Augusta Chronicle,* Aug. 7, 1993: 4A.
6. John Harwood, "In a Battle over the Trade Accord with Mexico, Clinton's Friends and Foes May Exchange Roles," *The Wall Street Journal,* Aug. 17, 1993: A16.
7. Rick Wartzman and Lucinda Harper, "Economists Expect Impact of Plan Will Be Limited, *The Wall Street Journal,* Aug. 9, 1993: A4.
8. Alan Brinkley, "The 43% President," *The New York Times Magazine,* July 4, 1993: 22.
9. Gerald F. Seib, "Budget Package Fails to Resolve Deficit in Trust," *The Wall Street Journal,* Aug. 11, 1993: A10.

Index

About the Author

As congressional reporter for *National Journal* since 1977 and staff member since 1973, Richard E. Cohen writes about both legislative and electoral politics and deals regularly with a broad cross section of members of Congress. He has been a frequent contributor to other publications, including the Sunday "Opinion" section of the *Los Angeles Times*, *The Baltimore Sun*, and *The Washington Post*. He has also been a regular guest on the C-SPAN cable network. He has written *Congressional Leadership: Seeking a New Role*, (Georgetown University's Center for Strategic and International Studies, 1981) and *Washington at Work: Back Rooms and Clean Air,* (Macmillan, 1992). He has served five terms as a member of the executive committee of the congressional periodic press galleries and chaired the committee from 1987 to 1989. Cohen was the 1990 winner of the Everett McKinley Dirksen Award for distinguished reporting of Congress.

Cohen graduated in 1969 from Brown University, where he was publisher of the *Brown Daily Herald*, and in 1972 from Georgetown University Law Center. During law school, he was an aide to U.S. Sen. Edward W. Brooke of Massachusetts. A native of Northampton, Massachusetts, Cohen and his wife, Lyn Schlitt, who is general counsel to the U.S. International Trade Commission, now live in McLean, Virginia; they have a seven-year-old daughter.